SERVER DISK MANAGEMENT in a WINDOWS ENVIRONMENT

SERVER DISK MANAGEMENT in a WINDOWS ENVIRONMENT

Drew Robb

AUERBACH PUBLICATIONS

A CRC Press Company

Boca Raton   London   New York   Washington, D.C.

Library of Congress Cataloging-in-Publication Data

Robb, Drew.
    Server disk management in a Windows environment / Drew Robb.
        p. cm.
    Includes bibliographical references and index.
    ISBN 0-8493-2432-7 (alk. paper)
        1. Hard disk management. 2. Client/server computing. 3. Microsoft Windows (Computer
    file) I. Title.

    QA76.9.H35R63 2003
    004.5'63--dc21

2003052460

Visit the CRC Press Web site at www.crcpress.com

© 2004 by CRC Press LLC
Auerbach is an imprint of CRC Press LLC

No claim to original U.S. Government works
International Standard Book Number 0-8493-2432-7
Library of Congress Card Number 2003052460
Printed in the United States of America 1 2 3 4 5 6 7 8 9 0
Printed on acid-free paper

Contents

Preface

Disks and disk health are given scant attention in the broad scheme of things. As you look over the computer press, you read plenty about CPUs, RAM, networks, integration, and the server wars. Hard disks barely seem to merit a mention, except perhaps once or twice a year whenever a bigger or faster drive comes out.

Hard Drives: The Biggest Source of Failure

Yet, disk drives account for more server failures and repairs than any other factor. According to the 2002 *PC Magazine* reader survey, hard drive repairs are by far the number one reason for server downtime among Windows-based servers (this holds true for UNIX servers, too, by the way). When several thousand server users were asked to name a specific cause of failure in servers, the results were surprisingly consistent (Exhibit 1). As you can see, hard drives account for half the reported failures. Other surveys have recorded similar findings, so it seems that more needs to be written about hard drives and disk management in general.

Why Windows Servers?

When it came to writing this text, I decided to stick to Windows-based systems. Why? Although Microsoft has about a 95 percent share of the desktop market, its server dominance has sneaked up on people quietly but forcefully. Currently, some surveys show Microsoft servers outnumbering other server operating systems by about 6 to 1. And, as Windows servers are still maturing, a disk management book in this area seemed to have more value.

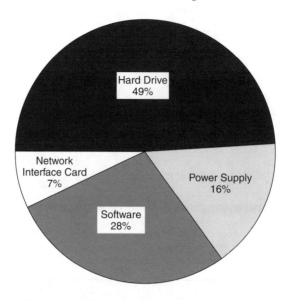

Exhibit 1   Causes of Server Failure

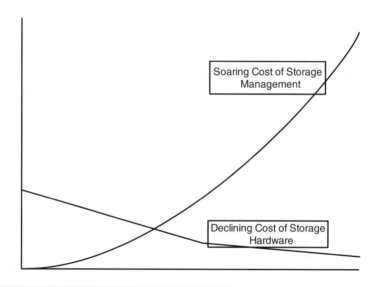

Exhibit 2   Storage Management Costs

Storage Management Costs

Another factor that drove the writing of this text was the terrific rise in storage management total cost of ownership (TCO) over the past decade. Ten years back, storage hardware accounted for the bulk of total costs, with management taking up only a small percentage of the total. The lines crossed around 1996 (Exhibit 2). Nowadays, the hardware accounts for a relatively small percentage of the costs, with management being by far the dominant cost. Think about it for a moment: Management costs include people, software, security, facilities, energy, hardware, and many other expenses. As the size and complexity of distributed computing environments have multiplied, so has the amount of management required. So, it appeared to be time to give the subject of disk management and, in particular, server disk management a little more attention.

What This Book Is *Not*

That said, there are a great many things that this book is *not*. An abundance of fine books are out that cover all sorts of related technical subjects in tremendous detail, and that is not the purpose of this text. Let us look, then, at what else this work is not:

- It is not a hardware treasure trove of details concerning hard disk hardware and configuration.
- It is not a detailed rundown of every command, GUI, and tab involved in every conceivable action an administrator needs to manage disks on Windows 2000.
- It does not go into intricate detail about all the Windows internal type of material that only the highest level technical staff can understand.
- It is not a compendium of storage management and storage networking information.

In reality, dozens of works in existence already cover these subjects adequately. In the bibliography at the end (Appendix B), I have endeavored to list a few of these texts. They go into far more detail, and some demonstrate far more knowledge of these areas than I will probably ever come to possess.

What This Book *Is*

So, rather than try to compete with some of the most brilliant minds in the field, in this book I instead decided to cover areas that appear neglected in modern texts. This work, therefore, stays focused on disks and disk management, particularly with regard to servers. What are the basic elements of a disk and various disk architectures? How do you manage the disks you have or plan to have? How do you keep them running well with a minimum of fuss? The book also discusses such key areas as:

- Windows file systems and operating systems
- Backup
- Disaster recovery
- Basics of disk management on Windows 2000

Perhaps even more importantly, though, it takes up areas that are paid scant attention among the books available on the market — vital areas such as:

- Disk quotas
- Fragmentation
- Optimization
- Hard drive reliability
- Asset management and software deployment
- Forensics

Vital areas, yet they are given a page or two at best in current literature. This book fills this gap with chapters addressing each of these areas, written in such a way as to tie them all together as essential ingredients of sound disk management.

In addition, I have pulled together a couple of more speculative chapters towards the end, going over disk and disk management trends that are likely to affect Windows-based systems in the near future. In addition to attempting to predict where hard drives themselves are headed, the book looks at the future for storage and how storage issues will affect those managing the ever-increasing number of disks at work in the modern enterprise, as well as taking a look at where the Windows platform is going with a chapter on .NET and 64-bit computing. Also included is a discussion of what Microsoft plans for the next few years on the server and desktop side.

Intended Audience

This book has been prepared in such a way as to provide value for IT veterans as well as less technically savvy individuals. For students, business executives, or less experienced IT staff, it gives plenty of definitions and explanations of the basics, including chapters on disk organization, file systems, and basic disk maintenance actions. In order to make it more accessible, technical words are defined and key concepts explained (and a glossary is provided in Appendix A). Veteran IT staff can skip those explanations and still find plenty of useful information on keeping disks rolling (or spinning) in the most efficient way and for maximum performance. But, be warned, IT vets. It never hurts to go over material again, and you should be wary of the dangers of thinking you already know everything. At the very least, the chapters on hard disk reliability, fragmentation, and optimization, as well as the trend chapters at the end, should provide plenty of food for thought and, more importantly, some material you can use to do an even better job.

Overall Direction

The overall direction that this material takes, then, is determining how best to manage and optimize the performance of the multitude of hard drives that exist within the enterprises of today. Important issues include server disk management, managing storage assets, backing up, managing free space, managing fragmentation, maintaining high disk performance, guarding against and preventing disk failure, and future developments with regard to hard disks. It is also important to note that this text concentrates entirely on Windows-based operating systems and file systems. Within that context, it speaks primarily about Windows 2000, as that is now the primary Windows server platform; however, the book also covers Windows 9*x*, NT, and XP in brief, as well as Windows Server 2003. In terms of file systems, NTFS is emphasized, but FAT and FAT 32 are also covered in some detail.

Software, Not Hardware

To further define this work, it takes a software approach and gives little attention to the hardware maintenance side (again, hardware is aptly covered in many other places, as listed in the bibliography section in Appendix B). I may reference some of these books but do not try to replace them. That said, the book does cover basic definitions and explanations of hard drive hardware in more than enough detail for the purposes of this text. In fact, an entire chapter is devoted to hard drive hardware and the different types available. In summary, then, this book has been written for those who want to know more about how to maintain their disks in optimum health, monitor them, and get the best out of them. It also highlights how IT managers can improve the efficiency of hard drives in the enterprise and how to manage them better.

Chapter Organization and Content

It all begins with an overview of the subject of server disks and their management in the Introduction. This section talks about the explosion in drive size and overall storage capacity and why that makes it more imperative than ever to take charge of server disks and disk management.

Chapter 1 covers the fundamentals of what a hard disk is and the basic definitions of terms such as cluster, tracks, platters, head, arm, spindle, controller, seek, caching, rotational latency, SCSI, IDE, and more. It includes plenty of charts and diagrams to make things clear. Though some readers will know all of this, some may be surprised to find at least a couple of basics concepts that have so far evaded them. By understanding *all* the basics, more understanding results. This translates into a greater ability to manage disks throughout the enterprise.

Chapter 2 goes over the various file systems for Windows, including FAT, what it is, and how it works, as well as NTFS and what it is, how it works, and how it compares with FAT. The chapter then discusses how data is arranged in these file systems and the various problems that can arise. I also address special file types such as the Master File Table (MFT).

Chapter 3 gets into an interesting area. Unexpected disk failure is an expensive proposition. It is not simply the cost of the drives themselves, but rather the cost of technical personnel time to replace and reload the disk that should be considered. Add in the user downtime, value of lost information, and, in the case of externally facing applications, lost customers and the amount of damage skyrockets. This chapter investigates the frequency of disk failure, finding it to be a far more common experience than many realize. It also discusses one of the most common measures of disk failures — MTBF — and debunks the myth that today's high MTBF ratings equate to disks that will last for half a century. Finally, it gives some tips, strategies, and tools that can be used to guard against disk failure.

Chapter 4 investigates the basic principles of disk management, including the difference between basic and dynamic disks, the difference between the volume types, and the various types of fault-tolerance schemes.

Chapter 5 encompasses the importance of backup. It gives a brief rundown on how backups work, how backups should be organized, the media involved, tools to use to speed backups, etc. The chapter takes a look at strategies for doing backups and restoring the data as needed and goes into depth regarding the backup functions that are preinstalled with Windows, as well as the use of third-party software, mirroring, and off-site replication. The chapter also addresses the special needs of backing up Linux in heterogeneous environments.

Chapter 6 explains the importance of disaster recovery planning (DRP) and how this ties into responsible disk management. DRP actually goes way beyond RAID and backup, and this point must be thoroughly grasped. Further, the chapter covers a subset of DRP, known as the contingency plan (CP), which addresses non-catastrophic failures due to accidental deletions, disk failures, and other potential data loss scenarios. By creating and implementing a CP, organizations are more able to eliminate significant amounts of data loss smoothly and relatively effortlessly.

Chapter 7 covers a tool — defragmentation — vital to keeping systems stable, improving disk performance, and maintaining them properly. It investigates what fragmentation is, the impact it has, safety considerations with regard to it, and the best ways to defragment networks. It also discusses manual defragmenters (such as the one built into Windows 2000), comparing them with third party products and showing benchmarks of their performance.

Chapter 8 explains the subject of disk optimization, which is said to reduce the time it takes to recover data from disks via intelligent placement of files in order to minimize head movement. But, how effective is disk optimization in the real world? Some say it produces great gain, but I am not so sure. For the average consumer on a low-end PC, optimization appears to produce some benefit. Where it may fall short, however, is in the enterprise. This chapter explains why.

Chapter 9 is all about another aspect of disk management that receives little attention in computer texts — disk quotas. Even though disk space seems to be nearly infinite (i.e., the amount of disk space and the sizes of disks seem to be getting bigger and bigger), the fact is that disk quotas are more important than ever. Pay no attention to disk quotas and in a short time your enterprise will be chock full of MP3s and other miscellany, and users will be screaming for more space.

Chapter 10 is all about the amount of hidden data that exists on disks and in documents. The area of computer forensics (recovering data from computers for use as evidence in a court of law) has grown in recent years. This chapter explains some of the basics of computer forensics, some of the main sources of hidden data, ways to retrieve it, and methods to get rid of it.

Chapter 11 covers changes being made by Microsoft and some of its partners that will make disk management in general much easier, particularly with regard to the management of storage assets. In particular, the chapter focuses on shadow sets and storage virtualization for Windows-based servers.

Chapter 12 addresses the trend toward consolidating multiple commodity servers into fewer large Windows boxes. It includes a discussion of scaling out the number of servers versus scaling up, which strategy to employ when, and the value of each approach. It also covers the ways to consolidate Windows-based servers, the hardware and software available, and the disk management advantages that can be realized; for example, instead of managing thousands of small disks, it is possible to streamline server operations into a few dozen large disks.

Chapter 13 begins with a brief discussion of the early days of Windows, then gets into Microsoft's first foray into server systems — Windows NT. Within a year or two, NT will begin to disappear as the vendor no longer supports it. Windows 2000 already dominates the Windows server landscape, and that domination will last another couple of years. So, lengthy coverage of Windows 2000 was essential to this book. This chapter goes into the basics of the Windows 2000 Server operating system, its various flavors (such as Windows 2000 Advanced Server and Windows 2000 Datacenter Server), and some basics on the Active Directory. Without an understanding of the Active Directory, your disk management skills are not going to get you very far on Windows 2000.

Chapter 14 is all about the main Windows desktop system of today — XP. Why have a chapter on XP if this book is more about server systems and server disks? Quite simply, it is impossible to talk about disk management without also getting into the desktop side of the equation. System administrators dealing with server disks must know all about XP and XP disk management, as they are going to encounter a lot of machines running the XP operating system. This chapter covers the essentials of the XP operating system, what is new, what is good about it and not so good, and how to manage it.

Chapter 15 covers upcoming developments. By the time you read this text, many of the items covered will already be in general release. Windows Server 2003 promises to add significantly to the gains made by Windows 2000 and certainly offers greater disk management capabilities than ever before. 64-bit computing will take a few years to become commonplace, but eventually 32-bit systems will become a thing of the past, as 16-bit systems are today. The chapter also investigates where Microsoft is going over the next few years in terms of server and desktop operating systems.

Chapter 16 covers an essential area of disk management that is given scant attention — asset management. Many organizations today have tens of thousands of hard drives and hundreds of applications running, yet they have no idea what machine runs what type of disk, what software is where, what version is running, or how all of this ties in to current licensing purchases. This subject, then, is not only an essential element of disk management, but it is also a vital organization basic when it comes to protecting an enterprise against attack from policing agencies that are increasingly on the prowl. Just last year, the Business Software Alliance levied big fines amounting to tens of millions of dollars.

Chapter 17 covers the ins and outs of distributing software in heterogeneous environments. Software deployment, or the lack of it, is actually one of the biggest sources of weakness in today's networks. A threat emerges and a patch comes out, but only a small percentage of companies actually distribute the patch in a timely fashion. This chapter, then, covers the threat and the steps that must be taken to avert it.

Chapter 18 asks such questions as: How prepared are you to meet the disk needs of the future in order to keep up with storage demands? Where exactly is the industry going and how big can disks get? Will disks be around forever? This chapter investigates what is on the disk management horizon and perhaps just beyond.

How To Read This Book

The chapters have been laid out in a general sequence that should make sense for most readers; however, they have also been written in such a way that if you want to find out about a specific subject, you can go into the relevant chapter and read it without much reference to earlier material. In whatever way you read it, though, heed this point: Make sure you know the meaning of the basic words being used. Contrary to common belief, it is bad practice to try to figure out word meanings from the general context. You will get it wrong more than half the time and end up with an incorrect idea. So, use the glossary at the back and crack open a dictionary or computer dictionary when necessary to clear up the definition of terms being used. That is the surest way to guarantee full comprehension.

Good reading!

Introduction

This section discusses the explosion in drive size, overall storage capacity, and why it is more imperative than ever to take charge of server disks and disk management.

Taking Hard Disks for Granted

Stripping away the tremendous complexity that can exist in regard to disks, the basic purpose of disks is very simple — to store data. That is exactly what hard disks have been doing since the 1950s when IBM worked out how to store 100 K on a 12-inch platter. This apparently tame event was actually a serious breakthrough, as it marked a move away from the cumbersome punch cards that had previously been the standard medium for data storage. Yet, despite the enormous expansion in disk capacity over the past fifty years, disks largely tend to be taken for granted. For many they are sort of a "black box" item. They spin away, buried inside little beige boxes that are usually gathering dust under desks or hidden in server closets. Most system managers hope they keep on going until it is time to replace all the hardware for the latest batch of bigger and better machines. In most people's opinion, disks are the last thing they want to worry about. And, anyway, if something does go wrong, you can just put in a new one ... right?

The Disk Is the Bottleneck

This out-of-sight, out-of-mind attitude toward disks, however, may be misguided. Consider the mechanics of disks with regard to one very important factor — system performance. A 2-GHz CPU means 2 billion operations per second. RAM operates at 20 to 30 million operations per second, sometimes faster. Now factor in the hard disk. Good ones take about 5 milliseconds to access data — that is only 200 operations per second (Exhibit 1). Some can

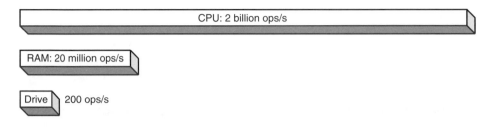

Exhibit 1   Relative Speed of Components

go faster, but not much faster. The point is that poor disk maintenance and disk management can mean that big powerful systems are held up badly by the sluggardly nature of the hard disk. So, it makes sense to know about disks and to be able to take action to avoid disks becoming a bigger bottleneck than they already are.

Disks Do Fail

After all, disks do fail. When an important one fails, IT has to scramble to replace it, while trying desperately to recover some, if not all, of the data, and this scenario plays out far more often than some manufacturers would like you to believe. A survey by San Jose-based Survey.com of 1293 IT staff and business executives, for example, revealed that the majority had experienced computer downtime in the previous year due to disk drive failure, and 30.3 percent of the time the computer was down for more than 24 hours. In addition to impacting IT staff and employees, one third of respondents said that these failures shut out customers. Thus, as well as the cost of the disk and labor, one must also factor in lost user time and the amount of business lost when customers are impacted by the failure. This survey discovered that most system administrators managed up to 500 disks on their Windows NT or Windows 2000 servers. The main actions performed to manage and protect data on the hard drive are backup, defragmentation, and hard drive replacement. When asked for the top problem with disks, most system administrators said drive failure and crashes, followed by running out of disk space.

Storage Explosion

This situation is made even more serious by the explosion in demand for disk space. According to META Group, Inc. (Stamford, Connecticut), storage capacity experienced 60 to 80 percent growth in 2002 and was expected to show annual growth rate continuing through 2006. Over the past year, in fact, more data has been recorded by mankind than in the entire rest of our history. To meet this demand, technology is utilizing two approaches: designing larger and larger disks and making it far easier to use more of them. The capacity of individual disk drives has already surpassed 180 GB, and IT research firm

Gartner Group (Stamford, Connecticut) foresees it hitting 1.44 TB in two years. Recent developments support the belief that bigger drives and more capacity are trends that will continue for quite some time. An industry group consisting of the likes of Maxtor, Microsoft, and Hewlett-Packard has announced a new ATA interface standard called "Big Drives" that allows drives to scale up to 144 petabytes. Seagate Technologies has also developed technology that permits a single 3.5-inch platter to hold up to 125 GB, three times the current level. And, the release of Microsoft's 64-bit Windows operating system ups the ante by making it possible to manage up to 16 TB of addressable virtual memory.

In addition to more and bigger disks, they are also being compressed into smaller and smaller spaces in terms of the number of disks per square server rack. The big original equipment manufacturers (OEMs), including Dell, Hewlett-Packard, IBM, and Sun, have followed the lead of, for example, nStor Technologies, Inc. (San Diego, California) in producing rack-dense servers. Take the case of the Compaq QuickBlade, which allows enterprises to fit 200 to 300 servers in a single rack, rather than the usual 42 servers.

Desktop Disks

It is important to note, though, that these trends are not limited to just the server market. A friend still uses my old desktop from five years ago, complete with its 500-MB drive, and it works just fine for what she uses it for — e-mail and word processing. These days, though, some desktop drives can exceed 100 GB, and multiple drives are becoming more and more common, so what is the upshot of this hard drive explosion? Manufacturing quality is hard pressed to keep up with the explosion in the sheer number of hard disks deployed and the quantity of data they hold. A recent white paper from a hard drive vendor was frank enough to say that the increase in the number of drives has resulted in a dilution of overall system reliability. It goes on to state that given the growth in disk sizes, each potential drive failure now puts more data at risk. So, ensuring the reliability of each drive has become more important than ever.

Neglect disks and disk management, then, at your peril. In today's disk intensive world, it is vital for organizations to take care of the basics of managing space quotas, monitoring disk performance, organizing disks and partitions properly, planning for future storage needs, taking care of backups, having an adequate Disaster Recovery Plan, and keeping disk I/O low by keeping volumes free of fragmentation. And that is what this book is all about. It will not turn you into an expert in every aspect and activity of disk management or hardware maintenance, but it will certainly give you a good overview of the subject and enough familiarity to make more qualified decisions when it comes to the overall health of your server disks and how you should best go about managing them.

Chapter 1

Hard Disks and How They Are Organized

While disk drives have been around since the 1950s, like anything else the technology keeps evolving. As a result, the assortment of options on the market available for data storage is expanding. Selecting the best disk drive for any particular operation and keeping it running at its best require an understanding of the hardware components, as well as how the data is stored and the terminology used by the manufacturers in describing their products. Only then can a correct comparison be made. This chapter provides details about the basic components and architecture of the hard disk and methods to improve its performance.

An understanding of the basic components of the hard disk and how they operate together — as well as the different paradigms for storing data and factors affecting disk performance — makes it easier to select the optimum storage solution for a particular project or installation. Following is a discussion of the basics of hard disks, including their physical components, how the data is stored, and factors that should be considered when comparing disk performance. Also examined are several tried and tested strategies that will help to improve overall drive performance.

Hardware Components of the Hard Drive

Any hard drive has several major components. Below, we briefly outline the core components; other items, such as cabling and connectors, are not covered here.

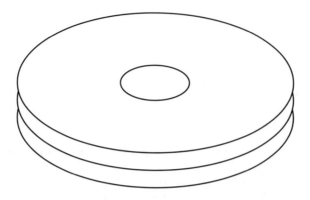

Exhibit 1   Platters

Platters

While the terms *hard drive* and *hard disk* are used interchangeably, hard drives typically contain multiple disks, or platters, stacked on top of each other (Exhibit 1). Personal computer (PC) hard drives generally have one to five platters, while servers will have up to a dozen. (The first disk drive, IBM's RAMAC, had a stack of 50 24-inch platters, each holding 100 K.)

The platter is the element that actually stores the data. It consists of a substrate coated with magnetic media. The substrate, made out of a nonmagnetic material, is there to act as a rigid support for the magnetic media. Traditionally, alloys made of aluminum have been used for hard drives, but to meet the demands of higher performance drives the industry is gradually transitioning toward the use of glass, magnesium, and other substances that provide greater rigidity, smoothness, and overall thermal stability. Switching to these newer materials allows manufacturers to create thinner disks and, perhaps more importantly in the long run, to operate them at higher speeds.

On top of the substrate goes a coating of magnetic media. Originally, this was a thin layer (less than 1 micron) of iron oxide. More recently, however, manufacturers have been replacing this by applying an even thinner coating of magnetic material using vacuum deposition, the same process used in manufacturing computer chips. The magnetic layer is then covered by a protective layer of carbon and a lubrication layer to prevent damage in case the head comes in contact with the platter surface. In most cases, both sides of the platter are coated with magnetic media. Why? The goal in coating both sides is to increase the "areal density" of the platter — the amount of data that can be stored in a given amount of space. Increasing areal density is what has continuously increased the capacity and brought down the prices of storage. A 3.5-inch floppy, for example, is the same size as the typical hard disk platter, but hard disk platters typically hold about 30,000 times as much data — 40 gigabytes (GB) — due to greater areal density, and this capacity will certainly increase even further in the coming years.

In 2001, for example, Seagate Technology demonstrated a drive with an areal density of 100 gigabits (Gb) per square inch. Such disks would make it

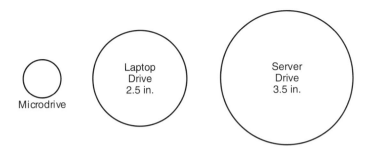

Exhibit 2   Disk Sizes

possible to store 125 GB of capacity on a single 3.5-inch platter. While drives built using that technology were not commercially available at the time of this writing, in June 2003 Western Digital released a 250-GB drive with over 80 GB per platter. It is only a matter of time before 125-GB disks are widely available on the market.

Interestingly, as areal density has increased, the size of platters has dropped. The typical server and workstation now have drives with a nominal 3.5-inch form factor, and the platters themselves are about 3.74 inches. This configuration has several advantages. Smaller platters are more rigid that larger ones, allowing the read/write heads to float closer to the surface. Also, the disks can spin faster, resulting in more rapid data access. High-performance drives, with speeds of 10,000 to 15,000 rotations per minute (rpm), achieve this speed by using even smaller disks (2.5 to 3.0 inches), thus trading lower storage capacity for quicker data access. Laptops, for example, typically utilize 2.5-inch platters, and the platter in IBM's Microdrive, which is used in devices such as digital cameras, is a mere 1 inch yet holds up to 1 GB (Exhibit 2).

Spindle/Motor

The platters are attached at the center to a spindle that is directly attached to the shaft of the motor. No belts or gears are used, as they could result in slippage and rotational speed variability; instead, the motors use a closed-loop feedback system to precisely control the speed.

Shock and vibration can cause the read/write heads to slap the disk surface, resulting in lost data and other damage, which is why spindle motors are specifically designed for minimal vibration. Even so, vibration is still a problem for manufacturers, one that worsens as rotational speeds increase. Newer rack-dense server installations, for instance, are beginning to experience vibration-related hard drive problems.

Fortunately, vibration is less of an issue in server installations thanks to some recent technological breakthroughs. In July 2002, for example, IBM released a new technology called Rotational Vibration Safeguard (RVS), which is designed to improve performance in large disk arrays by sensing the direction and intensity of the vibration on a disk and canceling it out. The first product to use RVS is IBM's Ultrastar 146Z10, a 148-GB drive running at 10,000 rpm.

While servers and workstations do occasionally suffer damage from shock, it is particularly a problem for portable devices. Mobile disks address this issue by adding cushioning to absorb and minimize impact, by stiffening components (including the spindle motor and head arms), and through design changes such as the use of smaller platters.

Head–Actuator Assembly

The head–actuator assembly consists of four principal components: the actuator, the arms, the sliders, and the read/write heads. The actuator is the device that moves the arms containing the read/write heads across the platter surface in order to store or retrieve information. While early disk drives used a stepper motor, and floppy drives still do, hard drives require something more accurate. Because platters now contain as many as 30,000 tracks per inch, precise location control is essential for locating positions on the disks. This is complicated by the fact that, given the tight tolerances involved, thermal expansion and contraction of components causes slight shifts in the location of the data. Today's actuators, therefore, are much more advanced than even recent predecessors. They consist of an electromagnetic positioning device coupled with a feedback servo mechanism to ensure that the heads are properly aligned to the disks.

The head arms move between the platters in order to store and access the data; however, it is important to understand that they all move together as a group, rather than each moving independently. At the end of each arm is a head slider. The slider is a block of material that holds the read/write head and acts as an airfoil to keep it positioned at the precise height above the surface of the platter. The lighter the arm and slider, the easier it is for the actuator to move them to the correct location, thus resulting in faster data access.

The read/write head converts the electronic 0s and 1s into the magnetic fields on the disk. Each arm used to have a single read/write head, but separate heads are now available to perform the reading and writing as distinct functions. The write head is the same type as used in earlier designs, but the read head is far more sensitive. From a design and manufacturing standpoint, this means that weaker magnetic fields can be used so that the data can be packed much more tightly together.

Logic Board

To run the various components that comprise the modern hard drive, disk drives contain their own logic boards. Mounted on these boards are a microprocessor, memory chips, and many other more minor components. The logic board itself is there to control the disk rotational speed and to direct the actuator in all its motions. In addition, it performs the process of transferring data from the computer to the magnetic fields on the disk. (This data is encoded rather than being a straight one-to-one translation due to the differing properties of electricity and magnetism.) One function that can lead to improved performance, particularly with servers, is optimizing the order in

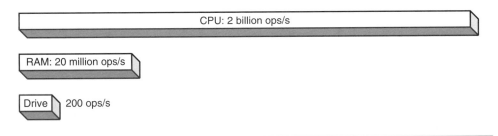

Exhibit 3   Relative Speed of Components

which data is retrieved in order to minimize the head movement and improve access time. This feature is less critical with workstations.

Cache

Even though disk drives are much faster than they used to be, they are still much slower than other components in the computer (Exhibit 3). Compared with the central processing unit (CPU) and random-access memory (RAM), the disk is a severe performance bottleneck in a computer. Even a high-speed server drive has a seek time of over 4 ms, which means it is able to perform fewer than 250 operations per second. While this speed is impressive relative to what used to be available, it is still way too slow when processors are running at over 2 gigahertz (GHz). A way to speed up operations is to store the most recently accessed data in memory; therefore, drives now come with several megabytes of cache.

Controller

In addition to the logic board contained in the drive itself, today's disks have controllers. These can come as either a controller card or an integrated controller on the motherboard.

SCSI versus ATA

Now that the basic components of the modern hard drive have been examined, it is time to take a look at the two main standards that exist for hard drives. Two different sets of interface standards have been developed for hard drives: advanced technology attachment (ATA) storage interface and small computer system interface (SCSI). (ATA is also known as IDE: integrated drive electronics.) ATA drives are generally less expensive and more common, while SCSI devices cost more and tend to be utilized for higher performance applications. However, within each camp is a move to change this situation. SCSI drives are finding uses in less high-end applications as their price comes down. Similarly, advancements such as serial ATA have allowed the ATA to move into high-performance disk drive applications.

Exhibit 4   SCSI Standards

Name	Maximum Bus Speed (megabytes per second)	Bus Width	Maximum Devices per Connection
SCSI-1	5	8	8
Fast SCSI	10	8	8
Fast Wide SCSI	20	16	16
Ultra SCSI	20	8	8
Wide Ultra SCSI	40	16	8
Ultra2 SCSI	40	8	8
Wide Ultra2 SCSI	80	16	16
Ultra3 SCSI	160	16	16
Ultra320 SCSI	320	16	16

Source: SCSI Trade Association (STA), San Francisco, California.

ATA Drives

"ATA" stands for AT Attachment, as it was first used for the IBM PC/AT computer ("AT" was short for "Advanced Technology" and was first used by IBM when it released the PC/AT in 1984). Other variants of the AT name include IDE (Integrated Disk Electronics), EIDE (Enhanced IDE), and DMA (Direct Memory Access), as well as Ultra ATA, Ultra DMA, ATA-66, and numerous other permutations of these terms. Such ATA drives were the first to incorporate a controller into the drive itself, rather than just having one on the motherboard, hence the name IDE. Originally, the drives sat on a card that was then plugged into an expansion slot, but due to various problems they were later put into a drive bay. ATA drives use a 16-bit interface, and each channel can support two drives. ATA standards are developed by Technical Committee T13 (www.t13.org), which is part of the InterNational Committee on Information Technology Standards (INCITS) and are published by the American National Standards Institute (ANSI). Ultra ATA provides for data transfer rates of 33, 66, or 100 megabytes (MB) per second. In 2001, a serial ATA interface was announced, and devices using this type of connection will be available before the end of 2003 according to the latest estimates.

Small Computer Systems Interface Drives

While ATA drives are primarily used for PCs, Small Computer Systems Interface (SCSI) is used more broadly for a wide variety of devices, not just hard drives. It is possible to use more than one SCSI device on a single interface. Like ATA, SCSI is published by ANSI, but it has been developed by INCITS' Technical Committee T10, rather than T13. An abundance of SCSI standards currently exists (see Exhibit 4), and new developments in the SCSI field show great promise. An industry association known as the Serial Attached SCSI Working Group is working on a specification for serial attached SCSI, which

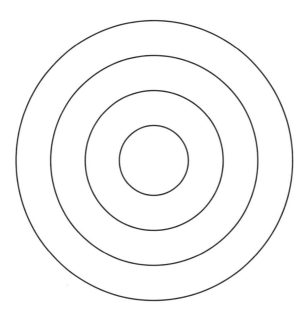

Exhibit 5   Tracks Are Concentric

will combine the serial ATA interface with some of the features of SCSI. Devices meeting this standard are expected by 2004 or thereabouts. The bottom line is that for workstations an ATA drive is preferable due to its lower cost, but for servers and mission-critical applications a SCSI drive is recommended. Even if the specs on ATA and SCSI drives seem similar, they are built for different types of usages.

What Is on a Disk

To develop an understanding of the need for formatting, this review now takes a look at what is on a disk in terms of tracks, cylinders, sectors, clusters, and extents.

- *Tracks* — A track is a concentric ring on the disk where data is stored. Hard drive tracks differ from compact disc (CD) tracks, which follow a spiral, as CDs are designed for continuous play and the head moves across the disk at a constant speed. Hard disks, on the other hand, are designed for random access to the data on a single track so concentric rings work better (Exhibit 5).
- *Cylinders* — Platters currently contain in excess of 30,000 tracks. On drives that contain multiple platters, all the tracks on all the platters that are at the same distance from the center are referred to as a cylinder. The data from all the tracks in the cylinder can be read by simply switching between the different heads, which is much faster than physically moving the head between different tracks on a single disk.
- *Sectors* — The tracks are further broken down into sectors, which are the smallest units of storage on a disk. With *x*86-based systems, the sector size

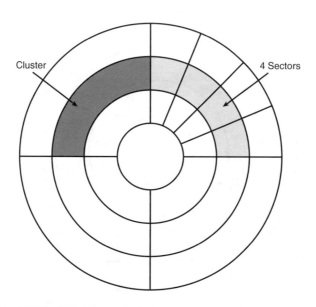

Exhibit 6   Sectors and Clusters

is set at 512 bytes. With earlier disk designs, each track had the same
number of sectors, but that is no longer true. Because a track at the edge
of a disk is about twice as long as one toward the center, it can potentially
hold twice as much data. In a system referred to as *zoned bit recording*,
a larger number of sectors are located on the outer tracks and progressively
fewer toward the center which results in higher storage capacity on a disk.
Because the outer tracks hold more sectors and the disk rotates at a
constant speed, data can be read faster from the outer tracks than the
inner ones. For this reason, it is generally better to store the most frequently
accessed data on the outer tracks (Note, however, that efforts to adapt this
technique to optimize file placement on disks have largely failed; particularly in an enterprise setting, efforts to place server files at specific points
are unworkable due to the presence of RAID arrays, virtual volumes, and
other advances that render file placement largely a lottery, a topic covered
in more detail in Chapter 8).

■ *Clusters* — Sectors are grouped together into clusters or allocation units
(Exhibit 6). As far as the operating system is concerned, all the sectors in
the cluster are a single unit. How does this work out on Windows operating
systems? When using Microsoft's Windows New Technology File System
(NTFS; available in NT, Windows 2000, and XP), the default cluster size
depends on the size of the partition. A partition (logical section of a drive)
that is 512 MB or smaller would have clusters each consisting of a single
512-byte sector, while a partition over 2 GB would have clusters consisting
of eight 4096-byte sectors. When creating the file system for a partition,
the administrator can create cluster sizes up to 64 kilobytes (KB). Setting
the clusters too small for the type of files on the disk results in the files
being split among too many clusters. Setting the size too large reduces
this problem but reduces the actual storage capacity of the disk. If a file
is smaller than the cluster, the rest of the storage capacity of that cluster

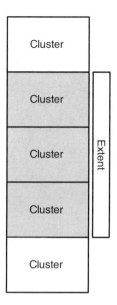

Exhibit 7   Extent

is unavailable. If the file is larger than a single cluster, the rest of the data is stored in one or more additional clusters.

- *Extents* — A set of contiguous clusters storing a single file, or part of a file, is called an *extent*. It is best to keep the number of extents for any file to a minimum, as each extent requires a separate input/output operation (I/O). Reducing the number of extents in a file using a process known as *defragmentation* greatly improves performance (Exhibit 7).

Disk Performance Definitions and Metrics

Some further definitions are provided regarding the performance of disks and their basic duties:

- *Seek* — To locate data on a specific part of a disk or to be in the correct position to retrieve data, program instructions etc., the head must move from one track to another. This action is referred to as a seek.
- *Seek time* — The time it takes for the head to move from one track to another is the seek time. It is the most important factor in determining the speed of a disk and can be broken down into three elements: (1) the time it takes to move the head from a stationary position until it is moving at full speed; (2) the time expended in moving the head from one track to another; and (3) the time required to stop the head. Note that if a file is fragmented, many additional seeks are necessary to open the file. Also note that, in its truest sense, seek time really only means the time it takes for the head to move across the disk perpendicular to the tracks (Exhibit 8).
- *Rotational latency* — It is much quicker to access data that is immediately under the head, in which case all the head has to do is move toward or away from the center of the disk to access it. If, however, the head has

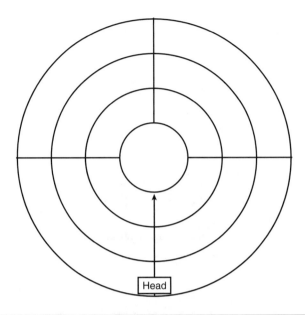

Exhibit 8   Seek Time

just passed the point on the disk where the data resides, it has to rotate almost a complete circle in order to access the data. This situation is known as *rotational latency*. For a disk spinning at 7500 rpm, it takes a little over 8 ms for the head to complete a 360-degree rotation on the disk; therefore, rotational latency can vary from 0 to 8 ms on such a disk and averages around 4 ms.

- *Access time* — A combination of seek time plus rotational latency. This gives the time it takes to access a cluster. Sometimes, people use the term *seek time* interchangeably with *access time*.

To apply these concepts, consider Maxtor's DiamondMax 80, which is touted as a high-performance drive and has a rotation speed of 5400 rpm. Seek time from track to track is 1 ms. When rotational latency is factored in, it takes the head an average of about 10 ms per seek, but it can take as much as 20 ms. Seagate's Cheetah drive spins at 15,000 rpm and has an average seek time (track to track) of 0.2 to 0.4 ms, with an average rotational latency of 2.0 ms. On average, a seek takes 3.6 to 4.0 ms. Interestingly, when you compare these numbers to the hard drives of ten years ago, the pace of advance is *much* slower than that for other components such as CPUs and RAM.

Disk Formatting

As discussed above, the substrate of the hard disk is coated so as to retain data; however, for data to be stored on a disk it must first be formatted. This is a three-step process. The first action, *low-level formatting* (LLF), is usually done by the manufacturer. LLF designates the tracks and sectors on a disk by recording markers on the surface that show where they start. After LLF of the disk, the second step is *partitioning* (or *initializing*). Partitioning reserves a part of a disk for a certain function, and the operating system considers each partition as a separate drive. Users who want the entire disk to be a single partition must specify just that. When using dynamic disks in UNIX or Windows 2000, the term *volume* is used rather than partition. The third formatting step, *high-level formatting*, consists of putting the file structure on the disk (file systems are covered in more depth in Chapter 2).

Grouping Disks: Stripe Sets and RAID

While a PC normally just has a single disk, in enterprise applications separate physical disks are frequently grouped logically for added performance, size, and reliability. Disks can be grouped in several ways to achieve this:

- *Stripe sets* — This approach involves using several disk drives and splitting the data between these drives to improve performance. Because the hard drives are slower than other system elements, using multiple drives speeds up the data access by allowing simultaneous access to parts of the file from more than one drive.
- *Logical drives* — Drives can also be grouped logically so that the operating system treats them as a single drive. For example, three 40-GB drives could be combined logically so that the operating system considers them as a single 120-GB drive.
- *Disk duplexing* — Two disks are operated by separate controllers and the data to both disks is simultaneously recorded for reliability and perfor-mance. When one disk goes down, the other can still be used for failover. A performance boost can be gained by setting it up so that a seek operation is sent to whichever disk offers the quickest turnaround at that time.

In addition, the various Redundant Arrays of Independent Disks (RAID) layers can be used. RAID is basically a disk subsystem that increases performance or provides some means of fault tolerance. The subsystem is composed of two or more disk drives as well as a controller. RAID is used mainly on servers but is now starting to find applications in PCs, as well.

Some of the various RAID levels are:

- *RAID level 0* — Uses striping for added performance but has no data redundancy. RAID-0 writes data to more than one drive to speed the process. Information is striped to one disk and then to others, back and forth, so the data is distributed among multiple disks. If one drive fails, the data is lost, as no redundancy is built into RAID-0
- *RAID level 1* — Uses full disk mirroring; that is, the exact same data is put on two or more disks. Read speeds are higher than for a single disk, as more than one disk can be read at the same time. Write speeds, however, are the same as for a single disk, as all the data is written to each of the disks. RAID-1 is expensive in that twice the storage space must be used to achieve redundancy. In comparison, RAID-3 and RAID-5 are less expensive.

- *RAID level 2* — Uses striping for performance and stores error checking codes (ECCs), which allow data errors to be detected and corrected; this is a relatively rarely used method.
- *RAID level 3* — Combines the speed advantage of striping, as for RAID-0, but with the addition of redundancy. Rather than doing full mirroring as in RAID-1, however, it takes the data from two disks, XORs it, and places the result on a third disk. In this way, it requires half as many disks as RAID-1 to store the redundant data. The acronym XOR stands for "exclusive–OR": A RAID system takes one bit from each of the two data disks. If both bits are the same (i.e., both 0 or both 1), it will record a 0 on the redundant disk; if the two bits are different (i.e., one is 0 and the other 1), it records a 1. This is also known as *parity.*
- *RAID level 4* — Does not use striping; stores parity bits on a separate disk. Like RAID-2, this method is rarely used.
- *RAID level 5* — Although similar to RAID-3 in terms of striping and replication, RAID-5 differs in that the redundant data is interspersed with the user data on the same disks rather than being stored on separate disks. The read speed is similar to that for RAID-0 and RAID-3, but the write speed is slower because both the user data and the redundant data must be written to the same disks. This is the most widely used RAID level
- *RAID level 10* — Actually RAID-1,0, in that it utilizes both striping (RAID-0) and mirroring (RAID-1), RAID-10 combines the improved performance of striping with the fault tolerance of mirroring.

The levels of RAID most commonly used for reliability are levels 1, 3, and 5. Several other RAID levels exist in addition to the ones listed above. Full specifications on all the RAID levels are available from the RAID Advisory Board.

Evaluating Disks

Having a good grasp of the different types of drives allows a user to make a better decision regarding which disk to buy for a particular application. All of the above data factors into this decision, but such choices basically boil down to the elements of speed, capacity, and reliability. Speed consists of seek time and rotational latency. As discussed previously, seek time is how long it takes for the read/write head to move to the correct track. A lighter head/actuator assembly, greater areal density, and smaller disk size all contribute to reducing seek time. Rotational latency is how long it takes for the disk to then spin to the spot where the desired information is stored, so it basically is a function of the disk revolutions per minute. Drive software can also improve the data access speed by caching the I/O requests and performing them in an order that reduces head movement. Keeping files defragmented, however, can have a greater positive impact than any of these factors. Even if, for example, the disk revolutions per minute are tripled, such an improvement does not begin to compensate for having to move the head to dozens or even thousands of locations to retrieve all the bits of the file. What about disk capacity? Capacity depends on areal density and platter size. The actual usable capacity can be reduced, however, by using incorrect cluster sizes, as discussed.

Mean Time between Failures

Reliability is expressed in the *mean time between failures* (MTBF) rating of a disk and can run anywhere from 300,000 hours to over 1 million. This figure does not mean that a disk is expected to last 1 million hours (114 years of 24/7 operation). As explained in the Seagate Technology Paper 338.1, *Estimating Drive Reliability in Desktop Computers and Consumer Electronic Systems*, the MTBF for a drive is defined as the number of power-on hours (POH) per year divided by the first-year annualized failure rate (AFR). In essence, this is an approximation for small failure rates and is intended to represent only a first-year MTBF. The figure does not indicate how long the drive will last, but it does reflect the odds that it will break down in the first year of operation. The higher the number, the less chance it will fail that year. This is explained in greater detail in Chapter 3.

While in an ideal world you would want to go for the highest possible rating on all factors, in reality tradeoffs are involved. For example, a higher rotational speed means quicker data access, but that speed boost is often achieved by reducing platter size and lowering capacity, so perhaps installing a higher disk cache would be better. Paying to get the highest possible MTBF rating might be a waste of money for a workstation that has all of its critical files stored on a server or for a single disk in a mirrored array that can easily be hot-swapped with a replacement if it goes bad. But, by knowing all the different components that go into disk performance and what effect they have on the overall picture, users can intelligently balance the features to get the best mix for their own operations.

Chapter 2

Windows File Systems

Windows server and desktop operating systems support several file systems. Although it would be simplest to have just one file system operating in an organization, most enterprises end up running several. This chapter explains the different types of file systems utilized in various Windows operating systems, the advantages and disadvantages of each, and how to get the most out of them.

Enterprise Windows

While Windows wrapped up control of the desktop market some years ago, it still has a long way to go before it achieves complete domination in the corporate server market. This is why the last few years have seen a rise in the number of server offerings from Microsoft as it moves toward higher end computing. Windows 2000 was a particularly important release as it represented a major improvement over Windows NT in terms of enterprise stability and scalability. Windows 2000 launched the Active Directory (AD), the Microsoft enterprise directory offering. The Windows Advanced Server Limited Edition offers 64-bit processing with up to 16 terabytes (TB) of addressable memory. At the high end of the Microsoft operating system spectrum, the Windows 2000 Datacenter Server with SQL Server 2000 supports up to 32 processors. Thus, Windows can now compete well in the mid-price server market, if not at the highest end. Along the way the company has also been upgrading its file systems to add the additional features, reliability, and security needed by corporate users. In this chapter, we look at the various types of file systems now supported by Windows.

Magnetic Disk Systems

Windows supports two file systems for magnetic disks: FAT (File Allocation Table) and NTFS (New Technology File System). The latter is the preferred system for Windows NT 4.0, 2000, XP, and Windows Server 2003, but these operating systems still support the older FAT file system for several reasons:

- Floppy disk use
- Backward compatibility
- Use with older versions of Windows in multi-boot systems

To take full advantage of the security, disk quota, and other features of the more recent versions of Windows, however, NTFS must be used.

File Allocation Table (FAT)

The File Allocation Table, or FAT, is the part of the file system that keeps track of where data is stored on the disk. The directory list, which contains such items as the file name, extension, and date, points to the FAT entry where the file starts. FAT was initially used with DOS, and the File Allocation Table file system now has three different versions: FAT12, FAT16, and FAT 32. The numbers used in these versions designate the number of bits used to identify a cluster.

- *FAT12* — The earliest version the file system, FAT12 allows a partition to contain up to 4096 (2^{12}) clusters. Because it supports clusters of one to sixteen sectors, the maximum partition size is 32 MB. Windows 2000 only uses FAT12 for floppy disks and for partitions of 16 MB or smaller.
- *FAT16* — FAT16 provides a 16-fold expansion in the number of clusters it identifies, supporting volumes containing 65,536 (2^{16}) clusters. It also expands the maximum cluster size to 128 sectors (64 KB) and maximum volume size to 4 GB.
- *FAT32* — To address the need for even larger storage capacity, Microsoft introduced FAT32 with Windows 95 OSR2. Following the pattern of the earlier versions of the file system, it uses 32 bits to designate a cluster; however the last four bits are reserved. Each volume, therefore, can contain up to nearly 270 million (2^{28}) clusters, which theoretically translates into an 8-TB volume composed of 32-KB clusters. In practice, however, while Windows 2000 will manage larger volumes created in other operating systems, it limits the size of new FAT32 volumes to 32 GB, as the file system grows quite inefficient beyond that size. To create a larger volume, the system can be dual-booted into either Windows 95 or 98, the volume established using that OS, and then the volume managed using Windows 2000.

The above types of FAT file systems have key architectural elements in common. Several sections actually comprise a FAT volume, starting with the boot sector. Following this are the File Allocation Table itself and, for protection,

Boot Sector	File Allocation Table	Duplicate FAT	Root Directory	Other Directories and All Files of the Volume

---

Exhibit 1   File Allocation Table (FAT) Volume

a duplicate File Allocation Table. Next comes the root directory and finally any other directories and files of the volume. FAT32 also stores a duplicate copy of the boot sector for added reliability (Exhibit 1).

The first three bytes in a FAT boot sector contain a jump instruction telling the CPU that the next several bytes are not executable. After that is an eight-byte original equipment manufacturer (OEM) identifier (ID) that identifies the operating system that formatted the volume. Next comes the BIOS Parameter Block (BPB), which lists the parameters of the volume. These include such items as the number of bytes per sector and sectors per cluster, number of reserved sectors, number of File Allocation Table copies (generally two), number of possible entries in the root directory, and number of sectors in the volume.

Each cluster in the volume has an entry in the File Allocation Table that indicates whether the cluster is bad, whether it contains a file, and, if so, whether it is the last cluster for that file. If the cluster contains a file that is continued in another cluster, the File Allocation Table entry will contain the number of that cluster. If the entire cluster is contained in a single cluster, or if that cluster is the final one for a file spanning multiple clusters, the entry will contain the value "0xfff", which indicates that it is the last cluster.

In FAT12 and FAT16, the root directory or root folder contains 512 entries, each one being 32 bytes. FAT32 permits an unlimited number of entries in the root directory, and that directory can be located anywhere on a hard disk. Each entry begins with the file name in 8.3 format (DOS format). Following this is the attribute byte, which contains six binary flags indicating if the file has been archived, if the entry is a directory or a file, if it is read-only, if it is a hidden file, if it is a system file, and if it is a volume label.

The next 11 bytes tell when the file was created, last accessed, and last modified. After these are 2 bytes identifying the location of the first cluster in the file (the locations of the rest of the clusters are stored in the File Allocation Table). The final entry is a 4-byte number giving the size of the file in bytes, yielding a maximum file size of 4 GB (2^{32}).

This root directory structure only natively supports file names using the 8.3 format. For long file names, it uses a truncated version of the file name (e.g., FILENA~1.EXE) for the main entry and assigns additional lines in the directory to list the long name using Unicode. Because the size of the root directory in FAT12 and FAT16 is limited, this reduces the total number of files or directories that can be listed in the root. This is not a problem with FAT32, however, as it does not have this directory-size limitation.

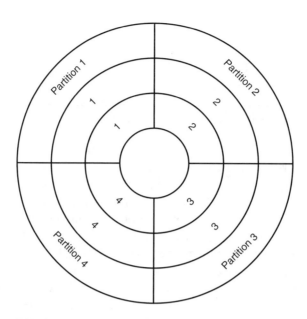

Exhibit 2 Partitions

New Technology File System (NTFS)

While each of the FAT versions represents an incremental improvement over its predecessor, NTFS takes a completely different approach to the way that data is organized as a result of Microsoft's desire to increase its share of the corporate marketplace. FAT was a very simple system that worked for PCs, but it lacked the management and security features necessary to compete with UNIX in a networked enterprise environment. The first attempt at a newer file system was the High Performance File System (HPFS) introduced with OS/2 Version 1.2. After the IBM/Microsoft partnership that created OS/2 fell apart, Microsoft created Windows NT, which incorporates some of the features of HPFS into its New Technology File System (NTFS). NTFS is the native file system for Windows NT 4.0, Windows 2000, and Windows XP operating systems. While these operating systems can operate with FAT, many of their features only work with NTFS, so NTFS should be used whenever possible. Fortunately, if one or more FAT partitions is running on one of these operating systems, it is a simple matter to convert them to NTFS without losing any data.

A log-based file system, NTFS addresses the reliability and recoverability problems of FAT. The clusters of a partition are numbered sequentially using a 64-bit logical cluster number (LCN). Theoretically, this system would allow access to 16 exabytes (16 billion GB), which far exceeds current storage needs. For now, Windows 2000 limits volumes to 128 TB, but later operating systems could take advantage of even larger storage capacities. Like FAT, it sets a default cluster size depending on the size of the partition, assigning a size of 4 KB for anything over 2 GB. Also like FAT, administrators can override the defaults and use a drop-down box to specify sizes up to 64 KB (Exhibit 2).

Partition Boot Sector	MFT	Duplicate MFT	File System Data

Exhibit 3   NTFS Partition

An NTFS partition is divided into four sectors: the Partition Boot sector, Master File Table, Filesystem Data, and a backup copy of the Master File Table. The two sections of the Partition Boot Sector occupy the first 16 sectors. The first section holds the BIOS Parameter Block, which contains information on the layout of the volume and the structure of the file system similar to what was discussed previously for FAT. The boot code to load Windows NT/ 2000/XP resides in the second section.

The next section contains the Master File Table (MFT). When creating an NTFS partition, the system allocates a block (the MFT Zone) that contains 12.5 percent of the capacity of the volume (Exhibit 3). This size is the amount considered necessary to support a volume with an average file size of 8 KB. If the volume will contain a large number of files in the 2- to 7-KB range, the size of the MFT Zone can be increased with the *fsutil behavior set mftzone* command. This command offers four options: setting 1 is the same as the default, setting 2 reserves 25 percent of the disk, setting 3 reserves 37.5 percent, and setting 4 reserves 50 percent. When the size of the MFT Zone is increased, NTFS does not immediately allocate additional space. But, when the original space allocated to the MFT Zone fills up, additional space will be allocated. Because this results in MFT fragmentation, thereby inhibiting performance, it is best to set the desired size before creating the volume. Keep in mind also that resizing the MFT Zone setting will affect all the NTFS volumes on the computer; it cannot be done for just a single volume.

The MFT consists of a series of 1-KB records, one for each file in the partition. The first 16 entries are reserved for the NTFS system files. Record 0 is the MFT itself, and the next 10 include a changes log file for system recovery, information about the volume, the index of the root folder, and a bitmap showing cluster allocation information. The final 5 files are reserved for future use. The MFT is followed by the non-system files of the volume and then by a backup copy of the MFT.

Two types of attributes — resident and non-resident — can be used to describe a record. Resident attributes are ones that fit within the MFT, while non-resident attributes are ones too large to fit in the MFT record. Each resident MFT record contains four types of attributes. The first, standard information, includes such file attributes as the archive bit (which indicates whether or not the file has been backed up) and time stamps that show when the file was created, last modified, and last accessed. The second attribute contains the file names; each file can have multiple names (for example, both a long and a short name), and both would be listed in this space (NTFS supports names up to 255 Unicode characters). The third, the Security Descriptor, contains the

Access Control List (ACL) data for the file. The final attribute, data, includes the data of the file itself; small files, under 1 K, can fit entirely within the MFT which speeds up access because the system does not have to first read the MFT to find the location of the desired file and then go fetch the file from elsewhere on the disk. Instead, it is all done in one rapid action.

Most files, however, are far too extensive to fit into the MFT record because the file itself is too large or the ACL is too big. In such a case, the data section of the record contains the locations in the main data portion of the volume where the file contents may be found. Each of these locations is defined by a virtual cluster number (VCN), logical cluster number (LCN), and number of clusters. The VCN is a sequential number relating to each extent of consecutive clusters on the disk that contain the file, and the LCN refers to the location of the first cluster of each extent. If, for example, the file was fragmented into four pieces, the MFT record would list four VCNs (1, 2, 3, 4). If the first extent begins on cluster 6097 and includes clusters 6098 and 6099, then the MFT would have VCN = 1, LCN = 6097, Number of Clusters = 3. The other extents would be similarly numbered. If the file becomes severely fragmented, additional records in the MFT will have to be used to list the additional extents.

Additional NTFS Features

In addition to supporting larger volumes than FAT, NTFS contains other features that make it better for corporate operations:

- *Reliability* — A drawback to using FAT is that if a computer goes down it can be difficult to repair the file system. For speedy recovery, NTFS maintains a log of every transaction that affects the file system. These actions are logged before they are performed. Then, when a problem occurs, any incomplete transactions can be completed or changes can be rolled back.
- *Mount Points* — All Windows versions assign a different drive letter to each partition or volume on a disk, a procedure that limits the number of accessible volumes to the 26 letters of the alphabet. Mount Points let the administrator attach other partitions to an empty directory within an already mounted NTFS volume. Rather than being limited to NTFS volumes, these additional volumes can also be using FAT16, FAT32, CDFS (CD-ROM File System), or UDF (Universal Disk Format), which expands the functionality of this feature.
- *Access Control* — The Security Descriptor function provides hierarchal access control for each file or directory in an NTFS volume. It is important to understand that the security features built into Windows NT/2000/XP work only with NTFS. If FAT is used instead, all security functionality is lost and the organization is at risk.
- *Disk Quotas* — NTFS permits assigning storage quotas on a per-user basis. It does this by tracking the Security ID (SID) of anyone who creates a file or directory. When the limit is exceeded, the system sends a "Disk Full" error report and logs it in the Event Log.
- *Encryption* — When the computer is running Windows 2000, NTFS includes Microsoft's Encrypting File System (EFS), which automatically encrypts and

decrypts files without user intervention. This is particularly useful for remote users, as laptops are frequently lost or stolen and one cannot rely on users to remember to encrypt their files.

These and other features are not available with FAT.

FAT versus NTFS

For most enterprise users, NTFS is the file system of choice. In those cases where there is some doubt, however, here is a summary of the key factors to take into account:

- *NTFS additional capabilities* — As discussed above, NTFS offers file access controls and permissions, as well as encryption.
- *Stability* — NTFS has much greater stability and resilience than FAT and allows users to roll back system states to earlier configurations after a crash. Having said that, FAT is stable enough for many users and conversion to NTFS is not easily reversed. Users who have a dual boot system that requires a FAT partition to run an earlier version of Windows will find it impossible to dispense with FAT without an OS upgrade.
- *Performance* — FAT has size limitations and restrictions that can sometimes lead to wasted disk space. NTFS tends to perform better, although it places more demands on memory and generally requires a larger amount of RAM than FAT does to run well. The better performance of NTFS shows up in such ways as speeding up searches through directories, which are much slower on FAT.
- *Partition size* — Today, with partitions growing to sizes larger than 32 GB, NTFS is essential, as FAT will not format partitions above that size. So, for large partitions, NTFS must be used; leave FAT alone.

Converting FAT to NTFS

Converting from FAT to NTFS is relatively simple to achieve and is something that users will need to know how to do, as some computer manufacturers ship systems preloaded with FAT32. Fortunately, Windows 2000 and Windows XP come with built-in utilities to help you with this. All the details are not provided here, as the topic is covered adequately elsewhere. Users can find out how to use these utilities in the Windows help files or just by typing "Converting FAT to NTFS" into a search engine, which will result in plenty of tips, cautions, and suggestions. Such a search may even uncover ways to convert NTFS back to FAT, although such pages are filled with cautions and warnings.

Optical Disk Formats

In addition to the magnetic disk formats, Windows 2000 also supports two different optical file formats: CDFS and UDF. The CD-ROM File System (CDFS) is based on ISO 9660, a read-only file system standard written by an industry group, High Sierra. The group got that name from its initial meeting in 1985 at Del Webb's High Sierra Hotel and Casino at Lake Tahoe, Nevada, where representatives of Apple, Microsoft, Sony, and others began cooperating on development of a non-proprietary file system format for CD-ROM. The initial standard was named after the group, but the International Organization for Standardization (ISO) requested that an international version of the standard be released. This version was formalized as ISO 9660 (Volume and File Structure of CD-ROM for Information Interchange). Macintosh, DOS, Windows, UNIX, and Linux all support the standard, which calls for 2048-byte physical sectors. Level 1 of CDFS, like MS-DOS, follows the 8.3 file name format. Directories are limited to 8-character names and 8 nested levels. Levels 2 and 3 permit longer file and directory names, up to 32 characters, and allow the use of lowercase letters. Microsoft developed an extension to ISO 9660, called Joliet, which is supported in Windows 95/98/2000/Me/NT4.0/.NET, as well as Macintosh and Linux. Joliet allows the use of Unicode characters in file names of up to 64 characters.

Universal Disk Format (UDF) is a later standard created in 1995 by the Optical Storage Technology Association and defined in ISO 13346. It permits 255-character names with a maximum path length of 1023 characters and can be used with CD-ROMs, CD-Rs, CD-RWs, and DVD-ROMs. While ISO 9660 calls for data to be written continuously to the disk, UDF utilizes packet writing. Windows 98 and later versions of Windows support the UDF format, although only for reading, not writing, files. To write to CDs or DVDs requires additional software.

Partitioning Strategies

With earlier file systems, partitioning was a means of avoiding the inherent size limits. Using a version of FAT on a large disk can still pose a problem, and partitioning is a way of addressing it. With NTFS supporting huge multidisk volumes, however, that is no longer a consideration. Other reasons to partition, however, include:

- *Multiple OS support* — This can include supporting multiple versions of Windows or adding a boot partition for Linux or another operating system.
- *Separating the operating system from the data files* — Putting these two in separate partitions can make it easier to administer them. Limiting access to the drive containing the operating system to those with administrative privileges, while letting users save and access the data files, can eliminate problems connected with unauthorized users accessing particular files.
- *Optimizing cluster sizes* — Having the properly sized clusters for the type of files can improve overall performance. When both large and small files reside on the same partition, it is difficult to determine the cluster size that optimizes performance. A large database or graphics file, for example, could benefit from using 64-KB clusters, as such a size would mean fewer

read/write operations and less fragmentation. A large number of text files, on the other hand, would do better with small clusters, as they would waste considerable space in a large cluster. Putting such files in separate partitions, with appropriate cluster sizes, would boost system performance for both types of operations.

Summary

In almost all cases, NTFS should be used in most enterprises, as it contains far more features and was designed specifically by Microsoft to add value to corporate systems. For Windows 2000, especially, NTFS should always be used to take full advantage of the security, disk quota, and many other benefits it offers.

Chapter 3

Hard Drive Reliability

Information technology (IT) departments are continually being asked to provide higher levels of uptime and reliability without increasing expenditures. One often overlooked way to fulfill these demands is to keep server, workstation, and laptop disk drives from crashing. This is becoming more difficult, however, as organizations strive to provide 24/7 service while being forced to extend equipment lifespan in the face of budget cuts. This chapter gives a basic rundown of the stats and surveys that exist on hard drive reliability, pointing out that drive failure is a far more serious problem than is commonly realized. It also investigates the consequences of failure these days and the various misconceptions regarding failure, particularly mean time between failures (MTBF). Most users think the MTBF statistic means that you will get 30 years of life out of every hard drive. Far from it. In addition to this misleading metric, the chapter covers the various systems and technologies designed to protect hard drives.

MTBF Explained

Given all the challenges facing IT departments, it is easy to become complacent about the subject of disk drive failure. Reading server spec sheets listing hard disk lifespan ratings in the hundreds of thousands of hours, one might assume that the drive will long outlast any use the organization may have for it. But, in actual fact, the alarming regularity of disk crashes in all organizations indicates a dangerous situation that cannot be ignored.

Many people, it turns out, have a misconception of what manufacturers mean when they provide the MTBF for their disks. MTBF, it turns out, can have two very different meanings. Some users assume it means "mean time *before* failure." If this definition actually applied, there would be no reason to worry. Most disks come with a 300,000- to 1,000,000-hour MTBF range;

many people who see this figure think that a disk with a 300,000-hour rating would run around the clock for the next 34 years before needing replacement. By the same token, a 1,000,000-hour disk would be expected to run for over a century.

Unfortunately, however, mean time before failure is not actually what the manufacturers are estimating. The correct definition of MTBF is mean time *between* failures, quite a different matter. According to Seagate Technology Paper 338.1, "Estimating Drive Reliability in Desktop Computers and Consumer Electronic Systems," Seagate estimates the mean time between failures for a drive as the number of power-on hours (POH) per year divided by the first-year annualized failure rate (AFR). This is a suitable approximation for small failure rates and is represented as a *first-year* MTBF. So what does that mean? MTBF relates only to the failure rate in the first year. Beyond that, the manufacturers really are promising nothing more than the usual three- to five-year warranty period that comes with any disk.

Now, of course, manufacturers are much too busy to do a full year of testing on a product before releasing it to market, so they take a batch of components and test them in a laboratory for a certain period, perhaps with a higher ambient temperature to accelerate the aging process. The actual tests themselves last only a few weeks. The aggregate number of hours that all the disks ran is divided by the number of disks that failed during the test, and the resulting numbers are run through certain formulas to estimate the MTBF.

As a comparison, an MTBF rating is similar to the J.D. Powers and Associates Initial Quality Survey to which automobile manufacturers refer in their advertising. The bottom line is that it is not based on real-world quality metrics. Similarly, the MTBF number obtained by manufacturer testing does not predict how long any one piece of hardware will last, but rather how many from a batch of disks are expected to fail within the first year. The higher the MTBF number, the fewer the predicted crashes. If, for example, an enterprise has 5,000 total workstations and server disks combined, with an average MTBF of 300,000 hours per the manufacturer's specs, it can be expected that one disk will fail every 60 hours during the first year — quite different from many people's perception of MTBF. If these boxes are running only 40 hours per week, that translates into a failure every one and a half weeks. But, when all the boxes are left on 24/7, one disk would fail, on average, every two and a half days. Now up the number of machines to 10,000, and about one disk will require fixing every day (Exhibit 1).

Remember, too, that this rating applies to only the first year. As the equipment gets older, particularly if someone is trying to stretch its usefulness beyond the first two or three years, disk failure rates rise alarmingly. At least the MTBF allows for comparison of the relative reliability between disks. For example, if one vendor offers a 300,000-hour MTBF and another 600,000, generally the disk with the higher rating will last longer and be more reliable.

When I explain the math of MTBF as above, I often hear cries of protest from experienced IT professionals who have been misled by MTBF propaganda over the years and do not accept the conclusions drawn, which perhaps contributes to why so little attention has been paid to disks. If they are going

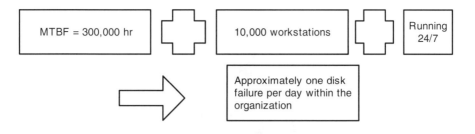

Exhibit 1   Mean Time between Failures

to run for over a century, why worry about them? But, for your own sake and for the sake of the organization, it is definitely advisable to worry about them.

Adding Up the Cost of Disk Failure

Another factor contributing to the fact that administrators tend to undervalue the problem of disk failures is that hard drive prices have decreased significantly in recent times, coming down to the $50 to $200 range. To many, it does not seem like a big deal to replace a disk when it goes down. Unfortunately, the hardware aspect is only the tip of the iceberg when it comes to costs. Add in the IT personnel time to replace the disk and, if replacement is done after a disk fails, employee downtime, the value of lost productivity, and potential loss of customers or loss of service to customers, and suddenly it turns into a very expensive proposition.

Inexpensive though disks may be, the data they contain is not, which is why most enterprises have some sort of backup and restore strategy in place. Although backup techniques have markedly improved over the years, relying on backing up as the sole solution to disk crashes is like saying that because medical technology has made great strides, we do not need to work to prevent automobile accidents or wear seat belts or install airbags in cars. True, doctors can do a pretty good job these days of piecing bodies back together, but it is a slow, painful, and expensive undertaking compared with preventing accidents in the first place. The same applies to hard drives. Preventing a crash — anticipating it, safeguarding the data, and replacing the disk before it fails — is far preferable to cleaning up the mess afterwards.

Do Not Rely on Backup

Certainly, relying on regular backup is far from a complete solution (see Chapter 5 for more complete details on Windows backup). To begin with, any data entered since the last backup will not be recorded on any backup tape or other media. In some organizations, this period can represent a day or even a week or more of data. For example, say a backup is done every weekend. Everything written to disk during the intervening week could be lost if a system collapse occurs before the next backup window (the following

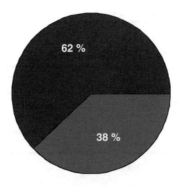

Exhibit 2   Tape Restore Failure

weekend). Also, one must consider human error, faulty media, and backup
hardware defects, all of which also result in data loss. One survey of 260 IT
professionals found that 62 percent of all tape restores failed; that is, 62 percent
failed to recover at least a portion of all the data that was sought (Exhibit 2).

According to research done at Pepperdine University's economics department, 6 percent of business PCs will have an at least one instance of data
loss in any given year, with an average cost of $2557 to fix. This figure includes
the costs of retrieving and recovering the missing information, lost productivity,
technical services, and the value of the data itself. Pepperdine states, though,
that that is a conservative figure as it does not include the costs of such items
as lost revenue or damage to reputation. Out of the total $11.8 billion in PC
data losses suffered by businesses annually, the study attributes 42 percent
($4.96 billion) to hardware failure. This figure does not include damage caused
by people dropping laptops, which is categorized as human error, nor does it
include natural disasters such as floods or lightning that result in hardware failure.

To this point, though, only the cost of data residing on PCs has been
considered. Most critical data these days is stored on servers, where the
consequences of lost data can be even more catastrophic. Complicating the
matter is the rapidly expanding mobile workforce where day-to-day operational data is stored on millions of laptop computers that simply cannot be
backed up daily. So, while backups do have their place in helping to safeguard
data, they should only be regarded as a last line of defense.

Do Not Rely on RAID

Realizing the shortcomings of backing up data, enterprises have turned to
using Redundant Arrays of Independent Disks (RAID) on their servers. RAID
has two main purposes: to speed up data flow by simultaneously reading
from or writing to more than one disk at a time (disk striping) and to preserve
data by replicating it on a number of disks so that if one goes down the
others will still be accessible. RAID can be achieved by utilizing either a
hardware or an operating system approach. Software RAID has the advantage
of being less expensive. Hardware RAID, on the other hand, is more expensive

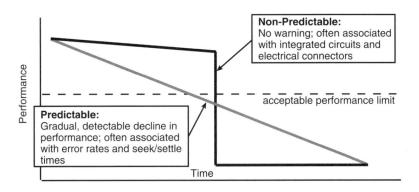

Exhibit 3   Sudden versus Gradual Failure (Black line shows non-predictable failure; performance remains good until a sudden failure occurs. Gray line shows predictable failure — steady performance decline over time.)

but faster. Because a separate RAID controller is doing the data replication and distribution, hardware RAID does not tie up the operating system and impact performance. (RAID is covered in more detail in Chapter 1.)

Although RAID is a significant improvement over relying solely on backups, it has its drawbacks. To begin with, it is expensive. Cost precludes its use in low end servers. Second, while RAID does prevent data loss, it does not prevent service loss. When a disk goes down in a RAID array, the system may keep running, but the faulty disk must still be replaced. During the hours it takes to add a new one and transfer data to it, performance takes a huge hit. Although one's employees are not likely to walk off the job during this time (they will just flood the help desk with calls), where customers are concerned it is a different matter. When service is slow on a company's Web site, its customers may very well click over to the competition. Numerous studies highlight the dangers of having a slow Web site and what it means in terms of losing out to the competition. The average consumer will put up with a delay of no more than eight seconds before deciding to leave a site. Such an encounter often leads to buying from the competition, never to return.

Predicting Failure

Recognizing the need for something more broadly functional than RAID, the server industry began developing methods to predict when a hard drive was going to fail so as to do something proactive instead of waiting until after the disk crashes. Most drive failures do not occur suddenly; rather, a slow degradation in performance can be detected, eventually culminating in total failure (Exhibit 3). By monitoring the status of drive performance indicators, then, it is possible to predict when a disk will fail and provide adequate time to safeguard the data, run diagnostics, and replace the drive if necessary before it completely fails. Disk monitoring also opens the door to being able to schedule disk replacement for slow times, perhaps during the middle of the night for servers that have to be up 24 hours a day. It is rather like watching the gas gauge on a car. The driver knows approximately how much fuel is left and can schedule a trip to the gas station whenever it is most convenient. Now imagine instead having to rely on the engine going dead before becoming aware that the fuel tank is empty. Who knows what kind of cargo the vehicle might be carrying, how far it will be from a gas station when the fuel runs out, or what time of the night it might be?

The first firm to address this issue was IBM (Armonk, New York), which developed a technology called predictive failure analysis (PFA). PFA monitors elements within a disk drive that are invisible to the end user but which eventually lead to failure. For example, as the spindle bearings start to wear out, the increasing friction leads to a rise in temperature. An upsurge in the number of sectors that need to be remapped also indicates a problem with the disk surface.

Self-Monitoring Analysis and Reporting Technology (SMART)

Compaq Computer Corporation (Houston, Texas) took this predictive failure idea and, in conjunction with other major manufacturers, developed the Self-Monitoring Analysis and Reporting Technology, or SMART as it is commonly known. With SMART, the controller takes data from sensors and provides that data, upon request, to the BIOS, operating system, or other software designed to monitor drives. The exact items monitored vary from one manufacturer to another but can include such things as head flying height (predicts future head crashes), disk spin-up time and temperature (disk motor problems), or the number or errors corrected. In total, SMART can monitor up to 30 different indicators. It rates each of these items on a scale of 0 to 255. Separate standards are available for ATA (IDE) and SCSI drives.

Even though system administrators have a vital need for such a tool, the solution turns out to be not quite as smart as it could be and unfortunately may have somewhat limited real-world usefulness. Why? When the hardware manufactures established SMART, they all agreed on the data format, but it appears that they could not agree on much else. Every manufacturer, it turns out, decides which elements to monitor and report and what thresholds are meaningful. This means that end users can neither monitor their own drives directly nor establish which thresholds should be set to ensure reliability.

The SMART protocol, in fact, defined 30 attributes to be monitored. Each attribute is placed on a scale between 0 and 255. When the monitored value goes too high or too low, warnings are issued. Each manufacturer can pick and choose which attributes suit them (some use only a handful, others use most of them), and each manufacturer decides which thresholds to set. The worse part of all this for users is that they have no idea which manufacturer monitors what attributes or how the thresholds have been set. If a user wants to change these settings, too bad; they are not available. Users, then, really do not know what is happening on their disks. For example, is SMART monitoring head flying height, the number of remapped sectors, ECC use and error counts, spin-up time, temperature, data throughput, or any of the other 24 possible attributes? As noted, it is up to the manufacturer to program in what is considered to be an acceptable range for any or all of the above characteristics, depending on what the manufacturer regards as threatening.

This situation can be verified by studying the fine print of the various industry pronouncements on SMART. According to an American Megatrends, Inc., white paper, for instance, no particular standard is associated with SMART or SMART devices. Just as different manufacturers' disk drives have different designs and architectures, the same is true when it comes to implementing SMART on those drives, and the degree of monitoring varies from manufacturer to manufacturer. No evidence exists, of course, to support the claim that manufacturers intentionally set SMART to make their own drives look good nor does evidence suggest that the manufacturers are more interested in drives lasting out the warranty period than in providing a truly useful monitoring system. Anyone saying so would have a difficult time proving it; yet, some believe this to be the case.

Steve Gibson of Gibson Research Corporation (Laguna Hills, California) states on his Web site that the idea of SMART may sound cool, but drives do not like to "tattle on themselves" because that would make them look bad. As a result, it appears that, because each manufacturer decides what their drives will report about themselves and because those manufacturers are competing with each other, the SMART system has turned out to be rather dumb.

The fact that each manufacturer decides on its own standards does not bode well for buyers interested in finding out when their drives have a problem. Suppose a disk is operating at 90 percent but will not completely fail until after the warranty has expired; it is likely that the consumer will not be alerted to the problem, particularly if the problem becomes observable only *after* the warranty has expired. From an economic standpoint, this makes sense for the manufacturers, whether or not any of them have actually utilized SMART in this fashion. But, it would seem that in some situations, manufacturers may be acting against their own interests when warning users about potential or inevitable reductions in performance.

In the defense of disk manufacturers, it is easy to see why they have taken this approach. Seagate, for example, makes a disk analysis tool available to people to test drives before returning them. In many cases, the company finds that returned disks are actually working fine and that users returned them due to some other problem. Seagate reports that 40 percent of the disks returned to the company do not have a hardware problem. Its SeaTools diagnostic software (www.seagate.com) runs a series of tests on the drive and, when the disk is not at fault, offers advice on sorting out errors arising with the operating system, file system, or partitioning. It is available for download in either a desktop or enterprise edition. IBM similarly offers Windows and Linux versions of its free Drive Fitness Test 2.30 and several other disk utilities at www.storage.ibm.com.

So, faced with this tendency of users to attach blame to the wrong component, who can really blame manufacturers for not wanting to advertise potential problems, particularly those that are not noticeable and may never seriously affect disk performance? It could be a recipe for disaster in a business that already has the slimmest of margins.

Getting back to the main point, the real problem with SMART is that it does not appear to be reliable. It is common for drives to fail without SMART giving any type of warning; yet, having SMART can lull administrators into a false sense of security, thinking they do not have to monitor disk status because SMART is supposedly minding the shop. This may even lead to more unpredicted disk failures than would occur without SMART because at least then administrators would know they needed to pay more attention to disk health and possibly seek out an appropriate tool for effective monitoring. Sadly, though, most system administrators remember the hype that surrounded SMART a few years ago. Vendors boldly stated that hard drive failures were now a thing of the past and that, with SMART-enabled drives, most kinds of failure would be spotted in advance, thus allowing IT personnel enough time to replace the drives before any catastrophic data loss occurred.

Anecdotal evidence from users, IT consultants, and IT managers, as well as data from the disk vendors themselves, points to a general lack of results from SMART. This failure stems from many factors, including:

- Failure to install SMART software to pick up alerts from drives
- Lack of interoperability of SMART data among drive manufacturers
- So many different implementations of SMART by manufacturers that users are never really sure what kind of alerts they might receive
- Perhaps most surprisingly, shortcomings in the technology itself

How Often Do Disks Fail?

How often do disks fail? Hard drive failures seem to be growing in frequency, possibly related to factors such as the size of modern drives and their utilization in so many mission-critical activities. This is supported by a recent survey by San Jose, California-based Survey.com, which found that a majority of 1293 IT staff surveyed had experienced computer downtime in the previous year due to disk drive failure. An even more worrying finding of the survey, though, was that less than 10 percent actually received any prior warning (Exhibit 4). This brings to light an important point. One oft-forgotten aspect of SMART is that it requires three elements to succeed:

- SMART-capable hard drive
- Operating system that accepts and relays SMART commands
- SMART application that displays these commands to the user

These days, the first two are often present, but the third is either omitted or inactive. Such has been the hype behind SMART, in fact, that many users and even a fair number of system managers think that just buying SMART drives is enough. They do not bother to read the fine print and even discard the CD that comes in the box. Many have failed to appreciate that a SMART drive

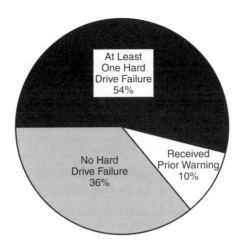

Exhibit 4   Hard Drive Failures Experienced in Past Year

itself does not generate any SMART alerts. The user must use software to check drive status for it to have any value. An IT manager in a Los Angeles legal firm, for example, experienced the unthinkable on RAID-5 — two disks going down. He failed to check his alert lights and missed the first drive going down. In hindsight, he believes it had been down for weeks before the second disk died, as he had noticed a slight dip in performance. Afterwards, when he wondered why SMART had not warned him, he was embarrassed to realize that he had not configured the software required to receive the alerts.

Not So SMART

Engineers at the Burbank, California-based disk management vendor Executive Software, Inc., also ran into trouble with the SMART technology when they tried to build a graphical user interface (GUI) to make full use of SMART. They created fail conditions for over 100 hard drives using a variety of methods. According to the director of research, even with disks being horribly mistreated and about to fail, not once did they receive a SMART alert. Steve Speregen, MCP, MCSE, a network consultant who runs the LA Windows Networking Users Group, has worked with virtually every type of system and drive over the past decade. During that time he has experienced or witnessed over 100 disk failures. As he sees it, SMART is all smoke and mirrors, and he has yet to see it work. He reports that he put in all the settings and used special motherboards but not once was he notified of any errors. In his view, the newer SMART II is not any better. Even some drive manufacturers will admit that SMART is not all they thought it would be. Maxtor Corporation's Web site provides a SMART Phase II white paper that states that SMART technology is only capable of predicting 20 to 50 percent of hard drive failures with sufficient time to allow a user or system manager to respond. This paper also states that one of the best kept secrets is that SMART is only an advisory service at best.

Products Using SMART

A few products have attempted to make the best of SMART as it is. EZ SMART by Phoenix Technologies (Louisville, Colorado) and Intelli-SMART by LC Technology (Clearwater, Florida) are two examples, but these applications are primarily one-machine products that are not meant for broad monitoring of multiple disks.

Compaq Insight Manager (CIM)

Compaq Insight Manager (CIM) offers enterprise functionality. CIM agents do a fine job of monitoring Compaq servers and, according to some user reports, actually manage to extract some value from SMART. CIM collects over 200 data items from Compaq Proliant servers (of which SMART accounts for only a handful of data items) in order to monitor the performance of disks, CPUs, and various other devices. When it comes to disk monitoring, though, it basically relies on the SMART standard. In this case, however, CIM is probably the best existing usage of SMART as far as actually extracting some real value from it. Through its more comprehensive diagnostics and use of agents, CIM seems to do a better job of gathering SMART data. Some users even report it has alerted them to drive problems in advance. The downside, though, is that it works best with Compaq server drives. Fortunately, the latest version, CIM 7, integrates better with parallel monitoring systems in Hewlett-Packard and Dell server drives. It is not so good with clone servers, though. Additionally, some users report that CIM 7 can be quite complex to run, and setting it up to work with rival manufacturer systems can be a challenge. Further, as it relies only on SMART, its dependability is suspect.

OEM Disk Monitoring Tools

Other vendors have put out products similar to CIM, although they are not as comprehensive. These include Dell OpenManage, HP TopTools, and IBM Netfinity Manager. CIM can interface with some of these tools and is able to monitor non-Compaq drives. Similarly, some of these vendor tools can pick up some of the information contained in CIM, but none of them does a complete job and most founder when it comes to monitoring anything at all on a clone server. This is particularly a problem outside of the United States where local hardware manufacturers hold a much larger market share compared with these big original equipment manufacturers (OEMs). Most of these OEM tools use either the Simple Network Management Protocol (SNMP) or the Desktop Management Interface (DMI). SNMP is a widely used network monitoring and control protocol. SNMP agents pass data about devices to the console that is monitoring them. These agents return data contained in a Management Information Base (MIB), a data structure defining what can be obtained from each device and the ways in which it can be controlled. Similarly, DMI is a management system that can monitor hardware and software components from a central console. Agents are used to gather data when queries are made. CIM uses SNMP, and Dell OpenManage uses DMI.

SpinRite

To avoid the frailties of SMART, Gibson Research's SpinRite tests drives by reading and rewriting data to the entire surface of a disk, removing any bad sectors as it goes. It issues alerts of potential drive failures and offers a nice set of recovery tools, too. This fine utility, though, has one drawback — it only works on FAT partitions, limiting it to Windows 9X and NT partitions running FAT. According to the Gibson Web site, a version will eventually be coming out that addresses NTFS and other file systems. It is hoped that when this version appears it will also be networkable, enabling companies to load it on their networks to monitor the health of every single server and desktop disk. Now that would be quite a product!

Hot Swapability

Though SMART drives have certainly failed to live up to early expectations, products such as CIM hold out some hope that the technology will not, in the end, prove less than useful. SpinRite offers a simpler and more effective solution to hard drive efficiency, at least for the individual machine. Some, however, might point to hot swapabilty as the answer. In theory, with a hot-swappable RAID array, when one drive goes down users can just replace it on the fly and they are up and running again. In the real world, though, it does not quite work out this way.

Say, for example, a Web server drive has been steadily but slowly deteriorating. On Friday, everything is fine, but first thing Monday morning it is discovered that one of the RAID drives is down. Due to RAID redundancy, the Web server has continued to function since the drive failed on Saturday morning, but performance has suffered badly. User complaints are piling up, and the boss is mad because the Web site hits are taking a beating. Even when the drive is quickly replaced, the company's troubles are far from over. Even after everyone is informed that the new drive is now online, the complaints do not let up and site usage bottoms out. Hundreds of thousands of dollars in business just went to the competition. What happened? Simply put, it takes many hours for a RAID array to rebuild after a new drive is installed. The more prudent approach, therefore, is to know about drive failures well in advance so appropriate action can be taken. Had the alert been received the week before, the faulty drive could have rebuilt during off peak hours, and the company could have continued to make a bundle in online sales.

Disks Will Fail

The one great truth in hard drive reliability, as told to me by someone in the HP Server Group, is that disks *will* fail. This gentleman characterized disks as being like light bulbs. If you are willing to pay more you might end up with one that lasts a little longer, but ultimately you should expect it to fail. The point is to have plenty of spares on hand and to be prepared and ready for that inevitable point when the disks do fail. Bottom line: In a data center of any size, hard drive failure is an almost daily occurrence. So, take steps to secure the data, safeguard against disk failure, and monitor the disks to avert failure before it happens. By doing so, IT moves away from an operating basis of putting out one fire after another to taking a proactive stance of maintaining disk health in such a way as to enhance overall organizational productivity.

Chapter 4

Disk Management Basics for Windows 2000

How exactly do you stay in control of your disks and manage them efficiently? This chapter looks at how an enterprise can control hard drive management and discusses the fundamentals of disk management, the different volume types, and the various disk arrangements employed in servers. It goes into detail about initializing and formatting disks, as well as creating volumes and fault-tolerant disk systems. With the advent of Windows 2000, in particular, much has changed in the land of disk management. Terminology has been adjusted, functionality has been enriched, and we now have a whole new element: dynamic disks, which promise greater features for disk management on Windows-based systems than ever before. For the IT professional, it is particularly important to understand the difference between basic disks and dynamic disks and what this means to system functionality.

The Importance of Disk Management

Disk management is one of the most important aspects of a system administrator's job. Without an understanding of the fundamentals of disk management, errors and catastrophes await. Although things were already complex enough, the advent of Windows 2000 has changed many things in the disk management landscape. It is vital to know, for example, the differences between a basic disk and a dynamic disk when deciding which one to employ. Also, many different volume types are now available; in fact, Windows 2000 changed some of the terminology previously used with regard to partitions and volumes. For some disks, the word *partition* applies, and for others the term *volume* is used. While this distinction may seem trivial, an understanding of the subtle differences between these terms is vital to Windows 2000 server disk management. This knowledge also very much relates to creating the fault-tolerant systems that play an essential part in everyday operations as well as disaster recovery.

Basic Tasks

A number of basic tasks, including disk initialization, disk formatting, volume creation, and creation of fault-tolerant disk systems, must be taken care of when Windows 2000 server disks (and workstation disks) are installed.

Disk Initialization

To initialize means to start anew, and when it comes to hard disks, initialization is necessary in order to prepare the disk for use. This means that the disk is configured into a maximum of four partitions, each of which is assigned a drive letter. Once initialized (or partitioned), the disk is ready to accept the file system and data. Each disk must be assigned a primary partition. Windows defaults automatically to the C: drive as the primary partition, but this default can be changed, if desired, to another partition. The primary partition contains the operating system (OS) and is the one used to boot up the system. As each partition functions as though it were a separate physical disk, partitioning helps to organize data. For example, the OS can reside on one partition, various applications on another, and data files on yet another partition. Such arrangements help simplify the task of finding files and organizing software.

Disk Formatting

With the disk initialized, each partition can be formatted with a file system: FAT, FAT32, or NTFS (see Chapter 2). Without a file system installed on the partition, data cannot be written to it. For Windows 2000, FAT is only available for backward compatibility, not for the formatting of Windows 2000 disks. Although the FAT32 file system can be used on Windows 2000, use of the NTFS file system is recommended instead, as it takes advantage of many advanced features, such as:

- Compression
- Encryption
- Disk quotas
- Mount points, which allow mounting of remote drives or folders onto any NTFS formatted volume, thus making data more accessible and adding additional disk space without affecting users
- Remote storage

Windows operating systems running DOS or Windows 9*x* do not have such features, nor do Windows 2000 partitions using FAT32 (see Chapter 2 for more details).

Volume Creation

In order to discuss the basics of volume creation it is first necessary to explain a few things. The advanced NTFS features mentioned previously also permit the creation of dynamic disks on Windows 2000. Dynamic disks allow the administrator to perform various functions without having to shut down systems or disturb users — for example, creating, extending, or mirroring a volume or adding a new disk without rebooting.

Basic Disks

Basic disks are no more than the partitions or logical drives that were creatable on Windows NT. Later operating systems, such as Windows 2000 Professional and Windows 2000 Server, both automatically default to the basic disks unless instructed otherwise. Alternatively, basic disks can be used initially, with a switch to dynamic disks later. When migrating from Windows NT to the Windows 2000 server, for example, it may be desirable to keep the prior NT configuration while getting used to the new functionality of Windows 2000. By doing so, users can stick to basic disks and make the migration relatively painless. When more familiar with dynamic disks, users can then make the relatively smooth transition from running Windows 2000 on basic disks to running the operating system on dynamic disks, which can be accomplished without losing much in terms of configuration while adding additional functionality. When should basic disks be used? Basic disks must be used to run earlier Windows operating systems and for dual booting. Basic disks also should be used on laptops running Windows 2000 Professional, because laptops have only one disk so the value of dynamic disks is lost. In addition, be aware that basic disks can make use of extended partitions and logical drives.

Extended Partitions

An extended partition is the part of a basic disk that contains a logical drive (i.e., it removes the restriction of four partitions per basic disk). Only one of the four basic disk partitions, though, can be extended. Note that extended partitions apply only to basic disks. For dynamic disks, which have no volume number limit, extended partitions are unnecessary.

Logical Drive

This is simply the volume created within an extended partition. Again, logical drives do not apply to dynamic disks.

Dynamic Disks

Dynamic disks in Windows 2000 provide far more management flexibility, fewer limitations (such as the partition size), and a greater feature set than do basic disks. Dynamic disks can run only Windows 2000 (and XP), not DOS or Windows 98/Me, and they do not permit the creation of partitions or logical drives. Dynamic disks:

- Make it possible to create or delete such items as simple volumes, spanned volumes, mirrored volumes, and RAID-5 volumes.
- Allow the user to extend a simple or spanned volume, remove a mirror from a mirrored volume, or split a volume into two volumes.
- Allow the user to repair mirrored volumes and RAID-5 volumes, as well as to reactivate offline volumes.

Note that, for dynamic disks, the term *partition* is not used; instead, the operative word is *volume*. With that in mind, the following text provides some of the definitions that are central to a full understanding of dynamic disks and how to utilize them.

Volumes

A volume is a portion of the physical disk that acts like a physically separate entity.

Simple Volume

Only one dynamic disk running on its own is referred to as a simple volume. Simple volumes contain no partitions or logical drives and cannot be accessed by DOS or Windows 9*x*.

Spanned Volume

A spanned volume is a simple volume extended onto other disks within the same computer. Unused free space of various sizes can be combined on a minimum of 2 volumes and a maximum of 32 volumes to create a spanned volume; however, note that deleting one part of the spanned volume deletes the entire volume. Similarly, if one of the disks containing a spanned volume fails, the entire volume fails. Spanned volumes can only exist on dynamic disks and cannot use FAT or FAT32. They are only visible to the Windows 2000 operating system (and Windows XP). Further limitations for spanned volumes include the fact that they cannot be mirrored or striped and they do not run in a fault-tolerant array. Thus, spanned volumes should be avoided if mirroring, striping, or fault tolerance will be utilized. Spanned volumes are particularly useful, though, for utilization of unformatted free space in different locations on different disks. Many different sizes of free space can be combined

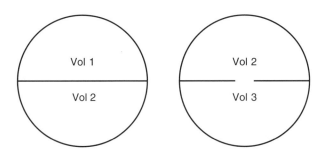

Exhibit 1   Spanned Volume (The volume extends onto other disks within the same computer.)

when creating the spanned volume (this is great for lots of relatively small pockets of free space, as it is possible to combine them all into one, easy-to-manage spanned volume). Spanned volumes can also be used to combine two or more disks into one large volume. NTFS can then be used to extend that volume again and again without impacting the data that already exists on the volume (see Exhibit 1). For those more familiar with Windows NT, NT referred to spanned volumes as *volume sets*.

Striped Volume

Striped volumes increase the capacity of volumes. Striped volumes combine areas of free space on anywhere from 2 to 32 disks into one logical volume. The data on each disk is divided into blocks and data is spread onto all the disks at the same time, thus reads and writes are faster — sometimes as much as 300 percent faster. Striped volumes, though, have no fault tolerance. If one disk fails, everything fails. Also be aware that striped volumes (also known as RAID-0 volumes) running Windows 2000 cannot be recognized by DOS or Windows 9*x*. Suppose, for example, that you have three partitions, each on a separate disk and each 500 MB. When they are combined into a striped volume, the file system regards them as a single 1.5-GB volume. This arrangement helps distribute the overall I/O load across many disks rather than bottlenecking at one disk and so adversely affecting performance.

Creation of Fault-Tolerant Disk Systems

While the disk arrangements discussed above have many benefits, none of them offers fault tolerance. What is fault tolerance? Basically, it means that the computer is able to tolerate a fault of some kind, such as data loss or the failure of one disk; despite such a hiccup, the system is able to continue without impacting the user community. To add fault tolerance, one must create mirrored volumes or RAID-5 volumes.

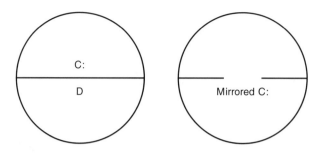

Exhibit 2   Mirrored Volume (The data on one disk in the C: volume is also written into a mirrored volume on another disk.)

Mirrored Volumes

Mirrored volumes (also known as RAID-1) are obtained by recording the same data onto two disks simultaneously. If one disk fails, the data is available on the other one, thus ensuring no data loss. This fault-tolerant arrangement has some disadvantages, however. To eliminate many of the potential problems, it is advisable to use only disks of the same size, model, and manufacturer. Further, when mirroring data, be sure to assign the same drive letter to each disk. Mirrored volumes aid throughput on high-load systems (see Exhibit 2).

RAID-5 Volumes

The RAID-5 fault-tolerant setup has data and parity striped intermittently across three or more disks. This arrangement provides better read performance, as data is read from three or more disks at the same time. Also, RAID-5 provides redundancy at a cost of only one additional disk for the whole volume.

Disk Management Console

The Disk Management Console is the tool used in Windows 2000 to configure any and all of the above disk arrangements and can be found within the Administrative Tools folder. The Disk Management Console displays information regarding the layout and type of every partition or volume, the file system, the status of the volume, its drive letter, its capacity, any fault-tolerant features, amount of available free space, and more. For example, if the user wants to know whether a volume is simple, spanned, or mirrored, this data can be found in the Disk Management Console. All of the volume types and fault-tolerant arrays mentioned above can be created via the Action Tab of the Disk Management Console. To configure or change a configuration, go into the Action Tab on the console and select the desired function. The Disk Management Console is basically a snap-in of the Microsoft Management Console (MMC), which is an interface for the use of the different management snap-ins. (A snap-in is simply a module of MMC that provides certain management capabilities for a specific device; every administrative tool in Windows 2000 is a snap-in.) Disks can be upgraded from basic to dynamic, for example, but make sure that 1 MB or more of unformatted free space is available at the end of the disk.

Converting a Basic Disk to a Dynamic Disk

Following are the steps involved in converting a basic disk to a dynamic disk using the Disk Management Console snap-in:

- Log on as the administrator or as a member of the administrator group.
- Click Start, and then click Control Panel.
- Click Performance and Maintenance, click Administrative Tools, and then double-click Computer Management.
- In the left pane, click Disk Management.
- In the lower right pane, right-click the basic disk that you want to convert, and then click Convert to Dynamic Disk. You must right-click the gray area that contains the disk title on the left side of the Details pane (for example, right-click Disk 0).
- Select the check box that is next to the disk that you want to convert (if it is not already selected), and then click OK.
- Click Details if you want to view the list of volumes on the disk.
- Click Convert.
- Click Yes when you are prompted to convert the disk, and then click OK.

Please note that access to the dynamic disk is limited to Windows 2000 and XP Professional; further, once basic disks have been converted to dynamic disks, the dynamic volumes cannot easily be changed back. Converting back to basic disks results in the loss of configuration and file data.

This is how the process works: To move from dynamic disks back to basic disks (say, to set up a dual-boot system running Windows Me), all dynamic volumes on the disk must be deleted before the dynamic disk can be converted back to a basic disk. What do you do if you want to keep your data? Back up the data or move it to another volume.

As you can see, it is possible to move back from dynamic to basic disks, although it is a decidedly more painful process. Whereas disk configurations can be maintained when moving up to dynamic disks, disk configurations are lost when the process is reversed. And, in most cases, it would be better to add a new machine running basic disks rather than disrupting the existing environment of dynamic disks.

Basic and Dynamic Disks and Windows XP

This section goes into more detail regarding how basic and dynamic disks relate to Windows XP. Basic disk storage uses normal partition tables supported by MS-DOS, Windows 9*x*, Windows Me, Windows NT, Windows 2000, and

Windows XP. As mentioned earlier, a disk initialized for basic storage is referred to as a *basic* disk. A basic disk contains basic partitions, such as primary partitions, extended partitions, and logical drives, as defined above. Such partitions also include multidisk partitions that are created using Windows NT 4.0 or earlier, such as volume sets, stripe sets, mirror sets, and stripe sets with parity. For Windows XP, however, it is important to note that XP does not support these multidisk basic partitions. Any volume sets, stripe sets, mirror sets, or stripe sets with parity must be backed up and deleted or converted to dynamic disks before installing Windows XP Professional. Like Windows 2000, Windows XP Professional does support *dynamic* disks. XP dynamic disks can contain dynamic volumes, such as simple volumes, spanned volumes, striped volumes, mirrored volumes, and RAID-5 volumes. With dynamic storage, disk and volume management can be performed without having to restart Windows.

What about XP Home Edition? Dynamic disks are not supported on Windows XP Home Edition or laptops running any version of XP. In addition, mirrored volumes or RAID-5 volumes cannot be created on Windows XP Home Edition, Windows XP Professional, or Windows XP 64-Bit Edition-based computers. However, a Windows XP Professional-based computer can be used to create a mirrored or RAID-5 volume on remote computers that are running Windows 2000 Server, Windows 2000 Advanced Server, or Windows 2000 Datacenter Server. The user must have administrative privileges on the remote computer to do this.

Be Dynamic, Choose Dynamic

Because dynamic disks do not contain partitions or logical drives, they do not restrict the disk to any kind of volume limit. Hard drives can be divided as the user sees fit and can evolve into very large volumes when small pieces of free space on various disks are combined into one volume. And, because rebooting is unnecessary when configuration changes have been made, dynamic disks are far more flexible than basic disks. In almost all cases, then, one should choose dynamic disks over basic disks, but if it is necessary to run a dual boot system using an earlier Windows operating system, if you are just getting your feet wet with Windows 2000 Server, or you are migrating from NT to Windows 2000, basic disks can be used initially with conversion to dynamic disks being relative simple later.

Chapter 5

Backing Up Windows Networks

Backing up data is nothing new. In fact, originally data was stored on punch cards, punched paper strips, or magnetic tape and only loaded into the computer when the data was needed. But, as storage capacities have grown, together with the need for constant availability, backing up the data has become a more complex, yet even more vital undertaking. This chapter takes a look at various strategies for doing backups and restoring the data as needed, and it goes into depth regarding the backup functions that come with Windows, as well as the use of third-party software, mirroring, and off-site replication. Because many Windows-based sites now have some kind of Linux added into the mix, the chapter also addresses the special needs of backing up Linux in heterogeneous environments.

No More Simple Backups

Backing up was once a simple enough affair. At night or on the weekends, an administrator would run a tape on the servers, and desktops were backed up by copying files onto a few floppies, but with the explosion in drive storage over the past few years this is no longer possible. To backup a single 60-GB drive, for example, would require in excess of 40,000 floppies — not a practical solution. But, as the problem has grown, so have the available options for backing up data and ensuring its availability. Before taking a look at some of those solutions, a few terms should be defined:

- *Backup* — In general English usage, the concept of a backup means a reserve or substitute, something extra. When used in computing, it refers to a copy of the data on various types of storage media or a copy of the data kept for safety or emergency purposes.

- *Restore* — A restore means retrieving a file from the backup. If data loss occurs but the data has been backed up, that data can be restored from the backup.

Windows Backup: What It Includes

Microsoft has included a backup utility with Windows for the last several years. VERITAS Software Corporation (www.veritas.com; Mountain View, California) wrote the backup applets for Windows NT 3.1, 3.5*x*, and 4.0, as well as Microsoft Exchange Server and Microsoft Small Business Server. VERITAS later provided the backup applet for Windows 2000. Windows XP Professional also has a backup utility, and one can be installed for XP Home Edition, although it is not part of the default installation. This product backs up and restores encrypted files and folders without decrypting them, so there is no breach of the security protocols.

For Windows 2000, however, things operate a little differently. Only administrators or backup operators with access to a domain controller can backup any file or folder within the domain, except system-state data, provided a two-way trust relationship exists. Local group administrators and backup operators have the right to backup any file or folder on their local server, and anyone with administrative rights to that machine can backup a workstation running Windows 2000 Professional. System-state data (registry, boot files, Active Directory database, etc.) can only be backed up locally.

The backup utility performs five different types of backups:

- *Normal* — Using the normal setting backs up all selected files and folders, whether or not they have been previously backed up. It clears all previous backup markers (archive bits) and creates new ones for all files showing they have been backed up. Doing this type of backup can be slow, but the restoration process is faster than when the other backup methods are used. This method would be useful when there is no shortage of time to perform the backup, but it is desirable to get the device back on line as soon as possible after a failure.
- *Copy* — A copy backup also backs up all selected files and folders, but it does not reset any of the archive bits.
- *Incremental* — An incremental backup backs up all files or folders that have an archive bit. When done, it clears the markers so those files are not backed up again when the next incremental backup is done.
- *Daily* — As its name implies, a daily backup backs up all selected files and folders changed that day. It does not look at or reset the markers.
- *Differential* — Finally, with a differential backup, only those files and folders that contain a marker are backed up, but the markers are not reset. The differential backup takes longer than doing an incremental or daily backup, but the restoration goes more quickly. If you performed a full backup over the weekend, the differential backup would contain all files created or modified since then. By doing a normal backup and then daily differential backups, only these two files would be needed for restoration,

Exhibit 1   Backup Types

Backup Type	Advantages	Disadvantages
Full (normal)	Easy to schedule Easy to restore Removes transaction log files Circular logging	Can degrade performance Time consuming Requires a lot of tape space and a large number of tape replacements
Incremental	Little impact on server performance Removes transaction log files Minimal tape space	More complex restore process Circular logging turned off

Differential	Little impact on server
	  performance
	Easy to restore
	Minimal tape space
		Does not remove transaction log files
		Circular logging turned off
		Requires more tape space than
		  incremental backup but less than
		  full backup

whereas if a daily or incremental backup is done, each of those backups done since the last normal backup would be needed to do a restore. So, if a disk went down on Thursday, you would need the normal backup plus each of the incremental or daily backups from Monday, Tuesday, and Wednesday.

The main backup types used are normal, incremental, and differential (see Exhibit 1).

To back up Windows 2000's Active Directory (AD), the normal backup method is used. When the AD is backed up, Windows Backup also automatically backs up all the system components and distributed services AD depends on, including the system startup files, the system registry, the class registration database of COM+ (an extension to the Component Object Model), the File Replication service (the SYSVOL directory), the Certificate Services database (if installed), the Domain Name system (if installed), and Cluster service (if it is installed). The directory by itself cannot be backed up.

Third-party software may contain additional methods to supplement the five types of backups used by Windows Backup. VERITAS Backup Exec, for example, includes an application called Working Set. This method backs up all files created or modified since the last normal or incremental backup. In addition, the administrator can specify a number of days back, and Working Set will backup all files accessed within that time period.

Obviously, one size does not fit all when it comes to backups. Most organizations will want to use a variety of methods to provide the optimum security and performance for their specific storage and operational needs, as well as methods geared toward their unique architectures. The built-in Windows utility provides basic backup functions and may be adequate for small installations, but most organizations will find the tool too limited. In this case, they will need to use a full-featured product such as VERITAS' Backup Exec or Computer Associates' BrightStor/ARCServe Backup.

Using the Built-In Windows Backup Utility

The various versions of Windows backup software are fairly similar, so the discussion here simply goes through the steps for backing up Windows 2000 Professional. Those using different Windows systems should be able to follow these steps with minor adjustments specific to NT or XP. Additional data on Windows 2000 backup features, as well as instruction for other versions of Windows, are available on Microsoft's Web site.

Windows Backup can be accessed through the Start Menu (Start → Programs → Accessories → System Tools → Backup), through a command prompt (*ntbackup*), or through a batch file. The Welcome screen has buttons for three wizards (backup, restore, and emergency repair disks). If you are already familiar with carrying out backups, skip the wizard and go straight to one of the other tabs (Backup, Restore, or Schedule) to set the backup parameters.

To change the defaults, click on the Tools menu and select Options. If a wizard is used, it first asks you to designate which items to back up: all files on the computer, just the system-state data, or particular files, drives, or network data. If you opt to backup only certain selected data, the wizard takes you to a Windows Explorer type of screen where you click on the boxes next to the items you want to backup. To backup data contained on a remote rather than local computer, click on the + sign next to the item titled My Network Places to open up a tree showing the other computers that can be accessed and backed up from that location.

The next page, Where To Store the Backup, has a pull-down menu to select the media type. Windows Backup supports local and remote hard drives, tapes, floppies, CD-ROMs, and Zip drives. Below that menu lies a window to type in the backup filename or media name. A button is also provided to browse to the backup location. Once the backup location has been designated, clicking Next brings up a screen summarizing the selections made so far. If everything is correct, click on Finish. For other options, click on the Advanced button. In the next window, you will be able to select the type of backup (from the five discussed above), whether or not to compress the data, and whether to append the backup to the existing backup file or overwrite it. You also have the option of scheduling a time for the backup to occur (e.g., once a day at noon or at midnight.) The wizard then takes you to the screen summarizing your selections. Click Finish to execute the backup.

Microsoft includes a backup utility as part of its Windows 2000 package that is a light version of the VERITAS Software Corporation utility. Like the defrag program that comes with Windows 2000, it is probably good enough for an individual at home but lacks key network functionality such as scheduling, compression, and encryption. For network use, utilizing the complete version of the VERITAS Backup Exec or another full-featured backup program such as Computer Associates' BrightStor/ARCServe Backup is essential.

Emergency Repair Disk and Restore Functions

Windows Backup has two additional functions — creating an emergency repair disk (ERD) and Restore. These functions are accessed from the same screen as the backup functions. Creating an ERD is extremely simple. After opening Windows Backup, just click on the Emergency Repair Disk tab, insert a 3.5-inch floppy, and click OK. The software will then copy certain settings and files to the floppy that might help start Windows after a crash. As part of creating an ERD, current system settings are saved in the systemroot\repair folder. Deleting or changing this folder may render the ERD inoperable. A new ERD should be made whenever any system changes are made, such as installing a new service pack.

Like Backup, the Restore function can be done using a wizard or by going directly to the Restore tab. Select the items to be restored and where to place them; the default calls for them to be returned to their original locations, but another address can be specified. The option of restoring existing files is also presented; the default is not to do this, as it will wipe out any changes made to the files since the last backup.

For domain controllers, data can be restored in three ways. When all the domain controllers are gone and the domain is being rebuilt from the backup, use Primary Restore. To restore a single domain controller when the other domain controllers are still active, select Non-Authoritative Restore. The backed up data may be out of date, but this method allows the restored data to be brought current by the other domain controllers; this is the default setting. A third option is performing an Authoritative Restore, which results in rolling back the entire network to the data contained in the backup.

Additional XP Backup Features

In addition to the standard backup and restore features, XP comes with several built-in disaster recovery options not found in previous Windows systems. Except as noted, these tools can be used in either safe or normal mode and operate through a graphical user interface (GUI). These tools include:

- *Last Known Good Configuration* — This is a startup option. If the system cannot be started in normal or safe mode following the installation of a driver or application, this tool allows the user to reverse the most recent driver and registry changes.
- *Device Driver Roll Back* — This tool allows the user to replace an individual device driver with the previously installed version.
- *System Restore* — This tool monitors and records changes to system files, certain application files, and the registry. It also allows the user to undo recent changes and revert the system to a previous state.
- *Recovery Console* — This is a command line tool for manual recovery operations when Last Known Good Configuration and safe mode did not resolve the problem.

■ *Automated System Recovery* — This is a last step before reformatting the disk and reinstalling the data when boot and system files become corrupt. It has a GUI to be used for creating a backup floppy, but the restoration is done in text mode. Using ASR does not reformat the disk, but it will at least restore the system settings and certain critical files on the boot and system partitions.

Beyond Basic Backups

Several new approaches have been developed in recent years to improve data security and reliability, but the discussion here covers only two of the more widely used ones: data mirroring and offsite backups.

Mirroring

Doing a backup involves taking a snapshot of the entire system at a given point in time and saving a copy of it, but mirroring is a more dynamic process. Every time a user changes a file, that data is recorded in more than one location — a process known as mirroring. That way, even if one set of the data goes down, the other set is available online. This can save a lot of time, because with a regular backup that data would be unavailable until it had been fully restored. Mirroring also has the advantage of being more current than backup because the data is constantly updated, whereas backups are usually done just once a day. The flip side, however, is that this benefit can sometimes turn into a liability. If a file becomes corrupted or is deleted, for example, it is no longer available at either location; therefore, the smart thing to do is to use traditional backups as well as mirroring to ensure data integrity and recoverability. The simplest way to achieve this is to have the data recorded in two partitions on the same disk. This system protects against the file being recorded in a bad sector but is of very limited value beyond that.

A step up is RAID-1, where two disks, run by the same controller, each record the data. This provides greater data protection than mirroring onto a single disk, but if the controller goes down, the data is lost. Disk duplexing provides even greater reliability by storing the data on two disks within the same system, but each with its own controller. Clustering, Network Attached Storage, or Storage Area Networks can also be used to provide redundancy.

Offsite Replication

Each of these approaches protects against a particular device failing but not against the data center going down. With remote mirroring, however, the data gets replicated to servers at another facility. The most famous recent example of remote mirroring occurred when a number of companies were able to operate despite their offices being destroyed in the World Trade Center attacks because their data centers were protected.

Among the several approaches to offsite storage, a company can simply purchase software such as LifeKeeper from SteelEye Technology, Inc. (Mountain View, California) or SnapMirror from Network Appliance, Inc. (Sunnyvale, California) to mirror files between their offices. The data can be updated on a moment-to-moment basis or synchronized on a set time interval. An alternative to running remote sites on one's own is to use a storage service provider (SSP). LiveVault Corporation (Marlborough, Massachusetts), for example, first performs a full backup of its customers' systems and then continually backs up changes as they occur. The data is stored at secure facilities managed by records storage firm Iron Mountain, Inc. The service works with Windows NT/2000 servers and requires a persistent connection of at least 128 kilobits per second (kbps). Clients who need to restore files can access the LiveVault backups via a browser and download the necessary files, or LiveVault will send the files on CD-ROM via an overnight delivery service.

Backup Cautions

With the array of tools and solutions now available, data can be backed up and restored with greater ease and reliability than ever before, but a couple of important warnings should be kept in mind. The first is that backup is a secondary, not a primary, security solution. Having to rely on a backup is an admission of failure. It does not replace tools that monitor the health of disk drives or other device components that can predict and prevent disk failure, nor does it eliminate the need for an undelete utility. While the big disasters attract all the attention, 90 percent of the time the files that need to be restored were accidentally deleted by users. Using an undelete utility is much simpler and quicker than restoring a file from a backup tape.

Another important point: The result you are looking for is not just a quick and easy backup, but a complete and accurate restore; therefore, a test restoration of data should be performed regularly, at least once a month. One company I worked for, for example, had dutifully made backup tapes for years. But, as the tape drive grew older, its drive belt started slipping which caused the tape to move at uneven speeds. It was not a problem to record the data, but later, when files had to be restored, the tapes would no longer synchronize. It is unlikely that such a situation will happen again, but always be sure that you will be able to get your data back when you need it.

Backing Up Mixed Windows/Linux Networks

Finally, I will address heterogeneous networks. One of the major problems with using a built-in Windows Backup utility is that it is limited to Windows machines. Although it would be simpler to have everyone using a single operating system, this simply is not how it works in the real world. In large part due to its price, Linux is now the second most popular server operating system, behind Windows, in terms of numbers of units shipped. But, the use of Linus and Windows both can cause problems for IT staff trying to keep everything backed up.

PCMall, an E-commerce firm based in Torrance, California, learned this when they started using Linux a few years ago. The company decided to open up a subsidiary, eLinux, and felt that it had better use the software internally if it was going to sell and support it. The company has about 800 users in four states operating in ten domains. The desktop environment is Windows XP/2000, but the server environment is quite a mix. The 60 servers run Windows NT/2000 and HPUX, as well as several versions of Linux — primarily Red Hat, Caldera, and Immunex. The first use of Linux at the company was for the E-commerce sites, but since then its use has expanded to provide additional infrastructure support for such things as NAT, DHCP, DNS, and IPChains. In addition, PCMall runs several open-source security products on Linux to monitor the status of its environment and to handle reporting. While the company was happy with the way Linux performed, no tool was available to backup the Linux servers together with those running on other platforms. The initial approach was simply to tar-ball the Linux systems up to tape or use AMANDA or some other open-source alternative that would work well for backups, but it was not possible to unify the environment.

Fortunately, as Linux has grown in popularity, so has the number of tools developed to support it in a heterogeneous environment. Legato Systems, VERITAS, Spectra Logic, Hewlett-Packard, and others now include Linux among the platforms they support with their backup products. Applicable to PCMall's case, Computer Associates started supporting Linux with its BrightStor EB software, so network-wide backups covering all of the machines can now be done, regardless of platform.

Storage Portal Case Study

As the world's leading manufacturer of motion and control technologies/systems, Parker Hannifin Corporation has annual sales in excess of $6 billion. Its Aerospace Group provides hydraulic, fuel, and pneumatic systems and components for virtually every airplane and aircraft engine manufactured in the Western world. The company's Control Systems Division–Commercial, based in Ogden, Utah, designs and produces flight control systems and components for commercial aircraft. Its product line includes primary and secondary flight control actuation equipment, steering equipment, and utility hydraulics.

Parker Hannifin Corporation's Control Systems Division began to experience backup difficulties when the number of servers expanded and the weekly backup volume mushroomed beyond 1.75 terabytes. As a result, IT staff wasted countless hours on manual backup tasks and had to cope with a weekend backup window that had grown well beyond 24 hours. The IT manager reported that over 80 man-hours per month were being spent on IT supervision for backup alone. Much of this time was spent going from server to server to find out why certain backup jobs had failed, to troubleshoot database problems that interfered with backups, and to format many backup tapes.

Parker Hannifin Corporation had been utilizing Computer Associate's small-office backup solution, BrightStor/ARCserve Backup, which had been working satisfactorily on the company's combination of Windows 2000, NT, AIX, and Linux servers. DLT tape was the primary backup medium. On weekdays, the company conducted a combination of incremental and differential backups, with two complete backups being carried out on weekends — one retained on site and another shipped offsite for safekeeping. This approach worked well until the number of servers involved and the amount of data became unmanageable. When the Control Systems Division reached 35 servers and weekly backup volumes grew to 1.75 terabytes, the need for change became apparent.

As noted, more than 80 man-hours per month were required to maintain the company's backup needs. Without any kind of storage automation available, the IT staff was forced to move from server to server to troubleshoot a constant array of backup and database problems. Worse, a complete backup on weekends took well over 24 hours. At this point, the company implemented Islandia, Computer Associates' BrightStor Portal, to provide centralized management of all its storage assets from one console. BrightStor Portal is an enterprise storage automation concept that permits enterprise customers to harness greater business value from massive investments in storage technology. The BrightStor Portal includes many integrated elements, such as BrightStor Enterprise Backup (BrightStor EB), which centralizes backup/restore throughout the enterprise, and BrightStor Storage Resource Management (BrightStor SRM), which ensures that business-critical information is always accessible and which minimizes network downtime in case of disaster.

As a result of this initiative, the Control Systems Division of Parker Hannifin Corporation has added significant power and scalability to its backup process. A complete backup, for example, was reduced from about 30 hours to less than 10 hours. In regard to recovery, the company reports that IT staff can restore applications in 90 minutes or less. Previously, restores were often unsuccessful yet consumed a significant number of man hours. This storage portal approach helped eliminate myriad backup problems, cut backup supervision to less than one hour per month, and reduced backup failures by 95 percent.

A storage portal provides the adaptable command-and-control capabilities necessary to effectively manage complex, heterogeneous storage environments such as storage automation and provisioning. The advantages of a storage portal include:

- A single point of access is available for all storage management functions, including replication, utilization, backup, restoration, and library management.
- The portal works with all the hardware that the company already has in place.

- The open architecture can adapt to and incorporate new technologies developed by storage vendors.
- The portal allows access to and utilization of the proprietary management features that storage vendors build into their products to get the maximum performance out of each device.
- The portal works simultaneously with all operating systems a company might be using, including Windows, UNIX, Linux, and mainframes.
- The portal supports laptops as well as fixed assets.
- The portal provides enterprise-wide reporting so managers do not need to manually assemble data from a variety of disparate sources.
- Integration with leading software and hardware products from Network Appliance, StoreAge, CacheWare, LXI, and others allows the storage portal to consolidate storage management tasks, thereby streamlining daily operations and improving management decision-making.

Chapter 6

Disaster Recovery and Disk Management

While disaster recovery planning (DRP) gets a lot of lip service these days, a surprisingly large number of organizations have failed to fully understand and/ or implement a comprehensive DRP. Simply put, every organization should have a sound DRP that will function if ever needed and that goes way beyond RAID and backup. Yes, the impressive capabilities of modern RAID arrays and the sophistication of backup procedures can make it appear that no matter what data loss occurs, IT is covered for all eventualities. Yet, there are gaping holes waiting to be exploited. This chapter takes a look at the many elements of DRP and how to implement one so that the data is safe and easily recoverable. Also discussed is a contingency plan (CP) that applies to non-catastrophic failure due to accidental deletions, disk failures, and other potential data loss scenarios. By creating and implementing a CP, organizations are better able to eliminate data loss and downtime due to non-catastrophic failures such as disk crashes and deleted documents. Further, a CP gives an organization a better understanding of the many intricate details involved in any DRP so that the eventual plan is more fitted to the real world and may actually function adequately in times of catastrophe.

Is Your Data Really Protected?

To hear some people talk, one would think that data protection is now an accomplished fact. With RAID on the servers, adequate backup, and a decent firewall, we can rest easy knowing our data is secure. Yet, the surprisingly high rates of disk failure in organizations and the associated high rates of data loss attest to the fact that, despite RAID and backup being in place, these tools appear to have been about as effective as throwing stones at a division

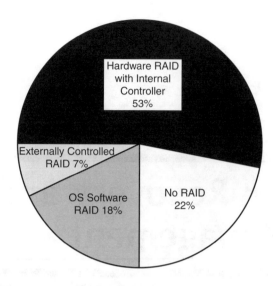

Hardware RAID
with Internal
Controller
53%

Externally Controlled
RAID 7%

OS Software
RAID 18%

No RAID
22%

Exhibit 1   RAID-Based Servers Shipped in 2000

of Panzer tanks when it comes to serving as a means of protection against data loss or worse, catastrophic failure.

Yet, the appeal of addressing data loss through built-in disk redundancy can be seen in the pervasiveness of RAID-based servers. According to Gartner Group (Stamford, Connecticut), 21.8 percent of all Intel servers shipped in 2000 had no RAID, 17.9 percent had OS software RAID (mainly Novell and MS systems), 53.3 percent had hardware RAID utilizing an internal RAID controller, and 7 percent had externally controlled hardware RAID. Breaking it down by market segment, today 100 percent of servers in the $10,000+ price range have hardware RAID, 98 percent of the $5000 to $10,000 server bracket have hardware RAID, and 45 percent of the sub-$5000 server range have hardware RAID (see Exhibits 1 and 2).

These statistics reveal the value placed on RAID technology. Not only does it accelerate I/O by simultaneously reading/writing to multiple disks, but it also preserves data by replicating it among disks. Although RAID is a great last line of defense, it has definite shortcomings. If a disk does go down, performance suffers badly until it is replaced and the data structure rebuilt. And, if more than one disk fails at the same time, the system is really in trouble. Further, RAID is largely a high-end server resource — 55 percent of low-end servers and close to 100 percent of workstations and laptops do not have RAID. Consequently, end-user hard disk failures are tolerated as a necessary evil.

Unfortunately, backup is not foolproof, either. For example, if a system is backed up every weekend, then any data newly written during the following week is subject to being completely lost; if the back up is performed on Sunday and new data is written on Monday and lost on Tuesday, then it is really lost, as it does not exist on any backup tapes. Even if the frequency of backups is increased, the same thing can still happen, just on a smaller scale. Imagine telling the boss that the 30-minute speech he spent all day writing

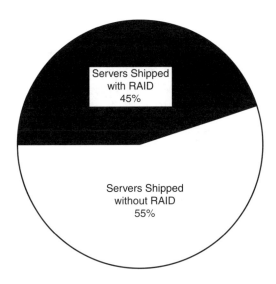

Exhibit 2   Servers Below $5000

then accidentally deleted is gone! And heaven help you if you have to rummage through tapes looking for specific documents. After hours of thankless work, you may end up finding the correct tape only to discover that the file being sought was not backed up or the media itself is faulty. A survey of 260 IT professionals found that only 38 percent of all tape backups retrieved all the data needed. Like RAID, backup is an essential system that everyone should implement, but it is far from the ideal solution for the problem of data loss and is only a small part of a comprehensive DRP.

Another problem with backup has arisen due to the tremendous growth of a mobile workforce. Over the years, companies have learned to keep critical information on servers rather than workstations and to back up servers daily; however, much of the day-to-day operational data is no longer on the network but is stored in the millions of laptops people carry around. Laptops might get backed up when they connect to the network, and maybe users will remember to back them up themselves, but then again maybe they won't. Given the abuse they take out in the field, laptops are more subject to drive failures than machines sitting in the office.

If backups were a total solution, then the market for data recovery software would not be so huge nor would so many companies be offering their services to recover data from hard disks and tapes. Although backup can be regarded as an essential element of data protection, it really is a last-line defense tool.

A Blended Approach to Data Protection

Protection now depends on more than one method. The nation uses a coordinated strategy involving ships, airplanes, submarines, ground troops, satellites, missiles, espionage, and law enforcement agencies to guard its borders. Cars have bumpers, seat belts, steel beams, and airbags to save passengers' lives.

Homeowners use outdoor lighting, watchdogs, door locks, and alarms to keep out thieves. When it comes to protecting an organization's computerized data, particularly in regard to DRP, a similarly blended approach is called for. Unquestionably one should always buy a reliable disk drive with RAID, back up data, and use a firewall and antivirus software. Each of these measures addresses a vital zone, but there is a lot more to it. It must be firmly understood that one can encounter two classes of disaster: non-catastrophic and catastrophic.

Non-Catastrophic Failure

Non-catastrophic failure is really a subset of a DRP and is addressed by a contingency plan (CP). The non-catastrophic category encompasses various types of failure, such as:

- Accidental deletion by a user
- Disk controller failure
- Hard disk/drive crash
- Network downtime
- Power surge

While RAID and backup are integral parts of any CP, they are far from sufficient. According to a conversation with Chip Nickolett, a disaster recovery expert working for Comprehensive Consulting Solutions, Inc. (Brookfield, Wisconsin), many of these issues may have already been addressed by hardware redundancy but this approach is not 100-percent foolproof. Non-catastrophic data loss, although disruptive to business operations, has the advantage that it is usually recoverable onsite within a relatively small time window.

Contingency Plan

As well as backup and RAID, CP tools include:

- Various undelete utilities, such as Executive Software Undelete, Quantum Software Undelete, Recover 4 All, and the Linux Files Undelete utility
- SMART-based disk monitoring utilities such as EZ SMART by Phoenix Technologies and Intelli-SMART by LC Technology
- Vendor tools, such as Compaq Insight Manager, which monitor disk health and other system parameters
- Non-SMART-based disk monitoring tools such as SpinRite by Gibson Research
- Network/system monitoring tools, such as Somix Technologies' WebNM and CA Unicenter, that can detect device problems and/or isolate hard drive issues
- Data recovery services that recover data lost in a hard drive that no longer functions (Ontrack is one example of such a service)

Although DRP gets more attention, a CP remains an essential element of organizational protection. In fact, it may well be that companies need to develop some competence with CP before being able to succeed well in any DRP initiative. Nickolett stated that his general recommendation to clients is to develop, test, and refine a CP before attempting a DRP.

In practice, much of the work of the CP will apply directly to the DRP, and the cost of refinement will be much less because work is done onsite. Most organizations tend to treat CP-related matters reactively. Generally, they do not plan for such disasters and, when one happens, someone in IT is called upon to handle the matter. Depending on the situation, this can mean hours of work to address a crucial issue or having to put users on hold for hours or even days while dealing with the problem.

Suppose you lose an important document due to human error. You may not receive a sympathetic ear when you call IT to say you just deleted a document you spent a full day compiling, and the response really depends on how prepared IT is for such an event and how high you are on the organizational totem pole. Oftentimes, IT has to turn away such requests, as the idea of hunting through hundreds of backup tapes for any vestiges of a document is daunting, and, of course, the likelihood is that recently created documents may not have been backed up since the last backup window. But, if it is the boss' PowerPoint presentation for tomorrow's show, IT will find itself searching and restoring whether it is a fruitless task or not.

An organization that is prepared for such a scenario would have instituted some kind of undelete function that made it easy for IT, and sometimes users, to recover data from accidental deletions. Further, Windows 2003 Server includes snapshot technology that makes it easy for users to recover lost files, without even disturbing IT.

The point is that the compilation of a CP forces companies to work out what they need to put in place and what processes they need to develop to deal with garden-variety data loss situations so that IT can deal with them with the minimum of distraction, cost, and downtime. When a hard drive goes down, instead of IT finding out about it a few hours after the fact and discovering that no hard drives of that type are in stock, disk monitoring software could have predicted the failure ahead of time and a stock of hard drives could always be on hand to replace faltering drives.

The CP, then, forces the organization to confront the multiple elements of potential data loss. The CP should be developed, tested, refined, and implemented. Doing so will educate the organization in regard to the intricacies of disaster recovery. As well as proofing the entire organization against non-catastrophic failure, this approach lays the foundation for a comprehensive DRP program. This method helps define a process that can later be modified for a full DRP. Further, in reality, the probabilities of non-catastrophic failure are many magnitudes higher than a full-fledged, catastrophic disaster.

Catastrophic Failure

Fires, floods, earthquakes, explosions, hurricanes, terrorist acts, and more constitute catastrophic disasters that can destroy an entire organization, or a portion or branch of it, overnight. This type of occurrence requires offsite facilities and data storage in order to ensure continuation of business activities. Design of such a facility must encompass such mundane matters as seats, desks, and office supplies, as well as IT systems and corporate data. Further, personnel will require telephone lines, network connections, and countless other items in order to function. The amount of detail, in fact, set down in any comprehensive DRP boggles the mind; yet, every single part of it is needed. Remember that if something horrible happens, normally reliable personnel may function poorly under stress and forget even the simplest of details. Every detail of every process should be recorded so that current and future staff can work through it effectively. Nickolett recommends checklists for everything; timestamp and initial every item and leave room for comments. In short, nothing should be left to chance.

Make the DRP Comprehensive

A word of caution about a DRP. It is extremely unrealistic to expect to work out a DRP in one meeting, write it up, distribute it to everyone involved, and then forget about it until a disaster takes place. This is a path to certain disaster, as the plan is not likely to function in the event of an emergency. According to Nickolett, most plans will experience some type of failure during their first execution, so it is very important to test the plan. Testing, retesting, and reconfiguring the plan on a regular basis will also expose one of the bugbears of many DRPs: A company might thoroughly work out a DRP — once. Then the company upgrades their equipment but experiences an annual 25% attrition rate. When an actual disaster strikes, much of the equipment is obsolete, and those who should be using it are not even familiar with it.

This brings us to another one of the pivotal points of DRP success: the assignment of responsibility. Place someone in charge of compiling and executing the DRP plan in time of need. This person should be held fully responsible for the organization's ability to respond to disasters small or large and should have a deputy; duties regarding the DRP should be a central element of the job descriptions of both these positions. During times of crisis, these people will work full time on disaster recovery execution, coordinating the activities of various personnel within the group, as well as communicating with outside agencies. Each department should also have its own DRP specialist, someone who organizes the department's activities during a catastrophe and who ensures the department's needs are taken into account when drawing up and testing the DRP.

The Economics of Disaster

Failure to develop a foolproof data loss prevention strategy could end up jeopardizing the company's data, profits, and future survival. After all, how much does downtime cost per user per day? Now multiply that by the number of employees and by the several weeks it might take to recover lost data. What about the lost sales, customers, and business or the cost of wages of all those employees unable to perform valuable work? Also consider catching up with the inevitable backlog when the system is running again — how much does that cost? The simple truth is that the potential costs of a disaster dwarf the price tag for even the most sophisticated DRP programs. Although events since September 11, 2001, have greatly accelerated the awareness of organizations regarding DRP, a surprising number still have not gotten around to actually addressing the problem. They still cling to the unrealistic hope that backup and RAID are enough. Obviously, backup is a key component of any strategy, yet many companies seek to cut corners by having redundant systems within the same building or next door. Case in point: Some companies within the World Trade Center actually located their disaster facilities in another part of the WTC. The moral of the story: Keep multiple backups in several diverse locations.

I have used a Zip drive for years to back up my key files and archives. It sits on top of my computer and is very handy whenever I need to retrieve data. While it has served its purpose well, I realized a while back that it did not protect me against disaster. One fire or flood or other disaster, and both my PC and Zip drive could be destroyed simultaneously. I found myself an online backup service so I have a record of my data files offsite. Proximity, then, is a key factor in DRP. Disaster resources should be located away from the main offices to create actual redundancy of files and resources.

Recognition of Mission-Critical Elements

A key element of effective disaster recovery is recognition of all aspects of critical operations. Whatever is necessary to function for the next month or three months must be identified and then established at offsite facilities. With particular reference to data, doing so includes mirroring data offsite. What else? As people tend to have tunnel vision regarding the definition of "critical" items, it takes input from all departments and many echelons of command in order to determine the exact recipe for DRP success. Which assets are most critical for the running of every area of the organization, right down to the fine details? It takes a lot of input to get it right. Outside help, then, is a very good idea. People who have experienced disasters, who have helped organizations work through them, and who have implemented DRP in dozens of similar organizations are good to have around when it is time to work out a disaster strategy. They can sort things out in an orderly process that moves smoothly from planning to implementation.

Drilling

Further, such people can help with an important component of DRP that is often neglected: drilling. Have you ever seen a really competent crew of seamen drilling? They do "man overboard," "abandon ship," and fire drills on board over and over. I even saw one crew, of the *Freewinds* out of Curacao, doing emergency drills blindfolded. Amazing to behold, but it drove home the point that these guys were ready for everything that Old Man Sea, Mother Nature, or human stupidity could throw at them. It is the same with corporate DRP. It is important to drill the plan thoroughly until everyone knows his part, what to do, where to go, and how to get back up and running quickly. Obviously, this exercise can be taken to extremes, but the consequences of not doing it become evident if we return to our nautical example. I have seen a crew fail to deal effectively with a small fire on board an ocean liner; they abandoned ship in a very shoddy fashion that endangered the passengers in the process and almost lost the entire vessel for no good reason.

Data Organization

Disaster recovery planning and contingency plans are now examined specifically with regard to data. Although alternate premises and physical logistics are vital elements, data is the heart and soul of any business. Here are some important points to take into account in order to cope better with data preservation and recovery.

Data Quantity

Although companies may have various replication scenarios in place, in the event of a disaster these plans may become overwhelmed by the sheer quantity of replication that has to be accomplished at once. You may have drilled replication with regard to a specific server, but what if the entire server farm has gone down? Any DRP, then, must include provisions for how exactly to replicate what might be tens of terabytes worth of data in a short time. The storage site, for example, had better have enough bandwidth to relay the data at the required speed. And, once the data has been received, can you use the images immediately or do you have to rebuild databases and cobble together multiple transactions until everything is complete?

Data Priority

Next is priority of data; that is, which systems and databases/servers should be restored first? If a disaster occurs, everybody will want this data restored *now*; therefore, it is important to have determined which data is most important and should be recovered first in order to get the business going again. Also, set up several phases of data recovery so that, even if the required bandwidth is lacking, at least the first phase can be pulled in immediately and effective action taken to minimize the delay in getting the company functioning. As part of this prioritization, determine an acceptable recovery window for each network or system. Some systems can perhaps be down as long as 48 hours without catastrophic affect on the business, whereas for other systems one hour may be too much downtime. Further, be realistic in your estimates. While it might be unreal to avoid any transaction losses, perhaps you can limit losses to as small a window as possible, but this depends on the type of business, which in turn determines the amount spent on minimizing transactional losses. Whereas a bank may have duplicate recordings of every transaction, a manufacturing company may decide it can afford to lose a day's invoices because it should be able to recover the information based on a few phone calls to the sales staff.

Data Medium

Next we consider the medium on which the data will be recorded. Most DRPs call for daily backup to tape, with a subsequent shift of these tapes offsite. The idea is that, in the event of a disaster, these tapes can be taken to alternative headquarters and the data loaded onto the servers, with the aim of getting the business up and running within a day or two. This is the preferred method for most American companies. Alternatives include electronic vaulting and mirroring. Electronic vaulting is backing up data across a network to an offsite location; this is typically far more expensive than tape backup but yields a faster recovery window. Mirroring data to an identical system can cut the recovery window to less than an hour, provided a remote operations center is available in the event of a disaster. Mirroring, however, significantly adds to cost. As a result, surveys of American enterprises indicate that 19 percent routinely use remote mirroring or continuous data backup procedures for enterprise servers. Gartner Group surveys found that 70 percent of Fortune 500 companies use replication-based backup systems for 10 percent of their data.

Hardware Issues

It is important to pay close attention to hardware issues such as machine types and configurations. Many elements, including disk capacity, device names, peripheral devices, RAM, and many more, must be considered regarding the subject of configuration. In addition to recording everything, it is also essential to consider exactly how the hardware is going to be replaced, detail by detail. According to Nickolett, another issue is deciding whether to use an existing preconfigured machine or to completely configure a machine (load the OS, initialize and configure the disks, determine the TCP/IP configuration and SCSI addresses, etc.). His recommendation is to plan for the worst case (i.e., complete rebuild). It might also be possible to reconstruct a new machine using a tape backup. Although this approach is somewhat inflexible in terms of configuration, it is a lot faster than a manual system reconfiguration.

Networking Issues

It is no good replicating all the hardware and software configurations if the necessary networking points are not taken care of. Are you running a LAN, WAN, or VPN? If so, what types of software and connections are necessary to replicate critical parts of the production environment in order to get back to work?

Software Issues

Software encompasses all manner of operating systems, applications, third-party software, customized code and applications, etc. It is important to have a complete inventory of all of these things, as well as a listing of what is really needed to resume business activity. Also, look into licensing. What happens if it is necessary to reload everything? Do your current licenses make it easy or difficult to do so? Find out what is involved and act before rather than after any emergency to ensure the process is smooth.

Test and Refine Some More

Many times in this chapter, the importance of testing and refining the plan has been emphasized. The two ways to do this are both valid:

- Validate the DRP and its inherent processes.
- Simulate an actual disaster to see how the plan performs.

Such tests should be run at least once a year to verify your readiness. For each test, keep notes of slows or failures and refine the DRP so each drill is better than the last. One always hopes that it will never be necessary to call on the DRP, but it is best to be prepared to do so. And, more importantly, CP processes that make IT extremely efficient at eliminating the slows and smaller data losses that plague every organization will be in place.

Chapter 7

Disk Performance and Fragmentation

Many turn to hardware upgrades in order to improve the speed and responsiveness of Windows NT/2000. From the latest hard drives and CPUs to more RAM, IT executives are constantly striving for upgrades that will open the door to increased performance. More recently, defragmentation techniques have gained popularity as an effective means of boosting performance at a fraction of the cost of hardware upgrades. Additionally, fragmentation is a significant factor in system instability. Users who keep their servers and workstations fragment free experience far fewer crashes, hangs, and system instability issues.

This chapter examines what fragmentation is, its impact, safety considerations, and the best ways to defragment a network. It also includes details on recent reports explaining the total cost of ownership (TCO) benefits of regularly defragmenting a network, how this may affect future hardware upgrade decisions, and the relationship between fragmentation and system stability. Finally, the chapter addresses manual defragmenters such as the one built in to Windows 2000 and how to use them and compares them to third party products.

History and Origins of Fragmentation

During the early days of Windows NT, it was believed that the design of NTFS would effectively eliminate concerns about fragmentation that had plagued earlier operating systems. Taking a look at the history and origins of fragmentation might provide a clue to the origins of this belief. Fragmentation first appeared about thirty years ago, right after that dark age when computers existed without disks or operating systems. By the late 1960s, disks appeared that were able to store thousands of bytes — a revolutionary concept at the time. One early computer, the PDP-11, had an operating system called RT-11 that introduced the concept of storing files in a formal file structure. The downside was that all files had to be contiguous. Disks with plenty of space, but lacking one free space large enough to accommodate a new file, were "full." With frequent file deletions, it was not unusual to have a disk reach the point where no more files could be created even though the disk was little more than half full. The solution was SQUEEZE, a command that compacted files at the beginning of the disk.

When a new operating system (RSX-11) came along that allowed multiple simultaneous users of the same PDP-11 computer, SQUEEZE became a problem as using it meant that all users had to stop working while it ran. This drawback led to the creation of a file structure that could locate parts of a file in different places on the disk. Each file had a header that gave the location and size of each section of the file, so the file itself could be in pieces scattered around the disk. Thus, fragmentation became a feature, not a bug, in these early systems.

The fragmentation approach of RSX-11 was carried over into the Open VMS operating system, and when its principle designers moved over to Microsoft, they built the NT file systems on this same fragmentation model. The problem, though, is that, as hard drive capacities and CPU speeds grew exponentially, disk speeds did not keep pace. In today's client/server world, where thousands of files are being written and deleted from disks repeatedly, the end product is files split into thousands of pieces that exert a significant toll on system I/O.

Does NTFS Suffer from Fragmentation?

The myth that NT and its file system NTFS do not fragment persisted for several years, causing people to believe that NT automatically selected the optimum position for files so as not to fragment them. Though NTFS did introduce better algorithms for cluster allocation, it quickly became evident that NT did fragment, and it fragmented considerably. Yet, for many years, Microsoft remained ambivalent about the impact of fragmentation on NT. Fortunately, there has been a change in stance over the past few years. In fact, the company now openly advocates regular defragmentation as a performance necessity and has included a "lite" defragmenter inside Windows 2000 and XP.

How Much Fragmentation Occurs in NTFS?

Just how much fragmentation occurs in NT and Windows 2000? For those doubters still clinging to the belief that these operating systems either do not fragment or effectively minimize fragmentation, try this experiment. Install a new version of the OS and MS Office, and then run an analysis of fragmentation. You might be surprised by the extent of fragmentation, especially for

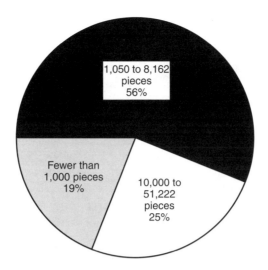

1,050 to 8,162 pieces 56%

Fewer than 1,000 pieces 19%

10,000 to 51,222 pieces 25%

Exhibit 1   Fragmentation on NT and Windows 2000 Workstations

NTFS. The results of such an experiment are supported by a fragmentation study conducted on 100 companies (ranging from small to large). This survey revealed that 56 percent of NT/Windows 2000 workstations had files fragmented into between 1,050 and 8,162 pieces. One in four reported finding files with as many as 10,000 to 51,222 fragments. For servers, an even greater degree of fragmentation exists. Half of the respondents discovered 2,000 to 10,000 fragments, and another 33 percent had files fragmented into 10,333 to 95,000 pieces. Although rare, it is possible to find the occasional file splintered into hundred of thousands and even millions of pieces (see Exhibit 1).

Detractors, however, argue that the performance hit from fragmentation is canceled out by a number of modern features. Disks come equipped with read-ahead and seek optimization technology, queued I/O requests are reordered to minimize head movement and revolution-time stalls, and a file-based cache bypasses disk access on commonly used files. Defragmentation vendors, on the other hand, counter with claims of increased speed and system performance, citing horror stories of crippled servers that take 30 minutes to boot up, only to move with the rapidity of frozen molasses. So, who's right?

Defining Fragmentation

Before we move deeper into the argument, though, we should define our terms. What does *fragmentation* mean? *File fragmentation* is the allocation of noncontiguous sectors on a disk; that is, instead of placing files in one location, parts of it are scattered all over the disk. Essentially, fragmentation means that files are broken into multiple pieces rather than residing in one contiguous block on a disk. When a file is opened, therefore, the head has to gather up all these pieces in order to display the file. Thus, the user experiences delays in waiting for a document to appear. If the condition is in an advanced state (it is quite common for server files to be splintered into thousands of pieces), it might even take as long as 15 seconds to open a document that previously was available in one second.

Stated simply, fragmentation is generated and accentuated by the multiple read/write operations of modern-day computing. When you write a lot of data, delete many files, write many more files, and delete some more, you end up with lots of small pockets of space and eventually not enough space to write large files into. As a result, these files have to be written into a series of smaller parts or fragments. It gets a little more complex than that, however. The very process of loading an application results in severe fragmentation of directories and files. Windows tends to scatter directories willy-nilly throughout a disk. As soon as you load the OS, in fact, you effectively have a badly fragmented system. Some users report 50 percent fragmentation after loading Windows 2000, Office, and a couple of applications — and this occurs on a disk that is three quarters empty. Try it. Take a brand new disk. Load Windows 2000 and see how much fragmentation exists.

Free Space Fragmentation

As well as file fragmentation, then, free space on the disk also becomes broken up, further aggravating the situation. When a new file is created, it may not be able to find a large enough block of contiguous free space, resulting in its being written to the disk in a fragmented state. As free space and file fragmentation takes hold, the condition worsens rapidly, and the user becomes aware of deterioration in performance. In addition to taking longer to open files, users begin to complain of overlong reboots and even backups taking much longer than before. A U.S. District Court site in Maine serves as an example of what can happen as a result of fragmentation. This site reported that a server was taking 20 minutes to shut down during reboot. The system manager said that years of experience had convinced him that system deterioration was a fact of life on NT and Windows 2000; however, when he loaded Executive Software's Diskeeper on all his servers and workstations, reboots returned to normal, performance sped up substantially, and reliability improved.

Fragmentation Adversely Affects Systems Stability

Windows has had a reputation in the past for crashing more than other operating systems (note that this situation is far less prevalent with XP and Windows 2000). It may well be that part of the problem has been user ignorance of fragmentation. While it is broadly accepted that fragmentation negatively impacts system performance, what is not so well understood is that fragmentation exerts a severe toll in terms of system unreliability and downtime. Simply put, a system is never in a more stable state than when all files are in contiguous form. The moment a file is broken into pieces, the door to a host of stability issues opens. A badly fragmented system will not only slow down considerably, but it will also be slow to reboot (or will not reboot at all in extreme cases), will suffer from far more crashes, will be slow to back up, and will cause file corruption, data loss, system crashes and hangs, program errors, memory issues, and even hard drive failures.

These consequences of fragmentation have been substantiated by hundreds of IT users of defragmentation products who have been interviewed over the past decade. About half or more have commented that their systems now rarely crash compared with before the defragmentation utility was installed. They attribute this improvement to well-maintained files and file systems, which in turn influence system stability positively.

Countless documents available within the Microsoft Knowledge Base (KB) address the subject of how fragmentation severely and insidiously affects system uptime and stability. Failure to understand the source of these problems forces IT staff to troubleshoot in the wrong areas which often leads to actions such as reinstalling software, re-imaging of hard drives, and expensive replacement of hardware, as well as an overworked help desk. These problems cut into company profits and lead to unacceptable levels of downtime by forcing system administrators to work reactively rather than proactively. At the root of many of these problems lies fragmentation. Fragmentation erodes stability and reliability in seven main areas, as follows.

Fragmentation and Boot Time

As mentioned earlier, fragmentation is a major factor in slow boot times. Many cases are on record of machines taking twenty or thirty minutes to reboot that previously took only a minute or two. This situation can deteriorate to the point where a machine will not boot up at all. This situation affects not only Windows NT, but also Windows 2000 and Windows XP. According to Microsoft, this issue can occur when the NTFS bootsector code contained in logical sector zero of an NTFS volume is unable to locate and load NTLDR[1] into memory because the Master File Table (MFT) is highly fragmented (see Microsoft KB article Q228734, http://support.microsoft.com). Why does this occur? The NTFS bootsector code locates and loads NTLDR into memory. This involves reading the volume's MFT to obtain the root directory. When the MFT is highly fragmented, pieces of the MFT and other metadata that must be read in order to locate the NTLDR may fall outside the areas of the disk that can be read by the INT 13 BIOS routine. Thus, the system fails to boot up.

Other Microsoft Knowledge Base articles discuss additional manifestations of similar problems. Microsoft KB article Q155892 discusses the situation when the allocation for NTLDR's $DATA attribute becomes so fragmented that the whole $DATA attribute is no longer in the base FRS (file record segment). Microsoft KB article Q176968 explains that when you attempt to boot with an NTFS system partition, the computer may hang after the power-on self test (POST), and you may receive an error message stating that a kernel file is missing. This can occur if the NTFS disk structure data contained in the MFT

---

1 NTLDR = NT loader: a program loaded from the boot sector that displays the startup menu and helps the OS load.

is fragmented (as described above), preventing boot up. It was thought that this bug had been eradicated in Windows 2000 and XP, as an updated bootsector code and NTLDR were made available for Windows 2000 with the intention of removing its susceptibility to this situation. Similarly, Windows XP includes "prefetching" of boot files and automatically defragments the boot sector to accelerate startup. However, neither of these fixes has eliminated the problem of systems failing to reboot periodically.

Fragmentation and Slow Back Up Times/Aborted Backups

Backup windows these days are shrinking. While IT used to have twelve or more hours available for backup and maintenance tasks, or even all weekend, they are now expected to perform such tasks in a shorter period. Yet, at the same time, the amount of data to be backed up is growing exponentially. This combination of circumstances leads to two problems. System administrators report that lengthy backups mean they do not have time for other routine maintenance actions. Backups have to be aborted when they take up too much time and threaten to encroach on the work day.

What does this have to do with fragmentation? Today's systems take a pounding that leaves most hard disks horribly fragmented within a very short period of time. Programs create and delete large numbers of temporary files, documents are written to disk and deleted continually, and, as a result, drives rapidly become fragmented. Documents are commonly found splintered into hundreds and even thousands of pieces. This adds to system overhead as it takes much longer for the computer to read and write fragmented files than contiguous ones. If fragmentation is not quickly addressed, the condition of the drive deteriorates rapidly (see National Software Testing Labs' white paper, *System Performance and File Fragmentation in Windows NT,* http://www.exec-soft.com).

In addition to slowing systems to a crawl, however, fragmentation multiplies the amount of time required for backup. If all files existed in a contiguous state, backup would occur relatively swiftly; instead, the head must thrash around gathering together numerous fragments before they can be consolidated into one piece and then backed up. The situation is compounded by the fact that most backup software creates a large number of temporary files. This results in even more fragmentation, further slowing the backup process.

This is why many users of enterprise-class defragmenters report backup times shrinking by several hours per night after instituting daily fragmentation of every server and workstation. By consolidating files into one piece before backing them up, a much shorter backup window is required, which allows system administrators to schedule other important maintenance tasks.

The IT analyst group IDC believes that, to maintain optimal system performance, companies need to schedule disk defragmentation on a regular basis for all their servers and workstations; otherwise, files can take 10 to 15 times longer to access, boot time can be tripled, and nightly backups can take hours longer. Similarly, if nightly backups are taking twelve hours (in a fragmented system) instead of four, not enough time may be available to complete a backup. Under these circumstances, IT would be forced to abort the backup before commencement of the work day. Fortunately, regular defragmentation eliminates these backup concerns.

Fragmentation and File Corruption/Data Loss

File corruption and data loss are two factors immediately traceable to fragmentation, as verified during recent tests conducted at the research labs of Executive Software. Both Windows 2000 and Windows XP were tested as follows. Technicians ran a utility designed to fragment an NTFS volume. Even though the drive was only 40 percent full, the files themselves were severely fragmented, resulting in the need for many more MFT records than usual. When they attempted to move a contiguous 72-MB file onto that disk, the result was the corruption of everything on the disk, including the 72-MB file. This occurred on Windows 2000 and on Windows XP.

Why does this occur? The presence of excessive file fragments on a disk makes it difficult for the operating system to function efficiently. When a large file is added, large-scale data corruption results. While nothing currently exists within the Microsoft Knowledge Base regarding this specific subject, documentation is available concerning other fragmentation-related corruption/data loss issues.

Receiving this message is not uncommon:

> Windows NT could not start because the following file is missing or corrupt:
> <Winnt_root>\System32\Ntoskrnl.exe.
> Please re-install a copy of the above file.

This form of corruption/data loss led to the inability to boot because some key files needed for booting the operating system were situated beyond cylinder 1023 on the volume. But, given the CHS (cylinder/head/sector) setup on the machine, the boot sequence could see only the first 7.68 GB of the volume during the initial boot phase. The needed file was situated beyond where the INT 13 BIOS interface could find it. Deleting the first file and replacing it meant that it fell within the first 7.68 GB. Regular defragmentation would keep system files from becoming too spread around the volume, preventing this situation from recurring. (This issue is covered in more detail in Microsoft KB article Q224526, http://support.microsft.com).

Fragmentation and Crashes

Many documented cases of errors and crashes on Windows caused by fragmentation can be found. Types of errors include system hangs, times out, failures to load, failures to save data, and blue screens. In one scenario, for instance, a crash takes place when attempting to run CHKDSK on a highly fragmented drive. According to Microsoft, when you attempt to run CHKDSK/F on a drive that is heavily fragmented or that contains bad clusters, Windows NT version 4.0 may halt with a kernel mode trap screen STOP 0x00000024 in Ntfs.sys (see Microsoft KB article Q160451). Another Microsoft KB article (Q165456) that highlights the reason for a system freezing considers the situation when the NTFS file system driver attempts to perform I/O to a fragmented file and does not correctly clear a required field, causing either a STOP 0xA or a deadlock condition. This causes the process to stop responding. What this means is that fragmentation can slow down I/O to the point where programs and processes cease to function entirely. With files in many pieces, they are unavailable to the system when needed and a crash takes place.

Fragmentation and Errors in Programs

Reports are also fairly frequent of errors in large applications such as Microsoft Outlook or Microsoft Word because the applications and/or associated databases are substantially fragmented. As in the previous section, this is related to the sheer size of such applications and the time it takes to physically gather all the parts in order to load properly. In some cases, fragmentation slows down the loading of applications, sometimes significantly, but in other cases the application times out or freezes. On Microsoft Word 2000, for example, an error message may appear stating that there are too many edits in a document. Users are advised to save their work or face data loss (see Microsoft KB article Q224029). This situation is caused by insufficient disk space on the hard disk containing the Windows Temp folder as well as by fragmented or cross-linked files.

Additionally, Windows 2000 can sometimes hang. During startup, this is related to the system hive file becoming too large due to fragmentation. According to Microsoft KB article Q265509, the system hive file is usually the biggest file that is loaded and is likely to be fragmented because it is modified often. If the system hive file is too fragmented, it is not loaded from an NTFS volume and the computer hangs. After startup, Windows 2000 can also hang due to the inability of the server service to keep up with the demand for network work items that are queued by the network layer of the I/O stream; that is, due to fragmentation, the server service cannot process the requested network I/O items to the hard disk quickly enough before running out of resources.

Compact disc (CD) writers and other media devices also experience problems caused by fragmentation. Such devices require data to be supplied sequentially in a steady stream. If the associated files are fragmented, this data stream is interrupted as the system struggles to gather together various fragments. This interferes with the quality of video playback and leads to a CD write aborting. Regular defragmentation heightens the reliability of such devices. According to Microsoft KB article Q306524 (*How To Copy Information to a CD in Windows XP*), CD recording may fail intermittently. The document provides several ways to resolve this issue, and the primary step is to defragment the hard disk containing the data destined for the CD.

Fragmentation and RAM Use/Cache Problems

Files often become so fragmented that they seem to take an eternity to be read into the cache. In addition to long delays, this situation can lead to system hangs. Similarly, a fragmented paging file creates system stability challenges. An "out of virtual memory" error message results, for example, on a primary domain controller, and data loss results. According to Microsoft KB article Q215859, the pagefile.sys file is either not large enough or is severely fragmented. This may also cause users to experience problems when they attempt to change their password or gain access to the network. As noted earlier, such memory issues are rooted in the fact that excessive overhead is required to compile files that are scattered around a disk in many pieces. By keeping files consolidated, these memory problems are eliminated.

Fragmentation and Hard Drive Failure

Fragmentation hastens the onset of hard drive failure by increasing the amount of head movement; consequently, regular defragmentation extends drive longevity. The reason for this is simple. When a defragmentation program is run, it attempts to move files, but if it uncovers bad areas on the disk, it directs the user to run CHKDSK. Without the running of a defragmentation utility, these bad sectors may not receive the attention they deserve. Over time, the number of bad sectors snowballs, leading to corruption of the entire drive.

Benefits of Defragmentation

What are the benefits of defragmentation? In the Maine District Court example above, instead of requiring twenty minutes to shut down a server, the process took forty-five seconds after defragmentation. File access times dropped from ten seconds to one to three seconds, and the MIS department reported many hours saved through faster backups. In addition, a study by IDC recently highlighted the fact that regular defragmentation enhances performance and can also lengthen the lifespan of a machine. IDC estimates that enterprises can add up to two additional years of life to the normal three-year usable life of workstations (see IDC white paper, *Disk Defragmentation for Windows NT/ 2000*, http://www.execsoft.com). Let us take a closer look at why regular defragmentation extends the life of hard drives. It takes the head one I/O to read or write a contiguous file. If a file is in 100 pieces, the head has to move 100 times to access it. If this is occurring every time a file is read or written to disk, the head and associated moving parts are effectively having to perform 100 times more work than would be required for a fragment-free file. The result is more wear and tear on the disk and an earlier failure.

Remedying Fragmentation

The remedy for these conditions, as well as for diminished performance on Windows-based machines, is simple enough: Defragment the affected disks. Defragmentation programs consolidate the various file fragments, positioning them on the disk contiguously (in one piece) and producing larger chunks of free space. Note, however, that the goal of a defragmenter is not to produce a pretty picture in the GUI when the program completes; rather, it is to increase performance and system stability without absorbing system resources. Some defrag programs take things to extremes and over-consume resources in order to produce a screen that shows one contiguous block of free space. In practice, this is not necessary, as long as most of the free space is available in a couple of large pieces.

How Defragmenters Work

Usually, defragmentation programs check each file on a disk to determine which files should be defragmented and which files should be moved to another location to provide more contiguous free space. If a file is to be moved online, then the defragmenter uses special applications programming interfaces (APIs), known as IOCTLs (input/output controls), that work in harmony with the file system to accomplish defragmentation safely. This special MoveFile API makes a contiguous copy of the file on the disk to the location specified by the defragmenter. Next, the MoveFile API changes the pointers to that file to point to the new contiguous copy of the file. Finally, the disk space of the original fragmented file is deallocated, but only after successful completion of the prior cycles. All this is conducted online by current-day defragmenters; files can be defragmented in the background, usually running at low priority so as not to tax overhead. As a result, the system does not have to be shut down.

Two file types in the operating system cannot be defragmented online using the special APIs. These are the paging file and, on NTFS, the MFT. On Windows NT 4.0, the directories also cannot be defragmented online. In Windows 2000, though, the APIs have been enhanced to move directories safely online during defragmentation. On XP, the APIs have been further enhanced to also permit online defragmentation of the MFT.

Preventing MFT Fragmentation

On NTFS, the Master File Table (MFT) is the map of each and every file on the volume and is itself a file. Every time a new file is made, a new record is created in the MFT file. As more files are added, the MFT expands. Unfortunately, files that are constantly growing, such as the MFT, are most susceptible to the extremes of fragmentation. Because the MFT is such an important file, to combat any tendency to fragment, Microsoft reserved space on the disk immediately after the MFT that is referred to as the MFT Zone.

Approximately one eighth of an NTFS volume is reserved for the MFT Zone. The theory is that the MFT Zone is reserved space on the disk for the MFT to expand, thus preventing or at least minimizing MFT fragmentation.

Despite this precaution, the MFT does fragment on occasion. This is because files still get written into the MFT Zone under certain circumstances. For example, when a disk is full, files are stored in the MFT Zone. Now, suppose that some files get deleted from this volume but *not* the ones stored in the MFT Zone. Despite space being available on the disk, files still reside in the MFT Zone. When more files are stored onto this disk, the MFT must expand to store these new files, but the files in the MFT Zone block the way. As a result, the MFT becomes fragmented.

Several attempts have been made to eradicate MFT fragmentation. One method is to bypass the operating system and the special APIs in order to defragment the MFT online (Microsoft technical authorities have told me that they consider this approach dangerous). A safer alternative is offline defragmentation during rebooting.

In addition, some tools actually work to prevent the MFT from becoming fragmented in the first place. If the MFT is fragmented when the defragmentation software is first installed on a machine, it is quickly defragmented at boot time. From that point on, a monitoring process works to ensure that the MFT does not again become fragmented, thus reducing the number of times required to defragment it. In practice, boot-time defragmentation will have to be run from time to time, but the frequency is something that should tie in with other maintenance actions that require reboot of Windows-based systems.

The MFT is actually the heart of the NTFS file system. It is essentially an index to all of the files on an NTFS volume, containing the file name, a list of file attributes, and a pointer to the file. The data for each file is contained in one record in the MFT, referred to as the file record. If a file is fragmented, then more than one pointer is required — one for each fragment, in fact. When the file system accesses a file, it must first go through the MFT to obtain the location of that file or the location of that file's various fragments, as well as that file's various attributes. As one might surmise, an additional MFT performance barrier occurs due simply to regular file fragmentation. In that the file system must access the MFT to obtain the location of every single file fragment and then locate the file fragments themselves, there is a lot of "double work" involved.

But, how does the MFT itself get fragmented and what can be done about it? First, it should be said that NTFS has a built-in feature that under some conditions prevents MFT fragmentation from occurring; for example, as noted previously, the MFT is created with a preallocated expansion space into which it can expand without fragmenting. Under a couple of conditions, however, MFT fragmentation does occur, one of which is very common.

Converting FAT to NTFS

The most common way in which the MFT gets fragmented is when a FAT partition is converted to NTFS. A FAT partition ordinarily is converted to NTFS when such a conversion is specifically needed or desired, but it also occurs automatically during Windows NT installation, if the NTFS format is chosen. The partition created during installation is a FAT partition, and even if the NTFS format is chosen during installation, the partition is still created as FAT and is only converted to NTFS after the first boot. When a FAT partition is converted to NTFS, an MFT is created. If the contiguous free space is large enough, the MFT is made contiguous, with contiguous preallocated expansion space. However, because the MFT itself plus the preallocated expansion space comprises about 12 percent of the partition, not enough contiguous free space is usually available and the MFT is created fragmented.

MFT and Full or Heavily Fragmented Disks or Partitions

One caveat about the MFT preallocated space must be noted. NTFS, having been developed to efficiently use every bit of space on a disk or partition, will utilize the preallocated MFT space for normal files if the disk or partition becomes full or heavily fragmented. Simply said, if the disk runs out of regular space for files or file fragments, NTFS will turn to the MFT preallocated space and begin writing files and file fragments to this space. When this occurs, the MFT can only expand by continuing its growth in another space on the disk, a space not adjacent to the MFT. Thus, MFT fragmentation begins; when that space runs out, another space will have to be found, and so on.

Effect of MFT Fragmentation on Performance

When the MFT is fragmented, access to directories and files slows down tremendously as the file system works its way through the fragmented MFT to access the pointers and file attributes necessary to access every file. Combined with regular file fragmentation, this is a performance nightmare — the file system has to make multiple I/Os to access the MFT and then make multiple I/Os to access the file itself. Until a couple of years ago, it was not possible to safely defragment the MFT, as it could not be moved safely online while the disk or partition was live and in use; hence, one could defragment a disk or partition and clean up regular fragmentation but MFT fragmentation would remain. (The author has personal experience with a medium-use disk that was regularly defragmented, yet ended up with an MFT in over 9000 fragments.) Before Diskeeper 5.0, nothing could be done about MFT fragmentation, and simply opening Windows Explorer, for example, could take two to three minutes. Diskeeper's Frag Guard feature prevents fragmentation of the MFT. For the first time, a defragmenter has taken a proactive approach to eliminating fragmentation.

Page File Fragmentation

Paging files present a problem for defragmentation software. Before going any further, though, let us take a look at what the page file is and what it does. NT, for example, supports up to 16 paging files on a system. These files are used for virtual memory; as Windows NT and its applications use memory in excess of the physical RAM, the Virtual Memory Manager writes the least recently used areas of memory to the paging files to free RAM. If a program accesses these areas of memory, the Virtual Memory Manager reads them from the paging file back to RAM where the program can use them. The paging file, then, is used to swap pages to and from memory to supplement the use of physical RAM; however, access to disk-based "memory" is quite slow compared with physical RAM — paging files operate in the millisecond range but physical RAM runs in nanoseconds.

Page-file fragmentation can impact system performance in a couple of ways depending on system configuration and use. It can prevent some files from being created contiguously. This is because the page-file fragments, being scattered all over the disk, may break up the free space so there is less space to hold the larger files. It can then take longer to write new files and read existing ones. Further, paging activity can be slowed down, depending on the degree of page-file fragmentation. If the page-file fragments are larger than 64 KB each, fragmentation is not a problem because only 64 KB (the system limit) is read at a time. So even if you have a 100-MB page file in one large contiguous location, it would still take 1500 I/Os to read the entire file. But, if the fragments are smaller than 64 KB, then multiple I/Os are required just to read one chunk of data. Additionally, the data itself is not necessarily contiguous; for example, if a program has 60 KB stored in the page file, the data may reside in three widely separated 20-KB pieces. And, with an extremely fragmented page file (say, 100 MB in size with 10,000 fragments), you will notice a very noticeable lag every time it is accessed, as each page-file fragment averages only 10 KB. Normally, however, a page file is fragmented into somewhere between 1000 and 4000 fragments, so this performance drag is not as drastic on an average system.

Defragmenting the paging file into a single location not only speeds up paging performance but also provides more consolidated free space to defragment the whole system; however, there is a problem. Once the system starts up, these files are always open and cannot be moved or deleted. At startup, the Windows NT system process duplicates the file handles for the paging file so that the files will always be open and the operating system will prevent any other process from deleting or moving them. For this reason, paging files are a challenge for defragmentation software. In order to safely defragment the paging file, defragmenters must defragment them at system boot time before the Virtual Memory Manager gets a chance to lock them down. While this is a desirable feature, regularly rebooting a system to defragment it is not a desirable situation, so the best solution is to keep the rest of the file system defragmented to mitigate any fragmentation problems caused by the existence of paging files.

As an active paging file is always held open by the NT operating system, it is impossible for online defragmenters to access it. Paging file fragmentation can be addressed either offline or by using Diskeeper's Frag Guard feature, which functions by monitoring the area on the disk at the end of the paging file and ensuring that enough space is available for it to expand.

Defragmentation Safety Issues

Definitely, then, a number of safety issues must be taken into account. Both Windows NT and Windows 2000 have APIs built in specifically to make safe online defragmentation possible. These APIs allow files to be moved safely online while the operating system is running. Defragmenters, therefore, must utilize the APIs or risk blue screens, system crashes, and file corruption. The only safe way to conduct online defragmentation on a Windows 2000 or NT platform is to go through the defragmentation APIs that the operating system supports. A defragmentation program manipulating data inside of the MFT or paging file unbeknown to the operating system or the file system could result in massive data loss.

While software could possibly be written to bypass the operating system in order to defragment the MFT and paging file online, the consensus is that it would be an extremely complex task fraught with danger. It is akin to changing the oil in a car engine while cruising down the freeway. Even if someone could figure out a way to do it, think about the ramifications. It is vital, therefore, that defragmentation tools be closely inspected before purchase. Use defragmenters that comply with the APIs.

Defragmentation Performance Testing

Surprisingly, until a couple of years ago, defragmentation had never been thoroughly benchmarked, an omission rectified by National Software Testing Lab (NSTL) of Conshohocken, Pennsylvania. Various reports have been done by NSTL on defragmentation performance testing. Since 1999, NSTL has conducted several benchmarks. The first focused on two of the most common NT configurations for that time, determined through a survey of 6000 system managers running Windows NT. A Pentium II 266-MHz workstation with 96 MB of memory and a 2-GB IDE hard drive, running Outlook and Excel, showed a performance leap of 74.5 percent with a defragmented drive. On a Pentium II 400-MHz workstation with 128 MB RAM and a 4.2-GB hard drive, the improvement rose to 80.6 percent.

Two popular server configurations also underwent testing. A dual Pentium PRO 200 with 128 MB of memory and five 4-GB SCSI hard drives, running RAID-5, Exchange Server, and SQL Server 7.0, recorded an increase of 19.6 percent on a defragmented drive. On a Pentium PRO 200 with 64 MB of RAM and two 4-GB SCSI hard drives, running Exchange and SQL 7.0, performance rose by a hefty 56.1 percent.

National Software Testing Lab tested the effects of fragmentation on files of all types and sizes. The Microsoft Outlook tests, for example, included opening 50 messages simultaneously; moving messages from the inbox to a separate folder; opening (and displaying the to:, from:, subject:, and date:) a large subfolder; a full text search of all messages in a folder for a specific string; and a filter that displayed all messages in a folder that contained an attachment. Each of these tests was executed on the system when the personal

Exhibit 2   Windows 2000 and Windows NT Defragmentation Benchmark Comparison

System Configuration	Windows 2000 (%)	Windows NT (%)
Pentium II 266 w/96 MB RAM, 5 × 2-GB IDC hard drive workstation running Excel and Outlook	85.5	74.5
Pentium II 400 w/128 MB RAM, 1 × 4.2-GB hard drive workstation running Excel and Outlook	219.6	80.6
Dual P PRO 200 Server w/128 MB RAM, 5 × 4-GB SCSI hard drives w/software RAID running Exchange and SQL	61.9	19.6
P PRO 200 server w/64 MB RAM, 2 × 4-GB SCSI hard drives running Exchange and SQL	83.5	56.1

folder was fragmented and defragmented. The SQL, Exchange, and Excel tests were carried out in a similar manner.

The results of this testing might exceed what some would have believed possible from defragmenting, but even if the real-world improvements are only half as good as NSTL recorded under laboratory conditions, these improvements represent performance numbers to rival many hardware upgrades.

Windows 2000 Tests

During the year of 2000, NSTL ran additional tests on Windows 2000. To compare Windows NT with Windows 2000, the same configurations were used. On a Pentium II 266-MHz workstation, for example, with 96 MB of memory and a 2-GB IDE hard drive running Windows 2000, Outlook, and Excel, an increase in system speed of 85.5 percent was recorded. On a Pentium II 400-MHz workstation with 128 MB RAM and a 4.2-GB hard drive, also running Windows 2000, Outlook, and Excel, defragmentation resulted in a performance jump of 219.6 percent (see Exhibit 2).

Examine the comparisons made in Exhibit 2. In the server category, a dual Pentium PRO 200 with 128 MB of memory and five 4-GB SCSI hard drives, running Windows 2000, RAID 5, Exchange Server, and SQL Server 7.0, showed an increase of 61.9 percent on a defragmented drive. On a Pentium PRO 200 with 64 MB of RAM, two 4-GB SCSI hard drives, running Windows 2000, Exchange, and SQL 7.0, performance rose by 83.5 percent. Windows 2000 scores were even higher than NT in each category.

During testing, care was taken to approximate real-world Windows 2000 operating conditions. The Excel 2000 test, for example, repeatedly opened and saved Excel files to the fragmented (or defragmented) partition. These documents (varying in size from 5 to 20 MB) contained formulas that the spreadsheet auto-calculated when it was opened. For SQL Server 7.0, testing focused on reading queries from a database and displaying the results from a variety of tables.

Upon completion of testing, NSTL published the white paper *System Performance and File Fragmentation in Windows NT,* in which it concluded: "Theoretical analysis and real-world performance testing demonstrate that fragmentation has an adverse impact on system performance. ... The best way to avoid these fragmentation problems, and to keep the system running at optimal performance, is to run a defragmentation program on a regularly scheduled basis." (The full text of the white paper is available at http://www.execsoft.com.)

XP Performance Tests

In *Defragmentation Performance Testing — Windows XP,* NSTL reported the results of tests that revealed the penalties imposed on Windows XP system performance by fragmentation. Their report documents on-average gains of 109 percent after defragmentation. According to Lloyd Holder, chief executive officer of NSTL, his company established significant performance gains through the use of cost-effective network defragmentation tools. In his opinion, in many of the cases tested, gains of this magnitude often surpass improvements realized through substantial hardware upgrades.

National Software Testing Lab also conducted testing on machines running common enterprise applications under Windows XP Home and XP Professional. The primary objective was to design and conduct a series of tests that would demonstrate the effect of hard drive fragmentation on system performance when common business applications are being run. Researchers used an IBM NetVista Type 6825–12U system with a 36-GB SCSI hard drive. It featured a Pentium IV processor running at 1.6 GHz. The system's BIOS was an IBM 20KT21AUS dated 10/10/2001. The system had 512 MB of SDRAM. The hard drive was an SCSI IBM Ultrastar DDYS-T86950N 36GB with an Adaptec 2916ON SCSI controller card.

Testing personnel partitioned the hard drive into two separate 18-GB partitions (drives C: and D:). They installed XP on the C: drive, and Excel and Outlook on the D: drive. A tool named FragmentFreespace.exe was used to create a 50% fragmented hard drive. The hard drive was filled to 20 percent capacity with approximately 3000 files. A hard drive imaging application was utilized to image this configuration, and it was used as the baseline for each test. NSTL then defragmented the drive using Executive Software's Diskeeper 7.0. To approximate real-world conditions, the Excel test repeatedly opened and saved several Excel files to the fragmented (or defragmented) partition. These files varied in size and contained formulas that were auto-calculated when a spreadsheet was opened. Outlook tests focused on its personal folder database, performing such actions as moving messages from the inbox to a separate folder and a full text search of all messages in a folder for a specific string.

Overall, NSTL found that a system defragmented with Diskeeper performed the tests significantly more quickly than a fragmented system. When running Outlook, researchers recorded an increase in performance of 67.90 to 176.10 percent after defragmentation. Excel tests showed gains of 83.67 percent.

Exhibit 3   Diskkeeper versus Windows 2000 Disk Defragmenter

System Configurations (GB)	Diskeeper	Windows 2000 Disk Defragmenter
9	32 minutes, 15 seconds	1 hour, 34 minutes, 9 seconds
30	3 hours, 13 minutes, 38 seconds	14 hours, 42 minutes, 58 seconds
150	6 hours, 19 minutes, 48 seconds	21 hours, 49 minutes, 44 seconds
2 × 60	3 hours, 9 minutes, 44 seconds	9 hours, 23 minutes, 30 seconds

Overall, test results show an on-average increase of 109 percent after defragmentation using Diskeeper.

Testing the Windows 2000 Disk Defragmenter

National Software Testing Lab recently took its testing a step further by comparing the results of using Diskeeper on Windows 2000 with those achieved by using the scaled-down defragmenter Windows Disk Defragmenter (WDD), which is built into the operating system. This investigation covered two key areas: speed and effectiveness. In all, four common enterprise configurations were used in the testing (see Exhibit 3). NSTL's Holder states that, after extensive testing, NSTL found that Diskeeper was between 300 and 500 percent faster than the WDD. (A copy of the NSTL report, *Comparison Testing: Diskeeper Vs. the Windows 2000 Disk Defragmenter*, is available at www.nstl.com.) In addition, NSTL discovered that Diskeeper scored three to five times faster than the "lite" defragmenter that is built in to Windows XP and Windows 2000. Holder believes that, of the three operating systems, Windows 2000 was found to be the most severely affected by disk fragmentation.

Running the Windows 2000 Disk Defragmenter

Although the WDD is not recommended in an enterprise setting, a brief explanation of how to use it is provided here. Depending on the version of XP/2000, WDD can be found in a couple of ways. Click on Start → Programs → System → Tools → Disk Defragmenter or open the Disk Management snap-in and click on Disk Defragmenter. When the WDD window appears, you are given a choice of Analyze or Defragment. It is advisable to choose Analyze first to discover exactly how fragmented a disk has become. A visual representation of fragmentation soon appears along with the Analysis Complete dialog box. This visual representation, though, is rather basic, consisting only of fragmented files being represented in orange, contiguous files in blue, system files in green, and free space in white. You can also view a report to see the extent of fragmentation in specific files. When you choose Defragment in the WDD, the utility works its way through the volume, rearranging files to make them contiguous. When the defragmentation run is completed, "before" and "after" images are displayed. In addition to NTFS, WDD supports FAT and encrypted files.

Anyone newly installing XP or Windows 2000 should immediately analyze the state of fragmentation on each volume as soon as installation is complete. While one would reasonably expect the disks to be free of file fragments, this does not turn out to be the case. Most of the time, considerable amounts of fragmentation are to be found because the installation process creates numerous files and directories that are soon deleted. This situation is exacerbated by installing a browser, Office, service packs, and other applications. Most users end up with a severely fragmented system no matter what they do to try to prevent it.

Users of the Windows 2000 version of the WDD were able to defragment only one volume at a time. If they wanted to address multiple volumes, they had to wait for the utility to complete, choose a different volume, and restart the process. For Windows XP, Microsoft added a simple scheduling script to give system administrators some means of scheduling defragmentation for multiple users/volumes. To use the scheduler:

- Click Control Panel → System → Maintenance → Scheduled Tasks.
- Double-click Add Scheduled Task, which starts the Scheduled Task Wizard. In the list of applications, click Defrag and Next.
- Select Task Frequency and click Next.
- Select the Time/Day when the Task is to run.
- Enter the name and password of a user with administrative privileges (a user who has control over the computer, can install software, and can change user passwords).
- Check the box to open Advanced Settings.
- In the Run box, add the letter of the drive to defragment so, for example, it looks like C:\windows\system32\defrag.exe c:.

The WDD can run only one volume at a time, so multiple partitions call for the addition of a separately scheduled task for each volume. In the Control Panel, open Scheduled Tasks, and in the File menu point to New and click Scheduled Task. Give the new task a name, and complete the necessary information. Be sure to schedule defragmenting sessions far enough apart so they do not overlap.

WDD Cautions

Several issues should be noted with regard to using the WDD.

Speed

According to NSTL, the WDD is three to five times slower than Diskeeper.

Scheduling

When it comes to scheduling many machines at once, the procedure for using the WDD becomes quite complex and involves the use of scripts and batch files. This may prove difficult to learn, manage, execute, and monitor for less experienced systems administration staff. Scheduling itself, for instance, largely depends on guesswork. As parallel defragmentation is not possible, defragmentation of one volume must be completed before another one can begin. The system administrator has to guess how long a specific volume will take to defragment, allow for more than enough time for it to complete, and set the times of additional volumes accordingly. However, as the WDD often hangs up or takes a long time to run on badly defragmented disks, on disks lacking free space, or on large disks, it is quite possible that the first defrag run will not be completed before the next run is due to start. On these occasions, the entire defrag schedule for that machine is aborted. As the scheduler does not allow for exclusion lists, it is impossible to specify files and directories that are to be excluded from the defragmentation process. On machines where a large number of temporary files are created and deleted on an ongoing basis, this feature would be particularly useful. One final point on scheduling bears a mention with regard to mixed Windows environments. The WDD can schedule only Windows XP machines; thus, a system administrator with a mixed Windows environment cannot schedule WDD on Windows 95, 98, Me, NT, and 2000 machines. As these operating systems are likely to form the bulk of user desktops in the foreseeable future, the scheduling capabilities of the utility are therefore minimal.

Priority Settings

Ideally, scheduled defragmentation processes should only run at low priority. This would ensure that all of the user's applications were serviced before the WDD. In practice, however, the utility contains no priority settings. Thus, the defragmentation processes compete with other applications for system resources. As a result, mission-critical applications run more slowly while defragmentation is being done. Obviously, one way around this is to schedule volumes to be run during off-peak hours. During such times, though, the defrag program may interfere with backup schedules and other off-hours maintenance processes. As the utility is slow and must complete volumes sequentially rather than in parallel, it is quite likely that resource conflict will occur during the course of the night.

Administrative Privileges

The WDD requires having administrative privileges in order to operate. This means that individual users, realizing that fragmentation must be slowing down their machines, cannot take action except to bring it to the attention of the

Exhibit 4   Thoroughness of Defragmentation

		After Defragmentation	
		Initial Total Fragmented Files/ Total Excess Fragment	
	Before Defragmentation		
System Configurations (GB)	Initial Total Fragmented Files/ Total Excess Fragments	Diskeeper	Windows 2000 Disk Defragmenter
9	805/3,934	0/0	76/1,603
30	15,387/56,785	5/4,289	1,718/9,274
150	49,847/325,608	0/0	24/318
2 ×60	7,361/18,417	0/0	26/998

system manager. Thus, everything relating to defragmentation must be referred to one person. The administrator then has to work out how to set up the scripts and batch files involved and know the names of all the systems and the volume configuration of the systems. This is no small task in a small network, never mind a major enterprise. If Windows 2000 machines are also present, the administrator has no choice but to walk from machine to machine to run defrag manually, volume by volume.

Free Space

The WDD requires a lot more free space to operate than do third-party defragmenters. A minimum of 15 percent free space must be available on the hard disk for WDD to run. The defrag program uses this space as a sorting area for file fragments. This does not take into account the MFT Zone, which accounts for another 12.5 percent of the disk, so over 25 percent must be free for the utility to function adequately; otherwise, it tends to thrash around for hours and either stalls or fails to complete properly. To increase the free space on a volume, delete unneeded files or move them to another disk.

Thoroughness

National Software Testing Lab tests on the thoroughness of defragmentation revealed that WDD does a far less thorough job than do third-party products. It tends to have trouble with large files, large disks, badly fragmented files, and volumes with a lack of free space. It also fails to address some types of system files (Exhibit 4). On the 30-GB drive, for example, the WDD left more than 10 percent of the files severely fragmented. Why this lack of thoroughness? It is due primarily to the inability of the WDD to take care of fragmentation in some system files such as the Paging File and the lack of a boot-time defrag function. With a consolidated Paging File, WDD has nothing blocking its redistribution of files or free space on a drive, but when fragmentation of the Paging File sets in, the amount of free space becomes restricted, eventually reaching the point where the utility finds it difficult to function. Users will notice a steady diminishing of performance over time.

The WDD does not address Paging File fragmentation for safety reasons. The defrag APIs built into the operating system are not designed to operate when the Paging File is in operation (i.e., whenever the machine is running). Third-party defragmenters take care of Paging File consolidation offline during boot-time defragmentation, but the WDD has no ability to conduct boot-time runs. For users of Windows 2000, the situation is even worse. The APIs used in Windows XP have been adjusted to allow defrag of the MFT and directories online, but the WDD in Windows 2000 safely defrags only the directories, not the MFT.

I/O Overload

The purpose of eliminating fragmentation is to handle the I/O overload at the disk level caused by files that are shattered into many pieces, but those attempting to deploy the WDD in an enterprise setting will end up costing the company far more in terms of administration expenses and productivity losses than the costs to license a reliable third-party defragmenter. WDD is probably adequate for most home users, but in the enterprise it fails to aggressively eliminate fragmentation, thus resulting in curtailed system performance. System administrators are advised to rely only on proven third-party, network-capable defragmentation utilities that are certified for use on Windows XP/2000 and that can function across all versions of the Windows operating spectrum.

Defragmenting a System

What is the best way to defragment an enterprise systems? Here is a brief rundown of steps to take to achieve maximum gains from the procedure. Note that although the features of the third-party products available on the market today vary, they are similar in many ways. The steps below are based on the use of Diskeeper. It has a 95 percent share of the enterprise market, and the steps generally apply to most other third-party defragmenters available on the market, such as those from Raxco, Winternals, and O/O Software.

1. *Installation.* Install the defragmentation utility across the network using Systems Management Server (SMS), a software product from Microsoft that permits the system administrator to do such things as remotely install and run software and hardware on a network. Alternatively, products such as Diskeeper now come with a PushInstaller feature that eliminates the high cost of deployment. Diskeeper Server version allows remote installation of the Diskeeper Workstation version through the network remotely in a few clicks.
2. *Analysis.* Before running the program, view the current state of fragmentation on the network by accessing the utility and clicking the Analyze button. You can choose which disks, partitions, or machines to view (Exhibit 5). Print the report to have a document to use for later comparison.

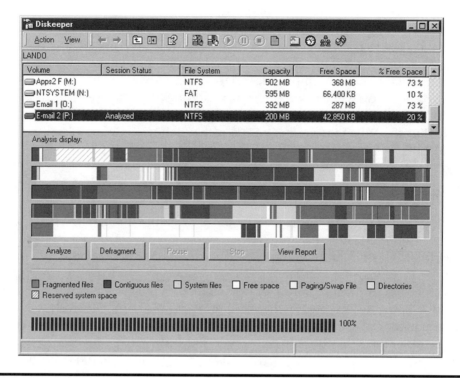

Exhibit 5   Before-Fragmentation Screenshot

3. 2a. *(Conditional) Create Enough Free Space.* If a disk is over 75 percent full, it is advisable to transfer data to another location or delete files. This creates enough room on the disk for the program to function optimally. Particularly when large database files are present, for example, this simple step can make a significant difference in how long it takes to complete defragmentation. Even though the latest defragmenters can now cope better with almost full disks, it is still advisable to run your machines with about 25 percent plus free space. Beyond that, you will begin to experience a noticeable drag on performance regardless of fragmentation.

4. *Initial Defragmentation Run.* After the analysis, select the disks to be defragmented and click the Defragment button. Even for brand-new machines, defragmentation should be conducted at once. When the operating system and applications are installed, the free space on a disk is often scrambled and results in fairly advanced levels of fragmentation. On the author's own new XP workstation at home, for example, despite having a largely empty C: drive, an average of 1.57 fragments per file was found, and the free space was 64 percent fragmented. After only a few weeks of use, one file ended up in over 2000 pieces. The initial defragmentation run may take a while, as a large number of fragments may have to be consolidated. It might even be necessary to run the utility several times for best results. Outlook, for example, gathers a massive database that can require a couple of defrag runs. A word of advice: When running manually, disk defragmenters normally automatically default to normal priority. To complete the process quickly, one can reset the default to highest priority by clicking on Actions and Priority. If overhead is a concern, however, set

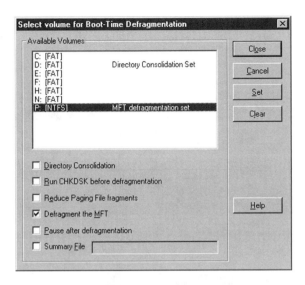

Exhibit 6   Boot-Time Defragmentation

the priority to lowest. The trade-off is that it can take longer for defragmentation to complete.

5. *View Report.* When the initial defragmentation is finished, click on View Report to view the condition of the disk. If high levels of fragmentation remain, it probably means that system files and directories are in a heavily fragmented state. For safety reasons, on Windows NT the MFT, directories, and Paging File should not be defragmented online. As these types of files are opened up early in the boot process, reliable defragmenters leave them alone and do not attempt to defragment them while online. Doing so can result in system crashes, blue screens, and data corruption. Changes to the defragmentation APIs on Windows 2000 and XP, however, have addressed these safety issues. On Windows 2000, the APIs now defrag directories safely online. On XP, both directories and the MFT are handled online. Only the Paging File remains unaddressed by the defrag APIs of Windows XP, and that shortfall is due to be addressed in a future release of Windows.

6. *Boot-Time Defragmentation.* For NT, the safe way to defragment the MFT, Paging File, and directories is by conducting boot-time defragmentation. This ensures the integrity of data files and prevents crashes. For Windows 2000, the MFT and Paging File can be defragmented during boot time; for Windows XP, the Paging File can be defragmented at boot time. Click on Actions and Boot-Time Defragmentation, select the disks to consolidate and then the types of files to address. Note that the Windows 2000 APIs have been updated to allow online defragmentation of directories (Exhibit 6).

7. *Set It and Forget It Scheduling.* Once boot-time defragmentation has been done, defragmentation should now be set to run automatically throughout the network using Set It and Forget It Scheduling (accessed via the Actions button). Select the disks to address, as well as the frequency, hours, and priority at which the program is to run. Note that Diskeeper now comes with Smart Scheduling, a refinement of Set It and Forget It Scheduling. Basically, the program adjusts defragmentation run frequency depending

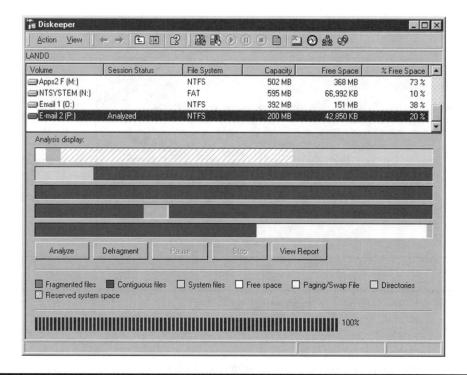

Exhibit 7   After-Defragmentation Screenshot

on the level of fragmentation experienced. If defragmentation is being done once a day and the system notices an increasing level of fragmentation, it will increase the number of runs accordingly until it finds the optimum level. Once this feature is in place, the user does not have to pay much attention to fragmentation levels (Exhibit 7).

Provided fragmentation is kept to a minimum and disks are not full, it probably will not be necessary to do boot-time defragmentation very often, if at all.

Hardware Upgrades versus Defragmentation

By following the above steps, performance on Windows NT, 2000, and XP can be maintained at a high level by keeping files and free space consolidated. As shown in the NSTL tests, it makes sense to keep Windows networks regularly defragmented. It may even provide a more economical alternative to an upgrade of system hardware, as discovered in an analysis by International Data Corporation (IDC) (Exhibit 8). According to Paul Mason, Vice President of Infrastructure Software Research at IDC, defragmenters are rising sharply in popularity as people realize that defragmenters often can deliver performance gains comparable to those for hardware upgrades at a fraction of the cost. He believes that this might be related to the apparently diminishing returns that hardware upgrades frequently provide.

Exhibit 8   IDC Comparison of Hardware Upgrade Costs versus Defragmentation Gains

	No. of Workstations	New Workstation Costs ($)	Staff Costs ($)	Total Staff and Workstation Costs ($)
Scenario #1	10	30,000	2,300	32,300
Scenario #2	1,000	3,000,000	230,000	3,230,000
Scenario #3	5,000	15,000,000	1,150,000	16,150,000

Source: International Data Corporation, Framingham, Massachusetts, 2000.

Exhibit 9   License and Installation Costs of Defragmentation Software

	No. of Servers	No. of Workstations	License Cost ($)	IT Staff Cost ($)	Total Costs ($)
Scenario #1	1	10	648	960	1,608
Scenario #2	10	1,000	23,000	960	23,960
Scenario #3	25	5,000	90,000	960	90,960

Source: International Data Corporation, Framingham, Massachusetts, 2000.

To compare hardware upgrade costs to defragmentation, IDC assumed a corporate average of hardware replacement every three years at an average cost of $3000 per workstation. After three years of operation, the original workstations would have steadily deteriorated in performance, due in no small part to fragmentation. With residual value estimated at 10 percent, this works out to $2700 over three years, or $900 annually per machine. IDC assumed that at the end of the three-year term, better workstations with faster CPUs, more RAM, and bigger hard drives could be purchased for the same price as before — around $3000. Further, the study carefully considered the time it takes to remove an older model and install a new one. In-depth investigation reveals that it takes approximately 2.5 hours to deinstall a workstation and another 3.25 hours to put in the new one, IDC rounded this up to six hours for each replacement at $40 per hour for IT staff. To simplify matters, the study did not take into account any expenses from the server side.

Exhibit 9 provides a summary of IT and new workstation costs. For the defragmenter side of the equation, IDC used Executive Software's Diskeeper for purposes of comparison, with NT workstation licenses costing $49.95 per workstation and $259 per server (list price at the time). IT time was computed at approximately two hours per month due to central controls and automatic Set It and Forget It Scheduling. Exhibit 9 also summarizes the cost of the defragmentation software as well as the cost of IT staff time. Based on these figures, IDC concluded that defragmentation may be able to delay the frequency of hardware upgrades by up to two years while at the same time delivering considerable savings. According to the IDC report, "As the level of

**Exhibit 10   Costs of Manual Defragmentation
for Each Scenario**

	No. of Servers	No. of Workstations	Annual Staff Hours	Total Staff Costs ($)
Scenario #1	1	10	572	22,880
Scenario #2	10	1,000	52,520	2,100,800
Scenario #3	25	5,000	261,300	10,452,000

Source: International Data Corporation, Framingham, Massachusetts, 2000.

server and workstation deployment increases, the cost effectiveness of defragmentation increases exponentially."

Total Cost of Ownership of Manual versus Network Defragmenters

This IDC study also reinforced the data provided earlier regarding the WDD versus a third-party defragmenter by using the same three scenarios as in the hardware comparison for the software comparison. Analysts allowed one hour to defragment server and workstation disks, taking into account the time it takes a system administrator to schedule the activity, move to the location, and perform the task on a weekly basis (at a rate of $40 per hour). Exhibit 10 highlights the high cost of manual defragmentation for each scenario. Network defragmentation, on the other hand, permits a system manager to schedule, monitor, and control defragmentation throughout the enterprise from one console. As well as offering significant savings, it allows system managers to efficiently schedule automatic defragmentation to maintain peak performance of the network. IDC found that centralized controls and automatic scheduling meant that system managers needed only two hours per month to adjust any defragmentation schedules. Regardless of the size of the network, therefore, annual IT costs worked out to be $960, considerably less than when employing manual defragmentation tools. Additionally, IDC made the point that TCO will be dramatically lowered when a network defragmenter is used to enforce an exact maintenance schedule across the enterprise. The report concluded: "Even though the actual numbers may vary from customer to customer, when considering the significant impact on TCO, it is difficult to find any argument to position manual defragmentation over network defragmentation."

Uptime Guarantee

The reports cited above demonstrate the performance impact of fragmentation. Conclusive evidence also exists that fragmentation is a primary factor in system unreliability; therefore, regularly defragmenting every server and workstation on the network is more than just common sense. It leads to greatly improved system stability and uptime, as well as a substantial reduction in help desk calls. And as networkwide defragmentation is fully automated, it represents one of the simplest, yet most effective, maintenance actions — one that equates to hard dollars in IT savings. Given the variety of problems that fragmentation causes — performance degradation, slow boot times, computers not booting up, slow or aborted backups, file corruption, data loss, crashes, hangs, errors in programs, memory issues, and a reduction in hard drive longevity — regular automated defragmentation is an obvious and proactive means of minimizing downtime and instability. Systems that are fragment free and are kept fragment free transparently by an effective network defragmenter will experience optimum levels of stability and reliability. Regular defragmentation, in conjunction with IT best practices, is a smart way to maintain uptime at a high level.

Chapter 8

Disk Optimization: Optimum or Not?

Some vendors tout a feature that is said to go beyond defragmentation. Known as *disk optimization* or *file optimization,* it is said to reduce the time it takes to recover data from disks as well as the time it takes to defragment. Disk optimization involves the intelligent placement of files on a disk in order to minimize head movement and process read/writes faster. It is an intriguing theory that software developers have flirted with for over a decade — improving performance by strategically positioning files. But, how effective is it in the real world? For the average consumer on a low-end PC, optimization appears to produce some benefit. Where it may fall short, however, is in the enterprise. The simpler the disk I/O model, the greater the potential for achieving some type of improvement in performance from optimization. With regard to RAID and enterprise environments, however, disk optimization begins to look a little shaky. According to some experts, optimization may sometimes reduce performance in the enterprise due to the resources used to optimize a disk as well as the complexity of modern disk architectures.

Hard Drives Are Slow

The relatively slow pace of disk rotation represents a serious performance bottleneck in modern systems. Just compare disk velocity to the rest of the key hardware components:

- *CPU:* Even low-end central processing units (CPUs) now surpass the billion operations per second mark. At the high end, they exceed 2 billion operations per second.

- *Memory:* Memory (or RAM) is calculated in millions of operations per second. Although it compares poorly with CPU velocity, the speed is already more than sufficient to serve up good-quality streaming audio and video over the Internet.
- *Hard Disk:* With good disks peaking at about 10,000 rpm, disk access is pinned at around 200 operations per second (five milliseconds per seek).

Thus, the CPU in a $500 computer operates almost one million times faster than the best hard disks on the market. It is no wonder, then, that anything that comes along claiming to improve disk performance is greeted with enthusiasm in the IT community.

Unfortunately, the liabilities of slow hard drives have much deeper ramifications due to fragmentation. Most operating systems are subject to severe fragmentation after several months of activity. It is quite common to find files that are in hundreds or even thousands of pieces. If a file is split into 200 pieces, for example, it takes one second to access a unit of information rather than five milliseconds. So, as the CPU roars on in the gigahertz range, fragmentation reduces the disk speed to a relative snail's pace.

The most time-honored solution to this performance hit is defragmentation, which consolidates file fragments into contiguous blocks, thus cutting down read/write times. Modern networkable defragmenters are able to produce gains on sluggish servers and workstations that are comparable to major hardware upgrades.

Enter Optimization

Optimization first reared its head in the 1980s during the heyday of the OpenVMS system. Since then, it has drifted in and out of fashion, often piggybacked with defragmentation software. The basic idea is that an optimizer is supposed to heighten defragmentation gains by taking the process a step further. In the normal course of running a system, files are split into hundreds or even thousands of pieces throughout the disk (Exhibit 1). When a defragmentation program is run, these fragments are consolidated into contiguous blocks, significantly reducing the time it takes to read and write (Exhibit 2). As you can see in Exhibit 2, though, system files and free space are not completely consolidated during defragmentation. This is where optimization comes in.

A disk optimizer attempts to go a step beyond defragmentation by grouping files according to how often they are accessed and modified. Although the optimization model varies from vendor to vendor, a typical model places system files, Internet browsers, and directories on the outer edge of the disk, followed by the often-used files, then little-used files, and finally free space. Frequently accessed files are usually placed at the beginning of the disk on the outermost tracks. Infrequently accessed files, on the other hand, are relegated to the end of the disk to free up space on the faster outside tracks (Exhibit 3). The Master File Table (MFT), for example, is often given top

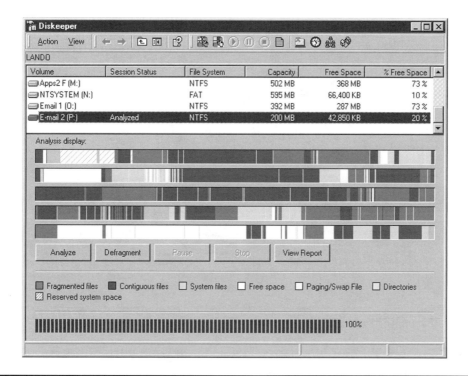

Exhibit 1   Before Defragmentation

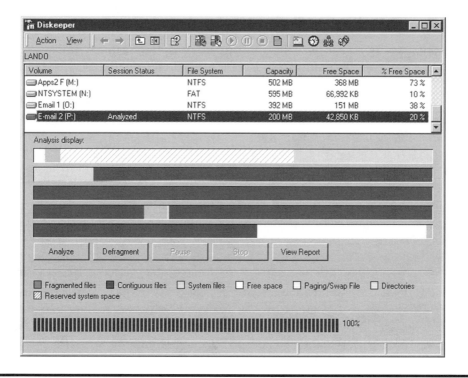

Exhibit 2   After Defragmentation

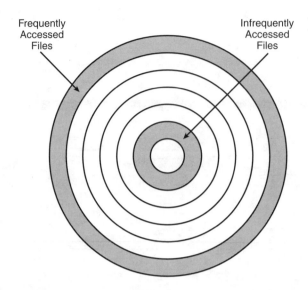

Frequently
Accessed
Files

Infrequently
Accessed
Files

Exhibit 3   Optimization

priority by optimization programs. This is an index file for Windows NT and Windows 2000 that is opened every time a file is accessed. Similarly, an Internet browser would be placed near the beginning of the disk.

Optimization Pros and Cons

In addition to increasing system performance, optimization is said to reduce the potential for file fragmentation over time. Where optimization does appear to add a small amount of value is in the individual desktop. Particularly in cases where the same types of files are accessed repeatedly while others are left dormant for long periods, optimization may reduce head movement. When the user is using the computer for only a couple of functions, such as browsing and word processing, optimization's reliance on access patterns may offer some potential benefit.

For the more sophisticated user, especially for the typical network, optimization is not likely to provide much return. A Microsoft program manager, who for many years was responsible for remote and distributed file systems as well as storage management on Windows enterprise systems, told me that the simpler the disk I/O model, the better analysis you can make for some type of improvement in performance from optimization. But, when you start moving to RAID and enterprise environments, disk optimization becomes very shaky. This opinion is shared by the National Software Testing Lab (NSTL), which reported on their investigations of both defragmentation and optimization. The NSTL paper states that file positioning is equally as likely to worsen system performance as to improve it. NSTL believes that even if the two conditions balance out at zero, the overhead involved can result in a net loss. (*Note:* The NSTL's *Final Report on Defragmentation Performance Testing* is available at http://www.execsoft, and the complete text of the NSTL white paper quoted in this chapter, *System Performance and File Fragmentation in Windows NT*, is also available at http://www.execsoft.com.)

Optimization Shortcomings

The following is a summary of disk optimization vs. defragmentation:

- *Potential for Gain.* Due to the mechanics of head movement and disk rotation, the maximum possible gain from optimization is only one or two milliseconds per seek, but only in the best-case scenario. With significant fragmentation, however, as much as 15 minutes can be added to boot time and files can take 15 seconds or longer to open, so the potential for gain from defragmentation is many orders of magnitude greater than anything that can be offered through optimization.
- *Overhead.* Apart from the fact that relatively minor returns are to be reaped, optimization also seems to consume more system overhead than a regular defragmentation utility. I tested this briefly using the Windows Task Manager, and the optimization programs run more slowly than regular defragmentation programs. After all, the process involves the analysis and repositioning of every single file on the disk to achieve what is believed to be an optimum file pattern. According to NSTL, the cost in resource overhead to accomplish such a task can result in a net loss to performance. I tried one vendor's optimization product and was discouraged with the length of time it took to reposition everything on my disk, far longer than a defragmentation run. Although future runs are supposed to take far less time, I never experienced much gain in the procedure and found it somewhat expensive in terms of overhead.
- *Safety.* The New Technology File System (NTFS) is a sophisticated, high-performance I/O subsystem that requires extremely close synchronization between the memory manager, the cache manager, and the file system. That is why reliable defragmenters are programmed to move as few files as possible. They work in close coordination with the applications programming interfaces (APIs) specially written to allow defragmentation on Windows NT and Windows 2000, moving only those files that absolutely must be moved. As a result, a minimal amount of overhead is expended, while gains are maximized and risks are minimized (about one percent of files are moved during defragmentation by the best utilities). Moving 100 percent of the files, on the other hand, provides 100 times the opportunity for error, greatly increasing the dangers of file corruption.

One optimization product I checked out was plagued with problems and has since faded as a marketing presence and is now included only within a utility suite. Users have reported problems with PowerPoint files after optimization, experiencing graphics degradation or files that will not open. Others have suffered from system slows with Outlook and other applications. To avoid the potential for sluggish performance or file corruption, the safest

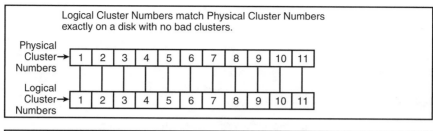

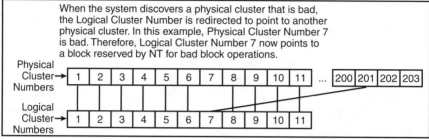

Exhibit 4   Logical Cluster Numbers

solution appears to be to shut down all other applications before running optimization software — perhaps possible for the individual consumer, but unworkable for most enterprises. It is worth noting, though, that Raxco's optimization product does *not* have a reputation for file corruption. The first run does take overlong, in my experience, but that company has managed to avoid the corruption problems associated with other optimization vendors.

Logical Cluster Numbers

To facilitate space allocation, disks are divided into clusters that represent the minimum space allocation quantity on any disk (on NT, this is normally 4 KB). When these disks leave the factory, however, it is quite usual for them to have a large number of bad clusters. Once the disk begins operation, further clusters can become damaged due to various factors. How does the file system cope with this phenomenon? Each file has a physical cluster number (PCN) and a logical cluster number (LCN). In the absence of bad clusters, the PCNs and LCNs match exactly, but when the system discovers a PCN that is bad the LCN is directed to point to another PCN. Thus, two consecutive LCNs may be widely separated on the disk (Exhibit 4); that is, where the file system *thinks* the data is does not necessarily correspond to where the data actually physically resides. LCNs, therefore, pose a serious problem for optimization. By specifying exact LCNs as the means of attaining an optimal arrangement of files, it becomes difficult to pinpoint exactly where many of these clusters actually reside on the disk. Where the optimizer thinks it is placing the files may not actually be where they end up. According to NSTL, optimization relies on assumptions about physical disk layout that are invalid in a large number of real-world environments. It makes assumptions about the behavior of software that are overly simplistic; in fact, the theoretical case that optimization can slow performance is at least as good as the case that it can improve it.

Multiple Partitions

With hard drives of 40 GB and more becoming the norm, multiple partitions have become a necessity. For better ease of management, each partition can be used for a different function. For the sake of simplicity, suppose that we have three equally sized logical volumes: C: hosts the operating system, D: is reserved for applications, and E: holds data files. Unfortunately, such an arrangement wreaks havoc with optimization. Instead of an exact physical beginning, middle, and end, one ends up with three logical beginning, middle, and end locations dispersed throughout one physical disk. Due to such an arrangement, all of these partitions can be accessed at more or less the same time. The NSTL white paper covers this topic in detail, but, to summarize, the user issues a command to the application (partition D: is accessed), the application makes calls to an operating system function (partition C: is accessed), and then the data is searched for and located (partition E: is accessed). The read/write heads are moving back and forth across the disk in a random pattern; thus, it becomes virtually impossible to place frequently accessed files on the "edge" of a multiple-partition disk.

Server Issues

Using optimization on enterprise servers has been likened by some to playing craps at Las Vegas — sometimes you win, more often you lose. In all probability, optimization is as likely to worsen system performance as to improve it. One reason optimization tends to fail to enhance server disk performance is its reliance on specific user access patterns. As soon as you add several users into the mix, patterns tend to become cloudy. Add thousands of users accessing dozens of programs, and the concept no longer sounds so impressive.

As noted earlier, the simpler the disk pattern, the better the chance that optimization may make a small difference, but, as progressive complexity enters in, it may actually become a performance liability. This becomes apparent when one looks at how optimization applies in a network run by a busy server. Instead of one user opening one document, the network has hundreds of users. Scores of applications are running simultaneously, and thousands of files are being accessed at any given time. In this random mode of operation, where does a disk optimization program place files, and will that placement have any impact on head movement? NSTL makes the point that even infrequently used files may be accessed enough that the effect on performance of strategic placement (optimization) is essentially immeasurable. Take databases, for example. Most people access a few specific entries, and it is rare that the entire database is accessed or updated in one unit of time; therefore, as databases are normally organized as one huge file, they contain both high- and low-frequency access

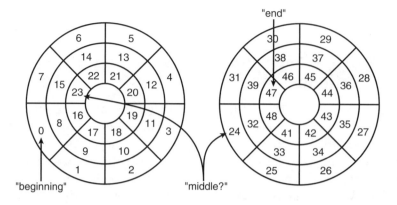

Exhibit 5   Two-Spindle Disk

information. So, where does the optimizer put them? Placed at the front of the disk, they take up a lot of space and could potentially slow I/O by pushing other frequently accessed files closer to the center of the disk. When positioned at the end of the disk, however, users could face delays in waiting for information that is called up constantly. Thus, most databases represent a lose–lose proposition for optimization programs.

RAID Arrays

A further complexity in the optimization picture comes in the form of hardware and software RAID. Although they make use of multiple physical disks, volume sets and stripe sets appear to the operating system as a single logical drive. Again, it becomes extremely difficult to predict the exact location of the center or outside edge of RAID arrays. While RAID employs as many as five platters, a highly simplified example of a two-spindle disk (Exhibit 5) is used here. The cluster numbers are shown, extending from 0 to 23 on disk 1 and then continuing from 24 to 47 on disk 2. With only two disks, the concept of a physical beginning, middle, and end begins to look questionable. Now add three more disks, and the concept becomes almost absurd. In the words of my Microsoft contact, you may be playing probabilities and perhaps you should think twice before gambling with user data and system performance.

Proven Disk Performance Solutions

With optimization appearing to fail to make the grade as an enterprise solution, what, then, are the proven techniques for improving disk performance?

RAID

Hardware RAID has a proven track record in the corporate world, both in terms of performance and robustness. Throughput is increased by handling logically contiguous disk operations in parallel instead of as one longer operation on a single disk. Although the adoption of RAID is widespread in large companies, its lack of use among small to mid-sized companies appears to be related to cost rather than reliability issues. But, if it can be made affordable, RAID represents an excellent way of increasing disk performance. In recent years, the cost equation has improved to where most mid-sized and even some small businesses are now able to take advantage of RAID. So, for better disk performance, hardware RAID is a good direction to go. Most companies that are looking for higher performance I/O go straight to RAID and are not overly concerned with disk optimization and data layout on the drive. NSTL notes, however, that RAID is just as susceptible to fragmentation as other disk configurations. According to NSTL, a fragmented file would not incur an I/O cost only if the file fragments happened to be in the same data stripe, which may not be likely. Usually, however, the effect of fragmentation on RAID is the same as on a non-RAID system: Additional head movement and I/O will be necessary in order to perform file operations. A safe and reliable network disk defragmenter, then, should be used regularly to keep RAID systems functioning optimally.

Caching

Caching is based on the principle that data that has been read or written is likely to be read again. Because memory access is many times faster than disk access, the caching of recently used files can significantly reduce I/O traffic. As a result, caching aids performance even in heavily fragmented systems. When NSTL tested the impact of fragmentation on a well-cached system, however, it still found that as little as 13 percent disk fragmentation exacted a definite toll on performance; thus, disk caching mitigates but does not eliminate these problems. Unless instructed otherwise, NT's Cache Manager caches all reads and writes on all secondary media. Cache Manager uses a number of aggressive techniques to improve performance. For example, it will attempt to read ahead in a file in anticipation of a program's requesting the succeeding data. It will also delay writes to the disk, so that if reads or writes of the same data occur quickly, they will be satisfied out of the cache rather than through a physical disk operation. Aggressive disk caching can mitigate the effects of disk fragmentation to the extent that data read by applications is read from the cache rather than from the disk itself. In fact, adding memory to a heavily fragmented system can improve performance on a fragmented system, although this is an expensive solution to a problem that can be fixed at little cost through software and good practices.

Defragmentation

Much like the importance of regular oil changes to vehicle maintenance, the tried and tested solution for disk performance problems on Windows NT and Windows 2000 is regular defragmentation. Independent performance tests by

NSTL have shown conclusively that defragmentation produces significant gains for both workstations and servers (see Chapter 7). With these results comparing favorably with most hardware upgrades, it is no wonder that network defragmenters are becoming the norm in large corporations.

Conclusions

Although disk optimization is an attractive theory that offers some potential benefit to individual PCs and low-end users, it does not appear to adequately address the complexity resulting from multiple partitions, multiple disks, and multiple users. Consequently, it is unlikely to produce significant performance benefits in an enterprise environment and may sometimes end up costing more in system overhead than it offers in return. Businesses, therefore, should put their faith in proven solutions such as RAID, caching, and defragmentation. If firms deal with reliable vendors, they will realize significant gains in overall network performance. As an enterprise solution, optimization has so many shortcomings that it is not about to replace or enhance network defragmentation any time soon. While it may result in a small gain on occasion under ideal conditions, it is equally likely to slow down a system by instituting arbitrary rules and idealized notions of head movement.

Chapter 9

Disk Quotas

Even though disk space seems to be a nearly endless subject in that the amount of disk space and the sizes of disks seem to be getting bigger and bigger, the fact is that disk "quotaing" is more important than ever. It is very much a case of build it and they will come — or, rather, put the space there and they will fill it, and quickly. The explosion in disk space has been closely paralleled by the growth of file sizes in recent years. Pay no attention to disk quotas, and in a short time any enterprise will be chock full of MP3s and other miscellany, and users will be screaming for more space. In addition to disk quotas, control of free space must be maintained. You do not want disks to fill up, and you want to be able to inform users ahead of time when they need to start thinking about deletions. Performance, in fact, suffers when disks fill up. So, here are the basics of the subject and some tools to help you stay on top of the disk space situation.

What Is a Disk Quota?

Disk quotas have been with us for quite some time. In mainframe and other legacy environments, for instance, they are a firmly established tool for staying in command of available space. Essentially, a quota is an assigned limit or amount for something. When it comes to disk space, the quota indicates the maximum amount of space assigned to a user or a directory. Disk quotas, then, control space consumption and prevent one greedy individual, for example, from consuming everyone else's space and causing system crashes and other situations.

Microsoft released Windows NT without any kind of disk quotaing features. It was left up to software vendors to develop the necessary disk quota management utilities to do the job. Even with the release of a built-in quota utility in Windows 2000, though, third-party quota products are still recommended as they have much more functionality and have greater flexibility than the scaled-down tool inside the operating system.

Basically, disk quota tools work by monitoring partitions/volumes, directories, files, and user space. They are used to set limits and warning thresholds for space and directory consumption. If users meet or exceed their space thresholds, various management actions can occur, including alerting users (and their administrators) that they have run out of free space or that they have exceeded, say, 70% usage of a disk quota. Users receive e-mails or on-screen notifications about quota-related matters. Administrators can view the event log as well as disk space reports and can alter the various quota thresholds.

Some tools allow the user to save the current document, whereas others leave users high and dry; as soon as a space quota is exceeded, the user is allotted no more space, thus losing the open document. Further, it is important to be aware that some disk quota tools merely alert users to the fact that the quota has been exceeded and can do nothing to restrict further disk usage.

Quota Terminology

Following are a few definitions regarding disk quota management:

- *Soft Quota.* Usage changes are monitored, but quota limits are not enforced. The soft quota mode means that quota violation events are not generated and file operations do not fail due to violation of a disk quota parameter.
- *Hard Quota.* Changes in disk/directory usage are also tracked; however, quota limits are enforceable, thus enabling the administrator to exert some control over user space consumption.
- *Quota Threshold.* A threshold is a point at which something is detectable or observable. In disk management, this can be either a point at which a warning is issued (such as x% of the disk quota has now been used) or the point at which the limit of disk space usage is reached. Different disk quota management tools permit various types and levels of thresholds. When a threshold is reached, it triggers specific actions such as e-mail or pop-up alerts, event log notifications, and restrictions.
- *User Quotas.* A user quota allows control over the amount of data any user can store in a directory or volume.
- *Directory Quotas.* Directory quotas make it possible to control the total amount of data that may be stored in a directory or volume, regardless of user.

Disk Quota Management

How does quota management work? According to Precise/W. Quinn Associates (Reston, Virginia; www.wquinn.com), a disk quota software vendor, several different approaches to quota management are available.

Using APIs

One method is to monitor file creation and allocation events after the file operation completes while utilizing operating system security features to restrict access. This approach harnesses WIN32 APIs that act on file system events and file operations after they have completed. When the quota is exceeded, users are prevented from creating additional files. The operating system detects changes in file size at the point when a file is written to disk. Because it is necessary to wait until after the I/O is complete, delays may occur; for example, if the system uses a lot of caching, the cache has to be flushed enough for detection of the exceeded quota to occur.

This approach, though, carries with it several disadvantages. As mentioned above, using APIs means that no action can normally be taken until a file is closed. Suppose that User X has a quota of 500 MB. He has already used 485 MB and then decides to create or copy a 1-GB file. That action would result in User X being almost 1 GB over the quota before any restrictions could be enforced. On the plus side, though, this feature does not expose users to data loss if they exceed their quotas by a small amount. In addition, using APIs can lead to other problems such as restricted access to specific directories and can result in changing security parameters, which should be avoided if possible.

Operating System Integration

Another approach is to integrate disk quota management with the operating system using a driver. This method, used by the built-in quota utility for Windows 2000, supports user quotas on volumes; that is, the administrator can control how much data each user is permitted to store on an NTFS volume. It does not, however, support directory quotas. But, on the plus side, administrators can generate reports and use the event monitor to track quotas.

Under this approach, when users exceed their quotas, they must delete some files, swap ownership of some files to another user, or obtain an increased quota allocation from the administrator. Each file's owner is directly tracked, and each user has an assigned amount of space; the administrator can set quotas for specific users on any volume or can set default quotas for new users. Windows 2000 also adds the ability to query the level of quota tracking, default quota limits, and the quota information for each user, a feature unavailable previously.

Windows 2000 administrators can set hard quotas, see who is using what, set warning thresholds, and more — quite an improvement over NT and its various third-party utilities. Quotas can also be disabled if desired, and the administrator can establish soft quotas in order to track quota usage without enforcement. In this arrangement, administrators at least know what is happening, although they are limited in what they can do about it. Alternatively, hard quotas can be set, tracked, and enforced.

What about quota thresholds? Various thresholds can be set to keep track of user quotas, not just to prevent them from being exceeded but to alert users and administrators when space limits are being approached.

While this approach integrates well with the operating system and NTFS file system, it has several disadvantages. For one thing, directory quotas are not supported. As these are important for controlling disk allocation in shared directories and for reporting on space usage by directory, most organizations require this functionality. Note that Windows NT quota tools provided this function to a greater or lesser degree, but typically did not support individual user quotas. Further, only one set of warnings is generated. If a quota is exceeded, an alert goes to the user and an entry is made in the event log. It is far better to initiate a scheme whereby a series of warnings are generated, starting at, say, 70% usage exceeded, then at 80%, 90%, and finally when the quota is exceeded. That way, users have a chance to delete files and exert some control over their allocations.

I/O Filters

Another method of setting quotas uses I/O filters. Such filters intercept I/O operations before they complete and so enable the monitoring of file creations and allocation changes on a real-time basis. By comparing this data to existing quota information, decisions can be made regarding space availability and space restrictions. This method has several advantages, particularly in that it allows both user and directory quotas, which can be set on both NTFS and FAT volumes. Further, system managers can utilize many configuration options to specify exactly how quotas and thresholds are to be enforced. In addition to the features of other approaches discussed previously, this method makes it possible for quota policy to be automatically adjusted in order to extend user quotas if needed. When plenty of space is available, the quota policy can be set to add space automatically when users exceed their limits.

Windows 2000 Built-In Quota Utility

Strengths

The specifics of Windows 2000 disk quota management will now be examined more closely. The built-in disk quota features of Windows 2000 represent a big improvement over Windows NT. Windows 2000 comes with the ability to set limits to disk usage that have already been preinstalled. These features are a part of the Profile Quota utility, which is built into the operating system. The administrator can set a limit to the amount of storage a user can take up on an NTFS volume. The default is set at 30,000 K, but this figure can be raised or lowered as needed. When a user exceeds that limit, Profile Quota will notify the user and the administrator and may or may not refuse to save the file, depending upon the configuration. Profile Quota improves storage management and control over earlier versions of Windows and will satisfy the needs of many users.

Limitations

Unfortunately, the Windows 2000 disk quota functions are too basic for enterprise users. For one thing, when disk quotas are enabled on a volume, all system users automatically are allotted the same amount of disk space, and it is not possible to assign quotas to specific folders or directories. Also, administrators are not able to monitor space consumption by user. Even worse, end users are not given notification as they consume their disk allotments; the only notification they will ever receive is "disk full." When users receive "disk full" notices when hard quotas are being used, they must delete files until they move below their assigned disk space usage. What is upsetting, though, is that users cannot save the files they were working on when they exceeded the quota. That work is lost. Let us just hope it was not the boss' 80-page PowerPoint presentation for tomorrow's keynote address.

These are just some of the drawbacks of this built-in quota utility. In addition, FAT drives cannot have quotas applied, nor can quotas be set on NT servers. Compression is ignored by Windows 2000 when it calculates disk space, and quota reporting functions are minimal. So, although Microsoft must be applauded for trying to respond to user requests to include disk quota and defrag tools, the utilities they installed have been found wanting and should be replaced in any enterprise.

I discussed this point recently with an analyst at Giga Information Group who validated Microsoft's efforts to license best-of-breed software tools in areas such as storage, defragmentation, and quota management from the leading vendors in these areas. The downside, however, is that the tools provided by Microsoft are bare-bones versions that typically do not meet the needs of most enterprises. The analyst's strong recommendation was for enterprises to immediately upgrade to the full-featured versions that include remote management and enterprise-class functionality. That said, Windows 2000 definitely does have greater disk quota capabilities than were possible with Windows NT, but recent user surveys have shown that the most desired functions missing in Windows NT and still missing in Windows 2000.

Third-Party Alternatives

Fortunately, various third-party utilities fill these gaps in functionality for Windows NT and 2000. Some of the best disk quota tools for Windows NT and Windows 2000 are NTP Software's Quota and File Sentinel and Precise/ W. Quinn Associates' QuotaAdvisor. (The complete versions of these programs may be downloaded and used free for thirty days from http://www.softwareshelf.com.) Penn State University's Chemical Engineering department, for example, wanted to improve their disk quota capabilities. Each of their 600 students needed guaranteed access to the network to complete assignments on a timely basis. Preventing overuse of storage resources, therefore, was critical. This higher education institution utilizes NTP Software's Quota and File Sentinel to graphically monitor and maintain storage requirements for all of the students. In addition, students are automatically notified when they are approaching their quotas. That way, students will not use up disk space unaware and undetected.

QuotaAdvisor

In this day and age, it is easier than ever for users to import vast amounts of "junk" into the files and databases of the modern corporation. Broadband has given users the ability to swiftly exchange large amounts of data with other employees, thus speeding up the decision-making process; however, it also makes it easier to clog up server space with downloaded MP3s and other large files. If unlimited storage capacity exists, this is no problem. For most enterprises, though, it is necessary to implement some type of storage quota system. The Windows 2000 built-in Profile Quota utility may be all right for some uses but is essentially of limited value. When additional functionality is needed, however, a third-party product should be selected. Precise/W. Quinn Associates' StorageCeNTral suite, for example, includes QuotaAdvisor for setting and monitoring quotas. Whereas Profile Quota only notifies a user when the storage quota is exceeded and expects the end user to figure out which files to delete, QuotaAdvisor takes active steps to prevent going over the quota and to assist the user in selecting which files to delete. QuotaAdvisor includes up to five configurable warning levels to notify the user when the storage limits are approaching. For example, an e-mail or on-screen message can be sent when the storage usage reaches 85 percent of quota, advising the user to delete some files or request more storage space from the administrator. When the limit is reached, users are still able to save their current files, even though they have exceeded the quota, so that critical work does not get lost.

Case Study: Premier, Inc.

Premier, Inc. (San Diego, California; www.premier.com), a firm that provides group purchasing and other services to over 1800 hospitals nationwide, uses QuotaAdvisor on its 350 clustered servers and Storage Area Network. Premier turned to Computer Sciences Corporation (El Segundo, California; www.csc.com) to manage some of its IT functions in 1999 when the company switched from Novell NetWare to a Windows-based network. As part of the switch, Premier asked that CSC install a disk space quota management feature. CSC configured QuotaAdvisor to alert users when they had reached 75 and 90 percent of capacity. The administrators also use the program's reporting facility to find out which employees are close to hitting their quota so they can contact those employees and determine whether they need more disk space. They can also provide the users with an HTML-based report showing the files in the user's home directory. The user can then click on the hyperlinks to view the files and decide whether to save, move, or delete them. Other useful features include the ability to run reports on files that have not been accessed in the last specified number of months, making it easy to evaluate and delete unneeded files and providing the ability to restrict the types of files that can be saved.

Conclusion: Upgrade to a Third-Party Disk Quota Tool

The bottom line is that Microsoft provides only rudimentary disk quota limitations and features within Windows 2000. For example, users do get volume-based quotas, but not directory-based quotas. Third-party products, on the other hand, add more flexibility to the disk quota function, including preventing users from saving files of specified file extensions — such as MP3 or various video formats. (I heard one story of a user downloading the entire Harry Potter film, consuming vast bandwidth and several gigabytes of space in the process.) It is also worth noting that, in addition to quota functionality, third-party products provide the detailed and valuable reporting capabilities that are an essential part of everyday IT life. Such reports are available for both managers and administrators and can be sent direct to users on a regular basis to inform them of the latest status with regard to their disk quotas.

Chapter 10

Hard Disk Forensics: The Hard Disk As a Source of Evidence

While the hard disk is a truly wonderful storage medium, it also has the capacity for storing information that can later come back to incriminate an individual or a company. The Federal Bureau of Investigation (FBI), for example, has become particularly skilled at gleaning evidence from computer disks. In many cases, agents can even recover data from disks that people spent time carefully erasing. In this chapter, we take a look at the subject of forensics in detail as it relates to hard disks. Just how many ways is data stored on the hard drive? What does it take to completely remove information from a drive? What are your corporate and legal responsibilities with regard to data, and what can you do to eliminate sensitive data that should never be seen by prying eyes? These questions and more are covered here (see Exhibits 1 and 2 for some statistics).

The Rise of Computer Crime

Computer crime is rising sharply. According to the Computer Security Institute (CSI), the threat from computer crime and other information security breaches continues unabated and the financial toll is mounting (see computer crime survey results in Exhibits 1 and 2). In response, the FBI has established the National Infrastructure Protection Center (NIPC) as well as regional Computer Intrusion Squads located throughout the country. The NIPC is a joint partnership among federal agencies and private industry. Its aim is to prevent and respond to cyber attacks on the country's telecommunications, energy, transportation, banking and finance, emergency services, and government operations infrastructures.

Exhibit 1   Joint Computer Security Institute/FBI Computer Crime Survey (2002)

Ninety percent of respondents (primarily large corporations and government agencies) detected computer security breaches within the last twelve months.

Eighty percent acknowledged financial losses due to computer breaches.

Forty-four percent (223 respondents) were willing and/or able to quantify their financial losses; these 223 respondents reported a total of $455,848,000 in financial losses.

The most serious financial losses occurred through theft of proprietary information (26 respondents reported a total of $170,827,000) and financial fraud (25 respondents reported a total of $115,753,000).

Most respondents (74 percent) cited their Internet connection as a frequent point of attack rather than citing internal systems as a frequent point of attack (33 percent).

Thirty-four percent reported the intrusions to law enforcement (in 1996, only 16 percent acknowledged reporting intrusions to law enforcement).

Respondents detected a wide range of attacks and abuses.

Forty percent detected system penetration from the outside.

Forty percent detected denial of service attacks.

Seventy-eight percent detected employee abuse of Internet access privileges (for example, downloading pornography or pirated software, or inappropriate use of e-mail systems).

Eighty-five percent detected computer viruses.

Exhibit 2   Computer Security Institute Survey Regarding Attacks on Web Sites and Web Servers

Ninety-eight percent of respondents had World Wide Web sites.

Fifty-two percent conducted electronic commerce on their sites.

Thirty-eight percent suffered unauthorized access or misuse on their Web sites within the last 12 months; 21 percent said that they did not know if there had been unauthorized access or misuse.

Twenty-five percent of those acknowledging attacks reported from two to five incidents. Thirty-nine percent reported ten or more incidents.

Seventy percent of those attacked reported vandalism (compared to 64 percent in 2000).

Fifty-five percent reported denial of service (compared with 60 percent in 2000).

Twelve percent reported theft of transaction information.

Six percent reported financial fraud (compared with 3 percent in 2000).

Attempts to deal with computer crime are also showing up in the criminal codes, which now specify computer crimes and their corresponding sentences. A decade ago, identity theft and hacking were vague and indefinite acts. Today, they are precisely defined and subject to heavy penalties. And, the long arm of the law does not pick up hackers only in this country (for example, the originator of the Melissa virus); it has also successfully tracked down people in Canada, Indonesia, and the Philippines for computer crimes against

U.S. companies. We will now take a look at two computer crime incidents, with particular attention on how the individuals were identified by using the forensics evidence resident on hard drives, which led to their eventual arrest and conviction.

Melissa

The Melissa virus was the first real celebrity cyber attack. When it struck in 1999, computers and the Internet were so much a part of everyday life that just about every media channel reported the Melissa story at length. And what a story it was. Damages from Melissa were estimated at half a billion dollars. This virus was first posted on a sex newsgroup using an AOL e-mail account. An AOL server then fed the virus to unsuspecting members of this newsgroup. They opened a file called list.zip and from that point on helped spread the virus across the United States and beyond. Once a computer was infected, the virus used Outlook to self-replicate. It e-mailed individuals in each computer's address book and incapacitated about 300 corporate networks.

To track down Melissa's creator, investigators relied on a tagging system used by AOL to identify newsgroup postings, as well as serial numbers embedded in various documents. The initial Melissa posting could be traced back to two Web sites. The FBI immediately shut these down. Both sites were linked to Melissa via an electronic fingerprint derived from a serial number found in documents created with various Microsoft Office applications. Forensics success in this case was assisted by a Microsoft document identification technology that assigns a unique serial number to files produced by Word, Excel, and other applications.

Using this data and other leads, the FBI seized a Web server in Orlando, Florida, belonging to an Internet service provider (ISP) and conducted an analysis of its contents. By this time, Melissa's creator was beginning to feel the heat and via e-mail asked a system administrator to delete his account and erase his files. This led the FBI to another ISP in New Jersey. FBI agents in New Jersey obtained a telephone number and arrived at the house of 30-year-old David Smith. Melissa, it turns out was the name of an acquaintance of Smith's   a stripper from Florida. He was jailed for five years, one of the first people ever prosecuted for spreading a virus.

I Love You

Within a few hours of being unleashed, the "I Love You" virus had spread to over 20 countries and was particularly destructive to radio stations, magazines, and advertising agencies as it targeted graphics and music files. One big publishing house, for example, lost its complete photo archives, as JPG and other graphics files were converted to ".vbs" files. The virus also spread throughout various U.S government and corporate sites. Damage estimates, taking into account lost productivity, damaged files, and the cost of updating antivirus programs, came to $10 billion worldwide. The I Love You virus spread in a manner similar to that for Melissa — via an attachment named "I Love You." When the attachment was opened, it then infected systems and spread via e-mail; however, it could replicate in not one but in three ways. In addition to spreading by e-mail attachments, it also could be spread via Internet Relay Chat (IRC) file transfers and shared drives on a network. It buried itself in the Windows directory and the system directory, and from there it modified registry keys so that on the next restart the user was sent to one of four Web pages linked to an executable containing the virus code. Any dial-up connection passwords were mailed to an e-mail address in the Philippines. In addition to creating HTML files on the hard drive to infect IRC members, it also spread to everyone in a computer's e-mail address book and destroyed music and graphics files. Unlike Melissa, which had plenty of time to spread, the FBI moved very quickly on the I Love You virus. A Philippine ISP was made to shut down access to the virus files within a few hours. Manila law enforcement agents traced those files to another Philippine ISP and eventually to a computer programming student.

Definitions of Computer Crime and Computer Forensics

While law and order may be catching up and the Wild West days of hacking may now lie behind us, further virus outbreaks can be expected in the coming years, as well as plenty more innovative ways for computers to be used with criminal intent. So what exactly is computer crime? *Computer crime* can best be defined as a criminal act in which a computer is essential to carrying out the crime; however, the definition is widening to include criminal acts where computers act as repositories of information about the crimes, although they may not be directly involved in perpetrating these acts. *Forensics*, in general usage, is the application of the tools of science, as well as specific scientific facts, to help solve legal problems. Television shows such as *CSI* and the Sherlock Holmes stories are all about forensics. What, though, does forensics have to do with computers? *Computer forensics* is the examination and analysis of data held on computer storage media such as disks, tapes, and other drives. It is basically the application of scientific, criminal investigation, and computer techniques to locate any data stored on or retrieved from media that can be used as evidence in a court of law.

As a result, computer forensics procedures have to follow prescribed procedures, rules of evidence, and legal processes. Just as you see detectives dusting an area slowly for fingerprints, computer forensics tends to move along at a plodding pace to preserve the accuracy of information without sacrificing the integrity of the evidence. This means that data must be carefully recovered and securely stored. It also means that investigators must become skilled at finding key pieces of data amid a massive volume of information. Make an error, and potentially successful prosecutions can fail based on technicalities such as unsatisfactory equipment, procedures not being followed properly, or inadequate presentation of evidence in court.

Uses of Computer Forensics

Computer forensics can be used in hundreds of ways. In the realm of serious crime, forensics is invaluable in tracking down the people behind acts of terrorism, murder, rape, blackmail, and money laundering. Forensics is also of value in such areas as theft of intellectual property, destruction or misappropriation of data, alteration of data, misuse of programs, use of unlicensed software, illegal duplication of software, and unauthorized access to a network or system. For human resources departments, forensics can prove useful in detecting unauthorized use of a company's computer for private gain, unauthorized access to confidential data, downloading and distribution of pornographic material, and misuse of e-mail, as well as in the resolution of employment disputes and dealing with hiring and firing matters.

Recovering Evidence

When looking for incriminating evidence in computers, the place to start is the My Documents folder. Less sophisticated criminals are sometimes caught because they kept incriminating material immediately accessible in such an easy-to-find location. Then, of course, the many records kept by e-mail programs can be accessed. The Microsoft antitrust trial, for example, focused on e-mailed statements from Bill Gates regarding its competitor, Netscape Communications. Since then, electronic discovery has assumed a vital role in many types of litigation. Groups such as Electronic Evidence Discovery (www.eedinc.com) estimate that 70 percent of corporate data exists only electronically and is never written down, up from 30 percent a few years ago. So the old notion of the FBI rolling in with several trucks and leaving with hundreds of file cabinets is changing. These days, they may still take some file cabinets, but these will be accompanied by dozens of servers and PCs.

Among the other places to look for evidence are Microsoft Outlook's Inbox, Deleted Files, and Sent Files. In addition to recovering e-mail from the desktop of the perpetrator, e-mail can sometimes also be recovered from corporate servers, backup tapes, ISPs, or the machines of recipients. Even data that has apparently been lost in deleted files can be recovered. If permanently deleted, it can still sometimes be recovered directly from the hard drive, provided it has not been overwritten.

Printed versus Electronic Versions

Rules of information discovery permit lawyers to receive printouts of computer data; however, this may not be the best way to retrieve data. Why? A computer-generated document is not necessarily the same as the printed version. Electronic files typically contain information that never appears on the screen or in the printed version of the file. This type of invisible material is known as *metadata* — information that the computer uses in processing files, such as when a document was created and by whom, when it was last modified and by whom, and on which computer it was created. Over 1000 bits of information, for example, travel along with each and every Microsoft Outlook e-mail. This type of data is kept as a record in the normal course of business but will never show up if someone provides only a paper copy of the document; yet, incriminating evidence may be stored away as metadata. Fortunately, lawyers and criminal investigators are getting wise to such things.

While the computer user does not actually create such metadata, other types of information *are* intentionally created but do not show up on paper. Deleted text is a prime example. When a person revises a document, deleted text may still be part of the file, even though it does not show up on the screen or when the document is printed out. In some cases, it is even possible to extract earlier versions of a document from the electronic version. I have seen this happen to someone who made some derogatory comments about someone and then deleted them in the final version of the document. Unfortunately, the deleted text was revealed when the Reject Deletion key under Microsoft Word's Track Changes function was used. In addition to Microsoft Word, database and spreadsheet programs also have collaborative features that retain deleted or revised text. All of these comments, as well as who made them and when, are also part of the electronic file, but not the paper version.

Microsoft Word Confessions

Over the past decade, Microsoft Word has become the most commonly used word processor in the world. Word contains features that allow users to collaborate, add graphics, and e-mail documents. These features, however, also open the door to security holes and can sometimes lead to breaches of confidential information. In addition, data can be disclosed unintentionally when sending a file by e-mail, saving it on a disk, or handing it over to someone. In the legal arena, in particular, this can be particularly damaging as far more information is given away than intended. As noted earlier, Microsoft Word and other programs that are elements of the Microsoft Office suite contain data that is not normally visible on the screen. This data can include such items as:

- Author name, initials, mailing address, firm name, names of earlier authors
- Comments made by others during review/revision, including the names of those making the comments
- Revisions made to the document
- Earlier versions
- Where document is stored
- Text formatted as "hidden"
- Hyperlinks to documents in the firm's computer system
- Names of people who received the document for review and/or approval

When a document created with Word is sent electronically to another person, that person can sometimes access this data. Revisions, for example, may be visible if the recipient uses an e-mail program to open the document rather than saving it and then opening it in a word processor. Some metadata can also show up if you open files using a text editor such as WordPad or Notepad.

Try this experiment: Open up a file using WordPad or Notepad (in Windows 98 or XP, click on Start → Programs → Accessories to find these text editors). Open one and use it to display a Word document. Alternatively, e-mail yourself a Word document as an attachment and open it using your e-mail program. You may well see at least some of the metadata that is regularly being relayed from user to user.

Preserving Confidentiality in Microsoft Word

This relay of unwanted data can be avoided in several ways. The first is to not send Word files electronically; instead, print them out and mail them, fax them, or even scan them and save them in another format. These are tried-and-true methods that will completely eliminate any hidden data. But, because Word is used by so many people, these approaches are not always workable. For those using Word, one good approach to eliminating the dissemination of unwanted data is this: Before e-mailing a document, open it up, copy and paste the information into a new, blank Word document, then send the new file. This successfully eliminates revisions, comments, and earlier versions of the document.

Another trick is to use Rich Text Format (.rtf), as this format preserves all the fonts and formatting while removing much of the hidden data. Click on File and Save As; instead of letting the save default automatically to a Word document, select the Save As Type box and scroll down to Rich Text Format and select it. Other ways to eliminate hidden data are explained in such places as the Microsoft Web site (http://support.microsft.com); for example, the Microsoft Knowledge Base article *How To Minimize Metadata in Microsoft Office Documents* (Q223396; http://support.microsoft.com/default.aspx?scid = kb;EN-US;Q223396) is an excellent reference that provides links to articles giving detailed instructions for specific versions of Word, Excel, PowerPoint, etc.

Finding Missing Files

Many people believe that when a file is deleted, it is gone. Others know that deleted files are often stored in the Recycle Bin but, if they are deleted from there, then they, too, are gone forever. But are they? In reality, deleting files and emptying the Recycle Bin may not actually remove the deleted document from the disk. It is similar to taking the label off a paper file folder and placing the folder back in the file cabinet. The folder may be more difficult to locate, but by leafing through the file cabinets you will eventually find it. The Master File Table (MFT), for example, keeps a record of where files are stored. When a file is deleted, the MFT entry is changed to indicate that the area is now available for reuse, but the data can sit there for hours or even weeks until it is finally overwritten by new files; that is, the deleted files remain on the disk until the computer writes another file in that same location. Thus, investigators have often found large volumes of data that had just been "deleted" from a disk in an attempted coverup, but even if some files are overwritten, earlier file data may not be completely gone. Remember back to when you used pencil and paper; if you erased what you had written and then wrote something else over the top of it, it might still have been possible to discern what was written underneath.

Even when the deleted file is actually unrecoverable, other versions of that same file might exist elsewhere on the disk. Windows makes many additional copies of files that the user never sees and is usually unaware of. On Windows XP, for instance, when I receive an attachment and open it, the default folder used is a temporary folder named OLK4. Sometimes when I have opened an attachment, made a few changes, and saved it without thinking, it gets dumped in OLK4 — and I have wasted hours trying to find that directory. It does not show up in any other folder. Fortunately, I have worked out how to solve this puzzle, but the point is that Windows has dozens of nook and crannies that even veteran IT professionals are unaware of, and each of these places can be accessed to recover lost or incriminating data.

For example, consider the swap file (or Paging File). This is a large section of the hard drive that the computer uses as additional memory space, and forensics experts can access this area to recover vital documents. Printer files are another source of hidden information. Whenever a document is printed, Windows creates an enhanced metafile (EMF) on the hard disk and sends that temporary copy to the printer. Even if the user never saves it, the printer version often sticks around on the disk, as one bank robber discovered in court. He had typed up his demand notes on a computer and printed them out without saving the files so he would not leave any evidence behind; however, investigators accessed the EMF files and he was convicted of robbery. It is the same with e-mail attachments. Windows creates a MIME file when sending files over the Internet, and these files may remain long after the original file is deleted.

Shredder Programs

Software to address this problem is known as a *shredder* program. When a file is deleted, these programs will repeatedly rewrite random data over that area to eliminate any traces of what was there previously. The Department of Defense, for example, requires the use of such programs and that an area be overwritten at least seven times. Shredder programs can be valuable when getting rid of old computers or sending people reused floppy disks; otherwise, you may inadvertently disclosure confidential information. If a shredder program is used, it must be used on a regular basis and set up to handle all of the extra and temporary copies of files that Windows creates. Such programs, however, can go too far; one is titled the "Evidence Eliminator." Since word leaked out about the document shredding done by Enron and Arthur Andersen, the law is getting tighter about such things as preserving corporate e-mail for three years. Interestingly, at Enron, all the shredding proved to be in vain as the data was discoverable in electronic form.

Forensics Software

While some companies have habitually tried to destroy e-mail records, others keep them in abundance, and that can be every bit as much of a problem as trying to track down deleted files. A company that has backed up on tape every e-mail sent in the last five years might initially appear to be evidentiary heaven. But, a single backup tape can contain 300 million e-mails — the equivalent of 360,000 banker's boxes of paper documents. While the evidence being sought may be there, it is almost impossible for individuals to wade through that volume of data to find the proverbial needle in a haystack. This is where forensics software comes into its own. Not only does it discover deleted files and expose metadata, but it can also help analyze, categorize, and manage all the different types of files on a disk. Here are some examples of forensics programs and other tools:

- Forensics Toolkit (Accessdata, Inc.)
- The Coroner's Toolkit (Computer Forensics Analysis)
- Computer forensics software, hardware, and services (DIBS Computer Forensics)
- DriveSpy and other hardware and software solutions (Digital Intelligence)
- Portable Linux Auditing CD (Fred Cohen and Associates)
- EnCase Software (Guidance Software)
- ILook Investigator Page (IRS Criminal Investigation Electronic Crimes Program)
- Broad forensics software site (Mares and Company, LLC)
- Forensics software and services (New Technologies, Inc.)
- Forensics tools and technology (Paraben Forensics Tools)
- Forensics software utilities (Tools That Work)
- The Ultimate Collection of Forensics Software (TUCOFS) (Cyber Enforcement Resources)

Guidance Software's EnCase, for example, simultaneously searches across multiple imaged hard drives, and it has built-in viewers for different file types so the user can go from looking at a fax to an e-mail to a photograph to a letter without having to switch between programs.

Another key element of forensics software is its ability to sort through all the documents and recognize duplicates. That way, when an e-mail with its attachment gets forwarded to everyone in the company, it is not necessary to look at the same document a thousand times, as it shows up only once in the index.

Chapter 11

Simplifying Disk Management for Storage Assets

A lot is changing in the subject of disk management as a result of the release of Windows Server 2003 (see Chapter 15). Most of the material covered in this chapter is part of Windows Server 2003. What we have to look forward to is greater functionality in the management of storage disks in the field of storage virtualization, as well as better management of data by users courtesy of virtual shadow sets. Further breakthroughs are a result of RAID-type snapshot technology that copies the complete contents of a volume in seconds, enabling transaction-heavy systems such as SQL Server to stay online while the data is being backed up.

Snapshot Technology

Snapshot technology is used now by many vendors. Essentially, a snapshot is an image or copy of a defined collection of data created instantly at a point in time. Copies are made almost immediately within the disk subsystem, despite the size of the volume. The primary use of a snapshot is to facilitate nondisruptive backups. Essentially, the snapshot image becomes the source of backup. After halting the application, the copy takes only a moment to create, so the user should not notice any delay. Implementations of snapshot vary from vendor to vendor. The two primary techniques are copy-on-write (loosely characterized as software based) and split mirror (loosely characterized as hardware based).

Copy-on-Write

In a general sense, copy-on-write can be characterized as software-based snapshots. Primarily, this application is used as server-based software, although the distinction of being software-only may be blurring as copy-on-write is now also being implemented inside intelligent switch or storage virtualization devices. Depending on the vendor, these devices may deploy software or firmware to provide copy-on-write capabilities. Basically, with copy-on-write, the snapshot is a logical copy of the data that gets created by saving the original data to a snapshot index whenever data in the base volume is updated. It provides efficiency by requiring only a fraction of the base volume disk space. Periodic snapshots can be made throughout the day. Sophisticated roll-back capabilities are being developed to instantly roll back a complete volume. Soon users will be able to select the time of the restore point and instantly revert to that moment.

Split Mirror

Split mirror could be referred to as the hardware-based approach to snapshots, but this is not strictly true. Just as RAID can be done via hardware or software, so can split-mirror technology be hardware or software based. Most vendors favor the hardware side, although some have software products that use the split-mirror method. The software involved, though, is primarily proprietary and works only with specific hardware from the same vendor and is included in the price. Split mirror is based on RAID/mirroring technology. In disk mirroring, two or more up-to-date full copies of the data are maintained. Every write request to the original data is automatically duplicated to other mirrors or copies of that data. The mirror may be contained in the same subsystem or may be between different subsystems, although these typically must be of the same subsystem model.

The mirror can be temporarily suspended — also referred to as a broken or split mirror — to create a snapshot or point-in-time copy. The disk subsystem is told to temporarily stop making updates to the mirrored copy, so the data is frozen at the point of the suspension. The split mirror can then be used for the backup process or other purposes.

Mirrors create an instant copy, or snapshot, of the data with the split capability. Unlike copy-on-write, a full data copy is available. In order to keep the disaster recovery copy available, a third mirror is usually established for the purpose of splitting. This requires three entire copies of the data volume to provide the protection and meet continuous processing demands for backup and other development needs. This setup has a primary and secondary real-time copy, as well as a tertiary point-in-time copy of the data. In the more sophisticated systems, the writes have been saved from the point of the suspension, they are applied to the mirror, and normal mirror operations resume; however, in some products, the entire mirror must be rewritten once the mirror is broken. In either case, the original data volume is not affected by breaking the mirror.

Products that utilize the split mirror to provide an instant copy or snapshot include:

- EMC TimeFinder (software included as part of the Symmetrix line of storage hardware)
- Hitachi Data Systems InstantSplit for ShadowImage (Lightning series of storage disk systems)
- HP SureStore Business Copy
- Sun StorEdge Instant Image (9900 server systems)
- XIOtech REDI (MAGNITUDE storage hardware)
- LSI Logic ContinuStor Director
- VERITAS Volume Manager and Volume Replicator

Hitachi Data Systems' ShadowImage technology, for example, has been incorporated into Computer Associates' BrightStor Enterprise Backup (EB) as well as the storage products of several leading vendors to create impressive results on the SQL Server platform.

SQL Server Backups

Mission-critical adoption of SQL Server has grown significantly over the past couple of years. According to a Gartner Group study, Microsoft has moved into first place in the Windows relational database segment with a 39.9 percent of the market, followed by Oracle with 34 percent. This growth has been driven largely by recent advances in data protection that reconcile the business needs of round-the-clock availability and high transactional throughput with the time demands of backup and recovery. Technical cooperation between Computer Associates, Microsoft, Hitachi Data Systems, and leading storage vendors has simplified and accelerated the backup and recovery process, resulting in the fastest database recovery performance ever recorded on any distributed platform: 2.21 TB per hour. This was achieved through the use of ShadowImage technology as well as heightened operational integration between the database, hardware, and backup/restore engine.

Breakthrough in Backup and Recovery Performance

Depending on the CPU and the size or type of backup being performed, processor utilization is often above 50 percent on critical systems during backup and restore operations. Some users even report utilization rates rising to 85 percent or more. During these periods, transactional traffic can grind to a halt and impatient users may go elsewhere to satisfy immediate needs. What is needed is an approach to storage that minimizes the bandwidth and CPU load during backup so transactional traffic continues unaffected and mission-critical systems stay operating at maximum efficiency. At the same time, the business-critical nature of the application is driving the need for rapid recovery, so this method must also provide a means of recovery for multi-terabyte databases at a far more rapid rate than is currently being experienced. These conditions have been satisfied by the BrightStor offering, a storage design for the Windows platform based on technology developed through the combined efforts of Computer Associates, Microsoft, and storage leaders such as Hitachi Data Systems, Brocade, Emulex, and Quantum.

This architecture was tested at Microsoft's Redmond campus using a 2.5-TB Microsoft SQL Server 2000 Enterprise Edition database. Technicians optimized these tests around the recovery performance of SQL Server, minimizing the impact on ongoing transactions during backup, and operational simplicity. These tests resulted in the following (see Exhibit 3):

- A 2.6-TB/hour archival backup speed
- A recovery rate of 2.2 TB/hour using 32 drives
- Average CPU utilization on the 8-CPU backup server of 26 percent during backup and 12 percent for recovery
- A time of 68 minutes to back up a 2.5-TB database to tape and 88 minutes to recover it
- Complete recovery of a 2.5-TB database in 11 minutes when done directly from a ShadowImage copy

Such impressive recovery and backup performance was achieved via automated integration and coordination of applications and hardware, in conjunction with implementation of ShadowImage technology. Essentially, a ShadowImage is a quick, point-in-time copy of data that allows databases and applications to remain online. Based on Hitachi Data System's split-mirror technology, extra mirrored sets of the data can be split off from the primary volume to create very fast backups.

SQL Server stabilizes the file system to allow a safe hardware snapshot, then BrightStor Enterprise Backup controls the entire sequence of actions, informing SQL Server to allow the ShadowImage copy and also controlling backup to tape. During the few seconds that a ShadowImage is being taken, SQL Server allows all database reads. Writes, though, are temporarily suspended for a few seconds. Upon completion of rapid point-in-time Shadow-Image copy of SQL Server, the database executes any queued writes and returns to normal operation. While taking the ShadowImage during testing, SQL Server processed 983 transactions per second consisting of a typical online transaction-processing environment.

Once the ShadowImage is completed, SQL Server continues and as far as it is concerned the backup is complete. As the data on the secondary volume is essentially a valid backup, this data can then be rapidly streamed to tape using BrightStor Enterprise Backup as an additional level of backup for archiving and long-term and off-site storage.

Performance is improved so markedly because this architecture accomplishes backup and recovery at a hardware, not a software level. Within the Hitachi Data Systems' storage subsystem, both the primary and ShadowImage volumes are replicated on demand to provide a point-in-time copy. By operating at a hardware level, it takes a few seconds to complete a snapshot

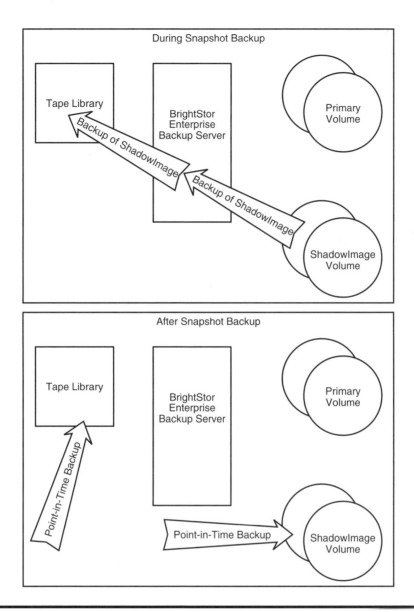

Exhibit 1   During and After Snapshot Backup

of the 2.5 TB of data using the ShadowImage technology. The ShadowImage volume can then be fed to tape directly by a backup server. Thus, a full backup can be taken without impacting SQL Server performance (Exhibit 1).

Similarly, when it comes to data recovery, the use of snapshots greatly speeds the process. If the required point-in-time copy already exists on the storage subsystem, for example, it is not necessary to recover the data from the tape library. During benchmarking, for instance, it took only 11 minutes to recover the 2.5-TB database to a point where transactions were running using a recent ShadowImage copy. Even when data had to be copied from tape to the ShadowImage volume, it took a total of 88 minutes to fully restore the database. In both cases, BrightStor EB ensures that the secondary ShadowImage volume and primary volume have been resynchronized before allowing SQL Server to commence recovery operations. These speeds are achieved due to the data being available to the database server almost immediately because of synchronization between the primary and ShadowImage volumes. Backup server CPU utilization averaged 12 percent during recovery.

In addition to greatly accelerated backup/restore and nominal overhead on the server, snapshots can be used in combination with differential and log backups providing the flexibility required to roll forward to a user-specified point in time, if necessary, while retaining the ability to backup large databases without disruption.

Storage Evolution

The storage-evolution approach to data protection has already been accomplished in BrightStor EB (Exhibit 2) and represents the probable direction of backup and recovery evolution on Windows in the foreseeable future. While it is already available for organizations using SQL Server 2000, it is currently being integrated with the upcoming releases. Windows Server 2003, for example, will include Volume ShadowCopy Service (VSS) and Virtual Disk Service (VDS), which allow interoperation and cooperation between storage hardware, storage software, and business applications. VSS lets vendors plug in snapshot, clone, and data replication solutions and allows integration with other applications. VDS, on the other hand, simplifies the configuration of direct-attached storage and storage area networks (SANs) by providing a standard way to interface with storage devices.

Further, everything learned by engineers and developers during the integration and benchmarking of the BrightStor offering (Exhibit 3) has been carefully documented. This information will be made available in a white paper that will be posted on Computer Associates' Web site (www.ca.com). Microsoft, Computer Associates, Hitachi Data Systems, and other storage leaders assembled some of the best minds in the field in one lab to figure out how to optimize Windows recovery speed and minimize backup overhead. In addition to the results disclosed above, these benchmark studies led to a large collection of lessons learned, which will soon be posted in the public domain, including in-depth research into how various parameters such as database size and the number of channels affect storage performance. The paper also offers insight into the various ways in which this architecture may be of benefit to smaller environments as well as non-Windows environments. While much of what has been discovered relates directly to large enterprises operating exclusively on a Windows platform, a surprisingly large number of best practices have been found to apply to small and mid-sized organizations.

The results of the research were achieved using Microsoft's SQL Server 2000 Enterprise Edition (consisting of 32 × 80-GB data files in one file group) running on a Unisys ES7000 Orion 230 server (divided into one database server partition and one backup server partition) utilizing the Windows 2000 Datacenter Edition operating system. A SAN used the Hitachi Data Systems

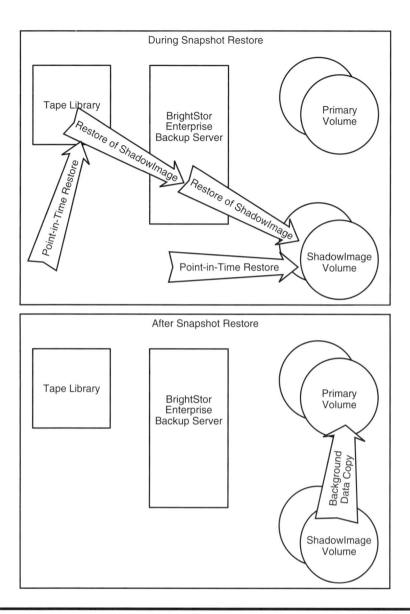

Exhibit 2   During and After Snapshot Restore

Lighting 9980 storage subsystem with Fibre Channel disk drives (32 RAID-10 volumes each consisting of 4 drives), four Brocade Silkworm 3800 fabric switches (2 Gb/sec), and two Quantum ATL P7000 tape libraries configured with a total of 32 LTO Ultrium tape drives connected to the Unisys server via 24 Emulex LP9002 Fibre Channel host bus adapters (HBAs; 16 HBAs on the backup server partition and 8 HBAs on the database server partition). Computer Associate's BrightStor EB and SQL Server Agent software exploited SQL Server's Virtual Data Interface (VDI), as well as ShadowImage technology from Hitachi Data Systems to ensure consistent snapshot backup and restore of the database (Exhibit 4).

Exhibit 3   BrightStor Offering: Fastest Ever Database Backup/Recovery Performance on Distributed Platform

Sustained throughput during backup: 2.6 TB/hour
Sustained throughput during restore: 2.2 TB/hour
Time to back up 2.5-TB database to tape: 68 minutes
Time to restore 2.5-TB database: 11 minutes
Average CPU utilization across 8 CPUs on backup server during backup: 26 percent
Average CPU utilization across 8 CPUs on backup server during restore: 12 percent
Average CPU utilization on database server during backup: 51 percent
Transactional load on database server during backup: 983 transactions/second

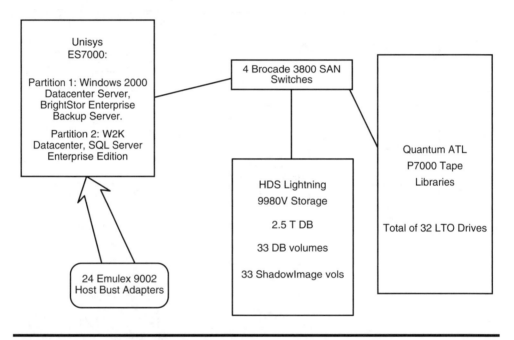

Exhibit 4   Test System Environment

While this white paper represents the release of a substantial amount of data, it is only the start. The next phase will be the issuance of a series of more detailed publications and services outlining best practices for the configuration and sizing of a wide range of storage environments.

Microsoft System Restore

Snapshot technology is not a new addition to Windows. Its first appearance was in the System Restore function embedded into Windows Me and XP as a means of restoring system configuration in the event of a problem resulting from the installation of new software or drivers. In that case, System Restore is used to go back to a previous point in time, and a good configuration is restored. System Restore technology is really a subset of snapshot technology as it does *not* take a snapshot of data files, only some system files and the Windows registry. System Restore requires a minimum of 200 MB of disk space and defaults at 12 percent of disk space. It is also a resource hog. Every time the system is started up, System Restore is actively taking a snapshot and writing data to disk of your current configuration. It takes a snapshot every ten hours and any time anything changes, so it makes loads of unnecessary copies and is not really of value as it discards old snapshots after a few weeks. For example, I decided to use it to remove an annoying message I could not get rid of that pops up after startup asking me to download the latest version of Yahoo Companion. This message would not go away no matter what I did. I decided to use System Restore to go back to the point in time before I downloaded the application that brought with it the annoying message. When I tried to revert to the previous system state, I discovered that I had about 100 snapshots available for my computer — one every ten hours for two months but none from three months ago when I had added the application in question to my system.

Shadow Sets

Microsoft is building VSS into its latest servers. Shadow copies of user file changes are stored and available to the user, so when users accidentally delete something, they can retrieve it simply by looking up the shadow copies on the server. These copies, in fact, contain only the actual changes made to files so they have a lower footprint; that is, this is a copy-on-write approach to snapshots, not split mirroring. A shadow copy is essentially a snapshot of the existing state of a working volume. Instead of copying every single bit, it is simply a log of changes at a specific point in time, changes made since the last system snapshot was taken.

The Windows Server 2003 family included VSS and many other improved management and storage functions. The Microsoft Management Console (MMC) is still used as the main management interface and incorporates Manage Your Server, a role-based management interface that organizes administrative tasks much better than previously. According to initial reports, it is simpler and more user friendly than the Configure Your Server interface of Windows 2000. Among the new core features of Windows Server 2003, storage has advanced the most. At a low level, the new operating system includes support for SANs and provides a unified management interface (including a new API) for hardware RAID devices. The most significant functional enhancements relate to shadow copies and federated file servers.

Advantages of VSS

When client versions of VSS are installed on remote desktops, users can recover lost data via the snapshots as the shadow copies are exposed to network users. Thus, when a document is accidentally deleted, the user goes into Windows Explorer, right-clicks the folder, and then selects the date and time of the snapshot from a list. *Voila* — the data is recovered without the user calling the help desk or requesting IT's assistance. Lost files can be recovered in moments, and the snapshot itself on even large drives takes about a minute without impacting server availability. Further, shadow copies of volumes are made at the time a backup is initiated. Data can then be backed up from the shadow copy instead of from the original volume. The original volume continues to change as the process continues, but the shadow copy of the volume remains constant. Users can refer back to earlier shadow copies, thereby retrieving earlier versions of documents that have been lost.

Volume ShadowCopy Service technology has many advantages. Servers and workstations can be backed up while applications and services are running, and open files are not skipped during the backup process. More importantly, the need to schedule a backup window where applications must be shut down is removed. VSS is much more thorough than System Restore. It completes data file snapshots so all the data is protected. As noted previously, it allows multiplatform interoperation and cooperation among storage hardware, storage software, and business applications; lets vendors plug in snapshot, clone, and data replication solutions; and allows integration with other applications. One warning, though: VSS and other approaches to snapshots must have temporary disk space available; if space is not available, VSS skips open files. This is another reason why you should always ensure your disks contain plenty of free space. Additionally, by virtue of the fact that snapshots make many temporary copies of a volume, the level of fragmentation is greatly increased. So, take advantage of snapshot technology, by all means, but be sure to support it with regular defragmentation.

One further warning is that VSS can be a space and resource hog. Default settings allocate as much as 12 percent of a volume to snapshots, and it runs many times during the day, thus consuming a significant amount of CPU time and RAM. It is probably best to select as little snapshot room as the system will allow, and do not expect to be able to go back 9 months to find a lost file. At best, a library of a month or two of files and file changes can be accessed.

Storage Virtualization

Another relatively recent advancement in the area of storage and server disk management is storage virtualization. The concept of storage virtualization addresses the complexity inherent in today's ever-expanding storage environments. Because more and more servers and storage devices provide greater capacity than ever before, management of disks and volumes becomes a difficult proposition. Storage virtualization holds the promise of being able to simplify the process so that you can locate space across a wide range of resources, collect it together into a virtual volume, expand storage resources on the fly, and logically push terabytes of data around in seconds without having to take systems offline.

Though Microsoft is not saying much about storage virtualization, it does appear to have entered into partnership with a Wisconsin firm, XIOtech, one of the leaders in storage virtualization. What is interesting is that, instead of the usual hype about what such partnerships promise, this one is being kept relatively under wraps. Almost nothing about XIOtech can be found on the Microsoft Web site, yet the company was recently named a Preferred Alliance Member, a program aimed squarely at the success of the Windows Server 2003 program. In a release on the XIOtech site, a Microsoft spokesperson indicated that Magnitude, XIOtech's storage virtualization platform, is an important resource.

The field of storage virtualization is a little muddy currently as every storage vendor claims to have virtualization capabilities. Almost all of them, in fact, have aggregation technology, not virtualization. At this point, it might be a good idea to explain such storage terminology, beginning with a look at the evolutionary history of the storage industry.

Storage and RAID

The early days of disk storage and RAID were covered in earlier chapters, so we will pick up the discussion shortly after the development of RAID. Some vendors cobbled together multiple physical RAID devices within one chassis, thereby sharing various redundant devices such as fans, power supplies, processor boards, caches, and switches. Further, these multiple RAID arrays eased the administrative burden by centralizing storage across redundant systems, centrally allocating capacity to a number of servers, and giving administrators the ability to manage data across many servers with one set of instructions.

While this approach greatly improved the ability to manage multiple disks, problems remained in terms of configuration, efficiency, and expense. The administrator, for instance, has to select stripe size and RAID type from the outset, configure the device, and then assign the storage. To increase storage capacity, it is sometimes possible to add drives (but sometimes not), but the system usually equates all drives to the smallest disk in the mix. With today's huge drives, in particular, this can lead to massive amounts of wasted space, which brings to light another problem. To gain full value for any large disks installed, that size of disk must be installed everywhere; otherwise, space is wasted. But, to upgrade disks is expensive and can mean upgrading services and other storage devices that are only a year or two old.

Other drawbacks can be mentioned in passing: problems encountered when changing volume configurations once they have been set, bottlenecks and hot spots, and the high cost of bringing in experts to reconfigure storage and remove complexity.

Server-Attached Storage

Today, the picture has been changed by such offerings as server-attached storage, Storage Area Networks, Network-Attached Storage (NAS), and SAN appliances. Server-attached storage accounts for many of the RAID systems deployed today. Even the highly touted NAS is really a hybrid of server-attached storage. The server-attached model is good for local uses but falls down in the enterprise. As the data is decentralized, it cannot be manipulated or analyzed easily. Further complicating matters for IT, the storage of every server has to be managed individually and backup traffic goes out on the network, absorbing bandwidth. Also, when it comes time to expand, another server will have to be purchased.

Storage Area Networks

Storage Area Networks resolved some of these issues by centralizing storage around a high-speed network. Multiple servers could connect to a storage pool and be managed far more easily, and storage could be added without having to buy more servers. Problems solved? Not quite. SANs remain somewhat complex, and they continue to be plagued with configuration limitations, inefficiency, and high expense, as well as performance bottlenecks. As organizational storage requirements have expanded greatly, the SAN has failed to provide the across-the-board simplicity required to manage enterprise assets easily.

SAN Appliances

Another attempt to solve the problem resulted in SAN appliances. Simply put, SAN appliances aggregate the storage on a SAN regardless of devices housing the data. This is what most vendors are now hailing as storage virtualization. While it does give a virtualized view of storage, the technique is really aggregation, which allows the user to more easily cobble drive space together. Further, users can perform LUN masking and LUN mapping using a SAN appliance box. LUN (Logical Unit Number) is the physical number of a device in a daisy chain of drives; each disk in a multiple-drive type of device can be addressed independently using its LUN. Because SAN appliances do not stripe data across all available disks, they are of limited real value. In reality, they do not remove installation and configuration tangles and have failed to arrive at storage virtualization in a true sense. So, what then is storage virtualization?

What Is True Storage Virtualization?

According to XIOtech, storage virtualization is basically the ability to stripe across and utilize all available space in a centralized storage pool, allowing storage to be centrally managed and shared with a heterogeneous server network. Actual virtualization offers many benefits. Storage management is greatly simplified, as the administrator has to deal only with storage requirements, rather than wrestling with all the details about size, type, and characteristics of the physical disk drives. While administrators today must know a

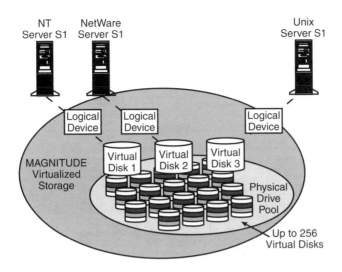

Exhibit 5   Virtualized Storage in a MAGNITUDE SAN Environment

lot about the system to tie various storage assets together, with virtualization they can quickly increase storage capacity by adding disk drives of any capacity or type. Further, administrators can configure storage resources to a specific environment, such as changing RAID levels on the fly. Different server operating systems can be running at the same time, sharing a centralized storage pool concurrently. But, the greatest benefits surround the virtual concept. Storage is allocated into virtual disks wherever the capacity is needed. If only short-term use is required, that capacity can then be thrown back into the storage pot for other uses, which means that volume expansion is greatly simplified along with data management. Instead of long, involved pathways, the system can manage, copy, mirror, and swap data within the storage box or across the SAN relatively effortlessly. What does this mean to capacity utilization? By striping data across all available drives, far more storage is utilized, and the system can be configured to maximize system performance by eliminating bottlenecks and hot spots.

XIOtech's Magnitude utilizes virtualization and stripes data across all available spindles, thereby utilizing all storage capacity in the system (Exhibit 5). Thus, it removes the limitations discussed earlier. It stripes across and utilizes all available space in a centralized storage pool and centrally manages and shares storage resources. Thus, the administrator can view one big storage pool and allocate data to individual servers as needed, which removes the user from involvement with many of the physical aspects of storage media. Effectively, administrators are able to move up from the device level, where they are managing hundreds of drives, to a true storage management echelon where they are able to manage storage pools from a central console without bringing servers down. From this position, administrators are able to (1) allocate storage to a server by creating a new virtual disk and (2) remove storage from a server and return the unused space to the free storage pool by deleting the virtual disk.

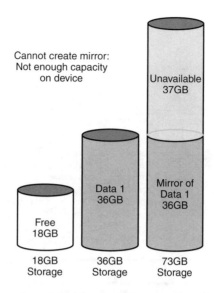

Exhibit 6   Inefficient Use of Storage Capacity in Aggregated RAID-10 Volume

Some of the advantages of virtualization include the ability to:

- Increase storage for a server through expansion of its assigned virtual disk.
- Create, change, or mix RAID levels on the fly.
- Add storage capacity to MAGNITUDE by plugging in another disk drive of any capacity; the system picks up the storage space and adds it to the free storage pool.
- Change the LUN of a disk to which the user wants to attach servers.
- Mask out a particular LUN to prevent undesired access by certain servers in a heterogeneous server network.
- Copy the data from one virtual disk to another to replicate volumes of data.
- Mirror volumes of data from one virtual disk to another.
- Migrate data from one virtual disk to another.

Virtualization Scenarios

Perhaps an example or two will illustrate this concept better. On a simple and small scale, consider a SAN appliance connected to a SAN with three disk drives or storage devices; one has 18 GB of storage, one has 36 GB, and the third has 73 GB.

- *Scenario #1.* The administrator wants to create a RAID-10 volume of 36 GB and uses a SAN appliance to put the data on the 36-GB drive while using the 73-GB drive as the mirror (Exhibit 6). What about the remaining 37 GB on the large drive? It is unused and, worse, is unavailable for future use. Further, the 18-GB storage device also goes unused. In such a scenario, the administrator would have to have an understanding of the physical characteristics of the storage environment to be able to set up RAID-10 successfully.

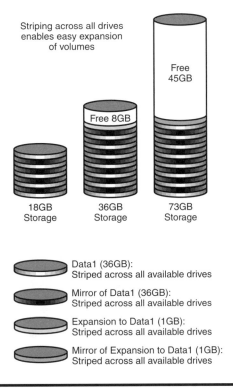

Striping across all drives enables easy expansion of volumes

Free 45GB

Free 8GB

18GB Storage 36GB Storage 73GB Storage

Data1 (36GB):
Striped across all available drives

Mirror of Data1 (36GB):
Striped across all available drives

Expansion to Data1 (1GB):
Striped across all available drives

Mirror of Expansion to Data1 (1GB):
Striped across all available drives

Exhibit 7   Flexibility of Virtualized RAID-10 Volume

- *Scenario #2.* A RAID device is used with the 36-, 73-, and 18-GB drives. It is not possible to create a RAID-10 36-GB volume, as the RAID device would only recognize 18 GB of capacity on each of the drives.

Now consider these scenarios in a virtualized storage environment equipped with the same 18-, 36-, and 73-GB drives.

- *Scenario #1.* With storage virtualization, the data and the mirror are striped across the 18-, 36-, and 73-GB drives, with some of the data going on each disk (Exhibit 7). What about the unused capacity? It is available for future use with no restrictions.
- *Scenario #2.* An extra 9-GB RAID-10 volume can be achieved simply by striping the data across all the spindles in the system. Free space on any partially used drives can be utilized with any new storage added to the system — true virtualization.

These examples can be applied to systems with hundreds of drives.

Virtualization and Windows-Based Servers

Gradually, this type of virtualization technology is becoming a part of Windows-based servers. When fully incorporated, it will signal a new dawn in server disk administration. Instead of fiddling around at the device level,

IT personnel will be able to manage their storage assets easily, thus leaving time to take care of other pressing matters. Further, this technology should make it possible to virtualize non-Windows-based storage resources within the enterprise and control them from a Windows server console. Until then, storage management will continue at its current level, and administrators will find themselves spending a lot of time managing an ever-growing number of disks and storage devices.

Chapter 12

Server Consolidation and Disk Management Simplification

One of the most challenging operational IT issues today is the management burden imposed by having to deal with hundreds of relatively small Wintel servers. Many companies have discovered the benefits of radically simplifying their data center infrastructure. In those enterprises where such an approach has been implemented, major improvements have been realized in their returns on investment (ROI), as well as overall business performance. Tremendous benefits, in particular, have come through server simplification and standardization. By consolidating the number of servers operating within the enterprise and optimizing that platform for the data center or for high-end and mission-critical applications, significant economic savings as well as greatly improved business agility are gained.

Harsh Economic Realities

The business landscape has changed significantly over the past several years. Where technology spending was once a mushrooming part of most corporate budgets, it is now subject to severe cutbacks. In 2001, for instance, IT expenditures actually fell for the first time in a decade. According to a study by Merrill Lynch, most chief information officers (CIOs) revised their budgets at least twice in 2002, and the deepest spending cuts were made in staffing, consulting, and hardware. Unfortunately, Merrill Lynch's prediction of three percent growth in IT spending in 2002 did not take place. Initial predictions

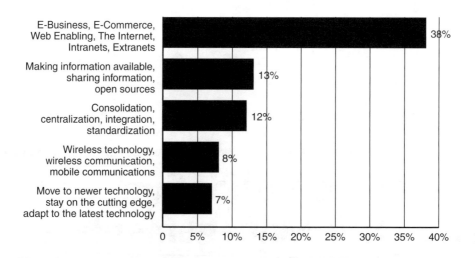

Exhibit 1   Most Important Strategic Trends

of twelve percent growth in 2003 were toned down, with many companies experiencing yet another year of slow or no growth. Yet, now is not the time to engage in another round of layoffs and further curtailment of IT budgets; rather, it is a time of opportunity. While continuing to search for greater internal efficiencies and far-reaching economies of scale, companies should find this to be an excellent time to prepare their IT infrastructures for future growth.

This viewpoint is backed up by a survey of 300 IT managers conducted by the Patrick Marketing Group of Calabasas, California. This survey reveals a lack of any clear-cut direction with regard to their planning for tomorrow. Although most can agree on the importance of E-business/Internet-related technology (38 percent), few other trends have clearly emerged to date as major drivers of change. Based on the survey responses, it appears that technology executives are focusing on information availability/sharing (13 percent), consolidation/centralization (12 percent), wireless/mobile computing (8 percent), and the nebulous issue of "staying on the cutting edge" (7 percent) (Exhibit 1).

Looking at this another way, most companies are simply waiting to see what happens. This is a total turnaround from the late 1990s' heyday of technology implementation just for the sake of staying on the cutting edge. While that period lacked any ROI demand for the substantial investment in technology, today's world is predominated by companies treading water. They do not want to risk anything. The scene is set, therefore, for forward-looking enterprises to achieve a competitive advantage by implementing strategically sound technology initiatives. In a year or two, the business press will be extolling the virtues of those few who stepped up to the plate and forged ahead with a technology vision rather than marked time like the rest of the crowd. But, even for those who cannot contemplate the slightest risk, server consolidation is a fairly safe bet.

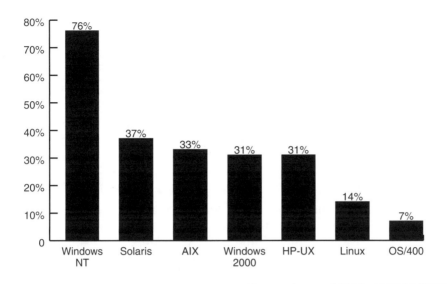

Exhibit 2   Operating Systems Run on Respondents' Servers

Assessing the Reliability, Availability, and Manageability of the Data Center

The typical data center has evolved into a complex multiplatform hybrid that has become difficult to manage and costly to run. Successive generations of technology are layered one on top of the other, cobbled together in a desperate attempt to cope with current demands. Most run some version of Windows *and* several UNIX variants side by side (Exhibit 2). This hodge-podge of technologies has resulted in greater complexity, thus raising the cost of doing business. Perhaps the most amazing offshoot of the steady advancement in technology, though, is the sheer number of servers in use. Many organizations are operating hundreds, and sometimes thousands of small distributed servers, a number that is growing by 10 to 20 percent with each passing year. While a distributed server model certainly offers economies of scale in typical business uses, the point comes when an abundance of servers adds an administrative burden. Organizations, therefore, must find the correct balance between economies of scale offered by distributed servers and management advantages afforded by a more centralized infrastructure.

Data Center Cost Analysis

Although well-worn clichés abound on the subject of the Internet and E-commerce, it is nevertheless true that the advent of the Internet has brought about a massive shift in the way business is conducted. Whereas the old way involved isolated information silos, each one operating independently, the new paradigm depends upon instantaneous information access and sharing. As a result, many legacy platforms have been exposed as no longer being adequate to meet the needs of the modern enterprise. Today's systems must be able to cope with Web-based technologies and applications and must be attuned to the demands of large numbers of customers and/or internal users; otherwise, the business consequences can be catastrophic. Witness the collapse of some prominent E-tailers after they failed to cope with demand during the 2000 holiday season. Delays due to system slowdowns, therefore, can be disastrous, and, unless an enterprise's systems and applications are geared toward immediate response across the Internet, Intranet, or Extranet, its future is in jeopardy. This is where the latest high-end Wintel servers running Windows 2000 Datacenter Server and Windows Server 2003 come into their own (see Chapters 13 and 15). The Unisys ES7000, for example, has achieved impressive benchmark results running Windows 2000 Datacenter Server.

Leveraging New Technologies To Streamline Data Center Operations

A year or more ago, it may have been prudent to tone down technology ambitions by placing upgrades and platform migrations on hold, but that logic no longer appears to apply. Many companies are waking up to the fact that savvy competitors have quietly upped their IT investment to achieve greater economies of scale and operational efficiencies. If they do not act quickly, they could shortly fall far behind. Those organizations that have already fallen behind, for example, cannot afford to let the technology chasm widen. They need to spend wisely over the coming months, particularly with regard to consolidation and standardization within their server operating environments. Those utilizing a Windows platform have two basic strategies for server deployment: scaling out and scaling up.

Scaling Out

Since the 1980s, computing environments have tended to become more distributed. Increasingly agile, powerful, and affordable low-end and mid-range servers became available. Easy to deploy and configure, such servers are now an established part of the IT landscape. As servers become overloaded or databases grow, additional servers can be added, or multiple functions residing on one server can be distributed over several others. This is known as scaling out or horizontal scaling. The purpose of scaling out is to improve performance (e.g., Web server farms) and availability (e.g., high-availability clusters) or to provide an immediate fix to a pressing IT situation. When it comes to increasing storage capacity, for example, scaling out offers a rapid and often cost-effective solution. Increasingly flexible, powerful, and affordable low-end servers have resulted in a scaling out in the data center to a more distributed computing model.

On the downside, though, an overabundance of small servers can create too much of an administrative burden, especially when hundreds of servers are present. Every server added to the data center requires space, power, telecommunications, and networking interfaces, storage capacity and connections, backup and restore systems, and an update to asset management inventories and supplier contracts. When taken to extremes, scaling out can result in fragmented databases and a series of disconnected, difficult-to-manage servers. Some servers end up underutilized while others are badly overloaded. In many cases, the proliferation of distributed servers within large enterprise organizations has proved to be an administrative money pit as well as a nightmare. As more systems are added to the network, the costs of administration and maintenance increase.

Horizontally scaled systems can be further characterized by multiple servers connected by relatively slow communication links. Although networks and cluster interconnects continue to improve performance in terms of high bandwidth/low latency, their speed is still dwarfed by the capabilities of bus and switch interconnects. As scaled-out systems communicate by message passing, the elapsed time to complete a task can sometimes increase markedly.

Additionally, each horizontally scaled server runs a copy of the operating system. This can result in synchronization challenges, not to mention trouble with the division of labor among servers. While the mantra in most enterprises is "one application, one server," distributed environments still tend to offer much coarser granularity when it comes to server management and workload planning. Costs, too, can mount up. Licensing costs, for example, for running hundreds or even thousands of small servers can be prohibitive, and managing these assets can turn into an administrative nightmare (see Chapters 16 and 17).

Scaling Up

By contrast, vertically scaled-up systems consolidate many small servers into one or more large servers. Systems that scale up are characterized by a single server with multiple CPUs running a single copy of the operating system. Although scaling out has become an accepted approach to modern computing, some consider it unsuitable for certain types of large-scale, enterprise-type environments, primarily because of the disadvantages discussed in the previous section. This is where the concept of scaling up or vertical scaling comes in. Systems that scale up are characterized by a single server with multiple CPUs running a single copy of the operating system. Scaling up decreases the elapsed time that it takes to complete high-volume tasks such as online transaction processing (OLTP) and complex tasks such as weather forecasting.

Which applications are most suited to vertical scaling? According to Aberdeen Group (Boston, MA), scaling up allows IT managers to run applications and databases that were optimized for a single environment, as is the case with many of today's most popular enterprise business applications, including Oracle, PeopleSoft, SAP, etc. These applications run best when they have access to plenty of local (nondistributed) processors as well as local data.

Large databases, ERP, and other single-threaded applications in particular are ideally suited to vertically scaled systems. Within data centers, especially, scaling up is probably the best strategy.

Server Price and Performance

Although scaling out may make sense in terms of performance, it may or may not be attractive in terms of cost; therefore, both price and performance must be considered before making any decision to carry out a server consolidation program. That said, many companies are going ahead with plans for change-outs in hardware. According to a survey by the Gartner Group, the chief factors precipitating the changes in server environment are cost concerns or cost-reduction requirements (27 percent) and a push for enhanced performance (21 percent). When it comes to higher end servers, though, priorities have shifted. With higher end servers, the most important issues and criteria that drive IT respondents' selection are reliability (53 percent), then cost (33 percent), then performance (27 percent). Clearly, for server consolidation on Windows to be a viable proposition, it has to offer greater reliability. If it offers higher reliability at a lower cost and better performance, then it becomes a very attractive option. So how does it measure up?

Wintel Servers Challenge Domination of Big Three

UNIX vendors such as Sun Microsystems, Hewlett-Packard, and IBM have long dominated the mid-range server market, but Wintel systems finally look like they are overcoming their desktop image. After almost a decade at the low end of the server market with ubiquitous NT boxes operating as file and print servers, Windows is now making a major play into the mid-range sector. The average data center these days consists of hundreds of Intel and UNIX servers — 230 servers to be exact, according to a recent survey of 300 data center managers by Patrick Marketing (Calabasas, CA). This survey highlights the dominance of lower end Windows NT and Windows 2000 servers (Exhibit 2). A server-management labyrinth is the result and can mean that adding a single application often requires adding three to five servers to the data center for production, development, testing, and backup. Further, many of these distributed servers run at very low utilizations. It has gotten to the point where, for many, the honeymoon is over with regard to the deployment of inexpensive, commodity-type servers for every function throughout the enterprise. The economics used to be attractive, but the licensing and administrative expenses may now be tipping the financial scales in favor of server consolidation.

This has been demonstrated in Gartner Group surveys that reveal a marked shift in attitude toward server consolidation in recent years. In 1998, 30 percent were already consolidating, 45 percent were considering the possibility, and 25 percent had no intention of consolidating. By the end of 2001, 69 percent were already consolidating, 25 percent were thinking about it, and only 6

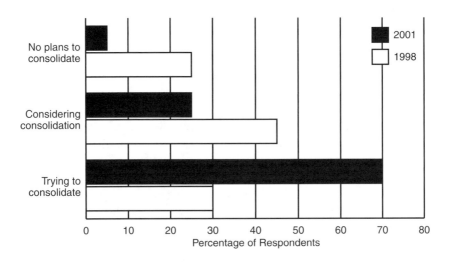

Exhibit 3   The Trend toward Server Consolidation

percent had no plans to do so (Exhibit 3). Based on a large volume of interviews with enterprise clients, Gartner Group now regards server consolidation to be one of the most important issues its clients are facing. The analyst group believes that consolidation and effective resource management within a single operating system can dramatically reduce TCO and improve enterprise flexibility.

Server consolidation was difficult with Windows NT, however, as the operating system struggled to overcome the 4-CPU limit, although some clustered approaches scaled higher. This effectively locked Wintel out of large-scale, demanding commercial computing applications. At the lower end, Wintel offered appealing price/performance characteristics, hence its widespread deployment as file, print, intranet, and infrastructure servers, but rarely was Windows NT used in core data centers and mission-critical business applications. That may be changing, however, due to the range of scale offered by the Windows 2000 Server family (and now the Windows Server 2003 family). Windows 2000 Advanced Server, for example, scales up to 8 processors. But, more importantly to the mid-range market, Windows 2000 Datacenter Server scales up to 32 processors within a single symmetric multiprocessing (SMP) server, putting it on a par with many UNIX systems but at far less cost. Factor in the improvements in CPU horsepower of late, and it can be seen that these servers perform well enough to be a serious rival to some mainframe machines. Windows 2000 Datacenter Server, in particular, has achieved some impressive scores using industry benchmark tests.

Windows 2000 Datacenter Server

The Datacenter Server is the most robust member of the Windows 2000 family. This operating system is designed to offer scalability and reliability for enterprise users. It provides companies with the ability to quickly expand to meet system needs while maintaining a high level of availability, as well as the opportunity to phase out smaller NT servers, replacing them with Datacenter Server clusters. Datacenter Server supports up to a 4-node server cluster, doubling the availability in any previous Microsoft operating system. It also supports network load balancing on up to 32 nodes. Perhaps the best news, though, is that it is impossible to purchase Windows 2000 Datacenter off the shelf; instead, it is available through only a handful of certified OEM partners, including Dell, Hewlett-Packard, Unisys, Compaq, and IBM. Each offers an approved Datacenter program that includes a package consisting of a specific hardware platform, Windows 2000 Datacenter Server, and the installation/ tuning/maintenance support needed to run a high-end Wintel server. Users must buy the entire package and can only obtain it from approved vendors who meet such standards as guaranteeing 99.9 percent availability, 24/7 support, on-site support, change management, and a minimum number of Microsoft certified professionals (MCPs) available in the support center. The whole idea is to hold these vendors 100 percent accountable for the system as a whole, as opposed to causing finger pointing between software and hardware vendors.

Unisys, for example, places a heavy emphasis on support services to maximize performance. A large group of support and implementation staff is available to walk users through the planning, prototyping, and deployment of the ES7000 server. Customers can take advantage of a wide range of services, such as setup and installation of Windows NT/2000, preinstallation analysis, hands-on sessions on the system management applications of the platform, capacity planning, Active Directory planning, customer training, benchmark services, and performance analysis.

Mid-Range Hardware for Windows 2000 Datacenter Server

One of the more attractive and sensible elements of the release of Windows 2000 Datacenter Server is that a person cannot just walk into a local Best Buy and purchase it nor is it available online. In order to position the software as an enterprise-only release, it can only be purchased from approved vendors, most of whom offer it on their own hardware platforms. Following are some of the main candidates. (*Note:* The specs have no doubt been upgraded in the time that has passed between writing this book and its appearing in print.)

Unisys ES7000

Leading the pack among the OEMs appears to be Unisys (Blue Bell, Pennsylvania), with its ES7000 Server. According to Gartner Group tests on online transaction processing, Unisys came out ahead of other vendor offerings. The analyst community in general seems taken with the ES7000. Giga Information Group (Cambridge, MA), for instance, feels that Unisys has brought the Intel world much closer to the high-availability, scalable, mainframe-class environment than any other vendor. In Giga's opinion the architecture developed by Unisys provides a far more scalable technology for multiple processor servers than the existing commodity Intel-based SMP servers.

Based on the cellular multiprocessing (CMP) architecture, the ES7000 supports server partitioning; offers process control, multiple operating systems, up to 32 Intel Xeon processors (as well as Itanium 64-bit processors), 4 to 192 GB of memory, and 8 to 160 PCI adapters for I/O; and is built to house the 64-bit Itanium processor. CMP also makes it possible to dynamically reallocate resources and offers mainframe-oriented crossbar technology that eliminates the bottlenecks associated with bus-based SMP architectures. Dedicated connections exist between memory, processors, and I/O components. CMP's support for partitioning enables administrators to create "servers within a server," thus executing multiple functions in heterogeneous operating environments within the same server.

Microsoft, for example, uses the ES7000/Datacenter server combination for Worldwide Marketing Database (WWMDB), an SQL Server 2000 database containing international and national sales and marketing data. The company initially established WWMDB on eight servers with four-way and eight-way architectures. Once the former database expanded beyond 1 TB, it no longer provided the necessary throughput. Processing levels were pegged at about 500,000 records per day. As a result, sales and marketing users experienced delays attempting to access information.

When Microsoft consolidated its eight servers into one ES7000 running Datacenter Server, the system moved up to processing more than 2 million records per day. Since that time, WWMDB has expanded beyond a 2.4-TB database with processing times increased by 53 percent.

Hewlett-Packard ProLiant DL7602G

Although Unisys currently appears to dominate the Windows 2000 Datacenter market, other vendors are attempting to close the gap. Hewlett-Packard's ProLiant DL7602G server (based on the ProLiant 8500), for example, has eight Pentium Xeon 2 GHz processors, 64 GB of SDRAM, and 11 hot-pluggable 64-bit I/O slots. It uses HP's F8 chipset architecture.

Investment banking firm Credit Suisse First Boston (CSFB), for instance, deployed two ProLiant 8500/Windows 2000 Datacenter Servers as parts of its overall plan to consolidate servers within its worldwide IT system. Currently, a blend of Sun/Solaris and Windows NT/Windows 2000 is being used for file and print servers, messaging platform, Web applications, and database and business applications.

The first implementation project of Windows 2000 Datacenter at CSFB involved file and print, using a four-server, split-site solution. The second was a two-node solution for Microsoft SQL Server 2000, using NetIQ's AppManager and AppAnalyzer products. Both run on ProLiant 8500 eight-way servers with Xeon chips. In terms of overall benefits, the company experienced better scalability across higher numbers of processors, very large memory (VLM) support, and improved performance running enterprise applications such as Microsoft Exchange 2000 and Microsoft SQL Server 2000.

IBM x440

The IBM x440 supports up to 16 Pentium Xeon processors. SDRAM memory is expandable to 32 GB.

Dell PowerEdge 8450

Dell's PowerEdge 8450, can link two sets of four processors in one server. It supports up to eight Intel Pentium Xeon processors.

Fujitsu Siemens PRIMERGY N850

Fujitsu Siemens Computers offers the PRIMERGY N850, based on an 8- and 16-way Pentium Xeon.

Fewer Servers

While mainframe and UNIX shops are not beating a path to their local Unisys dealer, the ES 7000/W2K Datacenter Server platform is gaining ground among existing Windows shops as an effective means of server consolidation. For example, Mark Anthony Group (British Columbia, makers of Mike's Hard Lemonade) saw its server population grow from 2 to 18 within a few months. That workload rapidly became unmanageable for a relatively small IT team. Mark Anthony Group implemented the Unisys ES7000/Microsoft Windows 2000 Datacenter Server combo which resulted in fewer servers to manage, simplified systems management, server load balancing, and gaining the ability to add processors to the server as business grows. The company was attracted to the system's mainframe-like stability implemented over a client/server environment. They can now run three critical applications in the same environment plus assign processors to meet changing demands. They can also add more processors over time without doing a forklift upgrade.

Server Consolidation at La-Z-Boy

More and more companies these days are now consolidating their Wintel servers. Furniture manufacturer La-Z-Boy, for example, launched its effort by consolidating 12 Compaq servers running Windows NT onto a single Unisys ES7000 running Windows 2000 Datacenter Server. The result was reduced administrative costs, lower resource requirements, and better hardware and software control. The consolidation allowed La-Z-Boy to avoid adding more full-time employees while managing an expanding IT portfolio. La-Z-Boy consolidated its distributed servers onto three partitions on the ES7000. It placed the general-purpose infrastructure servers (imaging, file and print, e-mail, Web, backup, etc.) on one partition. Another partition contains several SQL Server databases, which were formerly spread throughout the data center. Any new application, even if hosted on a commodity server, has its database on the ES7000. The company added a third partition to run MetaFrame thin client software from Citrix Systems, Inc. (Ft. Lauderdale, Florida). La-Z-Boy intends to add two more partitions: one to accommodate Microsoft Exchange Server 2000 and another as a test environment. The IT manager cautions that, although partitioning is relatively easy to do on these machines, it is always best to rely on Unisys tools and support to make it work well.

While remaining a firm server consolidation advocate, La-Z-Boy confesses to also indulging in some scaling out using small Windows servers. In the past year, the company added about a dozen commodity Wintel servers. This, however, is less than half what the company added the year before. These servers consist mainly of smaller machines to handle domain-name system and Windows Internet naming service functions. The reason that they were not consolidated into one larger server is that they appeared to add almost no administrative burden. Without an economic incentive to place them on the ES7000, La-Z-Boy decided to go ahead with a few small servers. Plenty of room for expansion remains on the ES7000, though. Despite an expanding workload and larger databases, the ES7000 runs at an average rate of utilization of only 6 to 8 percent.

Limits to Consolidation

While server consolidation is often a smart thing to do, do not just attempt to jam everything onto one high-end Windows server. It is important to understand that the degree of consolidation that can be achieved is limited due in part to geography, as well as limits that are inherent in some applications. For example, network capacity might restrict the ability to consolidate distributed Microsoft Exchange servers. DLL conflicts, applications with memory leaks, peak traffic load conflicts, and application conflicts are other issues that may have to be considered. In addition, different database products, such as Oracle and Sybase, will quite probably not coexist in the same partition.

Politics is another reason why it is wise not to think too big when it comes to server consolidation projects. Those who have been through server consolidation report that internal politics is probably the biggest reason for consolidation project failure. They strongly advise that it is far better to start small and achieve measurable results before making too many promises. And, even when small projects reap rich and immediate rewards, do not try to tackle cross-business consolidated projects without the support of senior management. Without the complete backing of top executives, most server consolidations are doomed due to the potential for conflict that may exist.

When Consolidation Makes Sense

Nothing is black and white when considering scaling up versus scaling out on Windows. Proponents on both sides can lay out a convincing argument either way for specific scenarios. That said, here are some situations when it probably makes most sense to consolidate many smaller Windows-based servers into a few more rugged Windows boxes:

- When a large number of distributed infrastructure servers handle tasks such as file and print, Web, and e-mail; however, this suitability varies from organization to organization. The bottom line is to base any decision on the administrative burden created by having to manage dozens of boxes.
- To consolidate multiple databases; some companies end up running many databases due to their servers being too small or are unable to scale enough to consolidate them. One large Windows 2000 Datacenter Server should be more than large enough for just about any database, with room to spare for many other applications.
- To manage more with limited resources; it is a whole lot easier to manage a couple of large servers than it is to manage a couple of dozen distributed servers.
- When application peak traffic periods are complementary; some organizations prefer small servers, each with enough capacity to cope with a specific application at peak load. Doing so, however, results in server utilization rates of 10 to 20 percent. Intelligently combining compatible applications on one server raises utilization much higher without endangering the organization.
- When application conflicts or DLL conflicts do not exist; some applications and databases just do not like each other. Test thoroughly ahead of time to eliminate conflicts.
- When the data center requires more space; one company went from a packed data center to a half-empty one by instituting server consolidation, which effectively bought the company two more years before having to expand by using fewer boxes to do more.
- When the volume of distributed servers becomes too great to keep up with routine maintenance, updates, etc., which is a very real situation these days. Virus updates, patches, and software upgrades are issued in a continuous stream (see Chapters 16 and 17).

These are just a few of the many situations in which server consolidation makes sense. By planning consolidation projects carefully, testing everything thoroughly, and bringing in some expert help, combining many small Windows servers into a few higher end servers is a smart way to minimize the management burden on IT. And, with far fewer disks to address, the administrator's job in disk management becomes a whole lot easier.

Chapter 13

Windows Past, Windows Present: Windows NT and Windows 2000

Over the past decade or so, Microsoft has introduced a great many operating systems as it has attempted to move from a strictly desktop company to one that could effectively service the needs of the enterprise. That road has certainly been a bumpy one, but the releases over the past couple of years, particularly Windows 2000 Server, indicate that the company is serious about establishing its enterprise credentials. In this chapter, we take a look at the various Windows operating systems of the past and present, focusing on those of most relevance to disk management and servers. The discussion covers Windows NT, Windows 2000, Windows 2000 Advanced Server, and Windows 2000 Datacenter Server. Windows 2000 Server is given the lion's share of coverage, as it is likely to be around for a long time to come. It represents a major shift up the server hierarchy for Microsoft due to its scalability, reliability, and manageability, as well as the incorporation of Active Directory (AD), which makes Windows directory management far easier than previously.

Windows NT

Windows NT marked the entry of Microsoft into the enterprise arena. It is a 32-bit operating system available in client and server versions and includes built-in networking and some multitasking capabilities. NT supports simultaneous multiprocessing (SMP), an architecture in which multiple CPUs in one machine are sharing the same memory resources. SMP systems provide scalability, as CPUs can be added when transaction volume rises. NT also has some enterprise security features and has added significant administrative capabilities to the Windows arsenal. The enterprise edition supports clustering and failover.

Although NT lacks sufficient reliability and has failed to scale high enough to be a serious threat to the mid-range and high-end of the server market, it has established a beachhead at the low end of the server hierarchy, principally as a file and print server and a Web server. Since introducing NT, Microsoft has steadily gained ground, and, before it was replaced by Windows 2000 Server a couple of years back, NT had captured a sizable portion of the low-end of the server market.

Windows NT in Action

NASA's Jet Propulsion Laboratory (JPL) in Pasadena utilized 150 Novell Net-Ware file servers in 1997. By 1999, that number had been cut in half, with the NetWare servers being replaced by 75 NT servers. This shift to Windows NT did not come about as a result of a senior-level policy decision; rather, it occurred as a gradual shift, primarily on a user-by-user basis. JPL's NetWare file servers were primarily used for file storage, print services, workstation backup, and hosting databases for such applications as cc:Mail. As the lab moved to a more standards-based, Standard Mail Transfer Protocol (SMTP) e-mail system, however, the need for NetWare servers diminished and they began to be phased out. Many have now been converted to NT servers, which run the same software and can double as application servers for the lab's Internet Information Server (IIS) (WWW and FTP services), SQL, and various custom-built applications.

During the period that NT was gaining ground at JPL, the application set it supported mushroomed. By the late 1990s, in fact, Windows NT came to support more applications than any other operating system. At JPL, even some of the UNIX-based tools used in engineering became available in Windows NT versions. And, as the Intel/NT combo gained in computing power, it became possible to duplicate traditional UNIX functions at a considerably reduced cost.

Why did JPL choose Windows NT? According to IT executives, Windows NT was perceived to be more stable, more secure, and less likely to freeze due to application failure. As a result, the NASA unit standardized its office, administrative, and financial systems, as well as e-mail systems, on NT. The e-mail consolidation was necessary due to the profusion of systems previously available at JPL — a jumble of proprietary e-mail packages, such as cc:Mail, Quickmail, WordPerfect Mail, MS Mail, and POP, each one storing, transmitting, coding, and decoding messages, attachments, and rich-text messages differ-ently. Although JPL used SMTP to handle correspondence between these mail systems, translation created a considerable loss of continuity. To resolve its e-mail woes, the lab adopted the MIME standard, as well as a NASA-defined set of data interchange formats for e-mail attachments and messages, word processing, spreadsheets, presentation graphics, and HTML extensions. As a result of this consolidation, only POP and IMAP are used for e-mail.

NT's Days Are Numbered

These days, JPL has largely phased over to Windows 2000. The majority of companies that adopted NT during the 1990s, it turns out, have already made the switch to Windows 2000. Those remaining on NT are advised to migrate as soon as possible because its days are numbered. The Windows 2000 Server has been out for three years now, and Microsoft has released the Windows Server 2003 line and has further server releases on the horizon. Microsoft will drop support for NT, and that day is coming very soon. Microsoft is phasing out support for Windows NT (and 9*x*). Critical users and applications should be migrated off these platforms before that date, and all users should probably be taken off these platforms by the end of 2004 at the very latest.

The Windows 2000 Server Family

While Windows NT was a good start, it failed to scale high enough to tempt most large enterprises to migrate mission-critical systems. As a result, Microsoft invested many years of research into its next major server operating system release — Windows 2000 Server. The Windows 2000 Server operating systems mark a significant upgrade over previous Microsoft products in terms of both reliability and feature set. Though based on the NT kernel, Windows 2000 is still a major upgrade, is far more stable than NT, and is designed to eliminate DLL errors when applications are installed (a problem in NT that earned it the nickname "DLL hell").

Windows 2000 Server has added Plug-and-Play support for the first time, making it much easier to add peripherals compared with its predecessor. More importantly, it has brought with it the release of Active Directory, which replaced NT's domain system and makes network administration much easier.

In sharp contrast to the relatively small download of NT (although three CDs were required), Windows 2000 Server represents around 30 million lines of code; consequently, it requires more than 1 GB of disk space and a whole lot of RAM compared with NT. It comes in a client version as well as three server versions: Windows 2000 Server, Windows 2000 Advanced Server, and Windows 2000 Datacenter Server.

Windows 2000 Server

Microsoft Windows 2000 Server is a multipurpose network operating system that can be used by businesses of all sizes. It is probably best suited for workgroup file, print, Web, and communication servers. It has improved management, reliability, and scalability features and can function as a multi-purpose network operating system for businesses of all sizes. The Windows 2000 Server operating system was designed with the intention of increasing the value of existing IT investments while lowering overall computing costs. It is easier to deploy, configure, and use because it provides centralized, customizable management services. The new management services also work well with most existing management solutions.

A Configure Your Server Wizard cuts the time it takes to build a server and minimizes errors. Other wizards make it easier to create Web sites and virtual directories and to manage security settings and security certificates. The Windows 2000 Server Resource Kit is also helpful in setting up Windows 2000 Server, reducing server configuration times and including plenty of ready-made scripts for a number of commonly used administrative functions, such as log-on scripting. Additionally, Windows 2000 Server has made it far easier to configure a network. In addition to providing support for Plug-and-Play network adapters, services that manage the trust relationships between organizational domains, it also provides automated replication and local caching of domain name system (DNS) and dynamic host configuration protocol (DHCP) information. Windows 2000 Server is also equipped with more powerful management services through AD (more on AD later) as well as such infrastructure tools as:

- *IntelliMirror*, which is a set of Windows 2000 features used for desktop change and configuration management. IntelliMirror allows data, applications, and settings to follow roaming users. Administrators can use it for total control over client data, applications, and system settings.
- *Group Policy*, which is based on AD and is a component of IntelliMirror. It allows control of user access to desktop settings and applications by groups rather than by individual users or computers. Group Policy lets an administrator define and control the amount of access users have to data, applications, and other resources.
- *Windows Management Instrumentation (WMI)*, which provides unified access and event services, providing the ability to control and monitor Windows-based environments, Simple Network Management Protocol (SNMP) devices, and all host environments that support the Web-Based Enterprise Management (WBEM) standards initiative of the Distributed Management Task Force (DMTF).
- *Windows Script Host (WSH)*, which allows users to automate and integrate common tasks using a variety of scripting platforms such as Microsoft Visual Basic, Scripting Edition (VBScript), Microsoft Jscript, and Perl. This includes direct scripting to AD and WMI.
- *Microsoft Management Console (MMC)*, which is also available on NT and is a user interface presentation tool to integrate all the necessary Windows-based and Web-based administration components necessary to fulfill a specific task.
- *Active Server Pages (ASP)*, which was first introduced on NT and allows organizations to create dynamic personalized Web sites. The implementation of Active Server Pages in Windows 2000 Server has been upgraded; it is faster, more reliable, scalable, and runs better on multiprocessor hardware.

Windows 2000 also includes integrated support for such developments as Extensible Markup Language (XML) and streaming media.

Certified for Windows 2000 Logo

Microsoft was smart enough to make its Certified for Windows 2000 program quite difficult for third-party vendors. Even though it took many months to qualify and was a far stricter certification program than Windows NT, thousands of business applications are now compatible to run on Windows 2000 Server. During the heyday of Windows 95 and NT, the Certified for Windows logo was little more than a marketing gimmick to broadcast the wide range of Windows-compatible applications available. As product qualifications were fairly lax, the program provided no worthwhile comparison of one third-party application with another. That all changed with Windows 2000. Microsoft has wisely revamped the Certified for Windows 2000 program as if to emphasize that Windows 2000 is *not* the same as Windows 9*x* and NT. Certification had vendors jumping through hoops trying to meet the stringent requirements. Seven months into the certification evolution, with the operating system already released, only nine workstation and nine server products had managed to meet the Windows 2000 application specification.

This application specification for Windows 2000 ensures that compliant products provide users with a more manageable, reliable, and secure experience. Only software that bears the logo is fully equipped to take advantage of features such as Microsoft Software Installer (MSI), component sharing, data and settings management, support for OnNow power management, user interface/accessibility support, and AD. MSI, for instance, permits installation without reboot, as well as comprehensive monitoring of all system installations, minimizing the types of DLL conflicts that occasionally crop up on Windows installs/uninstalls.

The tests for the Certified for Windows 2000 program were conducted for Microsoft by Lionbridge's VeriTest Labs. Initially, third-party software had to comply with each point of a 500-page checklist (for server applications, the checklist is around 200 pages longer). Those applications that met this new specification have been licensed by Microsoft to bear the Certified for Windows 2000 logo.

Although Microsoft issued three levels of certification for Windows 2000, two are mainly cosmetic, with only one having real value. At the bottom of the pile comes *Planned*, signifying nothing more than the vendor's intention to one day make a product compliant. Next comes the misleadingly titled *Ready*, which can mean anything from "we believe we are compatible with Windows 2000" to "submitted for approval" to "failed the VeriTest inspection." Officially, however, this designation indicates that the independent software vendor (ISV) has tested the application for Windows 2000 compatibility and will offer Windows 2000-related product support. Unfortunately, some vendors are capitalizing on consumer ignorance by advertising their wares as "Windows 2000 Ready" as though it carries some additional weight. The only classification that can be depended upon, therefore, is *Certified*, which confirms that the application has met all standards in the Windows 2000 Application Specification, has passed all Windows 2000 compliance testing by both the ISV and

VeriTest, and has been approved by Microsoft. Certified is the highest ranking and the only one that matters in product comparison or purchasing.

The value of Certified applications was highlighted in a recent Gartner Group study. Total cost of ownership (TCO) reductions of as much as $1675 per desktop were attributed to exclusive deployment of Certified applications on Windows 2000. Essentially, in creating a strong logo requirement, Microsoft has made the logo valuable to enterprises, which will be able to use certification as a condition for use of that application in the enterprise. Gartner Group states that enterprises that use only applications that conform to the specification have the potential to increase the stability of their systems and lower their TCO.

Microsoft eventually relaxed its hard-line stance with regard to Windows 2000 certification. Prior to the release, it emphasized the value of becoming certified, but after a few months the company toned down its message and appeared happy to have vendors assume the Ready label. This is a shame, as insistence on maintaining a Certified designation, with no Ready category option, would have gone a long way toward completely eliminating the DLL conflicts and inexplicable crashes that once were the bugbears of Windows.

Windows 2000 Advanced Server

Windows 2000 Advanced Server is somewhat similar to Windows NT Enterprise Edition in that it supports clustering and failover. This server operating system is basically designed for business applications and E-commerce. It includes all the features and application availability of Windows 2000 Server, with additional features that make it rugged enough to keep business-critical applications up and running under demanding conditions. It also supports larger numbers of users and data. Advanced Server lets users increase server performance and capacity by adding processors and memory (i.e., scaling up; see Chapter 12). Advanced Server also includes enhanced SMP support and better memory capabilities, with memory scalable up to 8 GB.

Two clustering technologies are available in Advanced Server: cluster service and Network Load Balancing (NLB). Cluster service is used to link individual servers in the performance of common tasks. If one server fails, the workload is shifted to another server. NLB, on the other hand, ensures a server is always available to handle requests. NLB spreads incoming requests among multiple servers linked together to support a specific application. As traffic increases, these servers can scale out to meet capacity needs.

Windows 2000 Datacenter Server

Windows 2000 Datacenter Server is the King Kong of the Windows 2000 family. It offers support for up to 32 processors and up to 64 GB of memory, enhanced native clustering (up to a 4-node server cluster), dramatic reliability improvements, performance that some analysts consider to be on a par with Solaris and other high-end UNIX systems, as well as greater support from the vendor community. It is specifically intended for high-end and data-center applications that demand high levels of availability and scalability. It is ideal for running mission-critical databases, enterprise resource planning (ERP) software, and high-volume, real-time transaction processing.

Before the release of Windows Server 2003, Windows 2000 Datacenter Server was the most powerful and functional server operating system ever offered by Microsoft. It supports up to 32-way SMP and up to 32 GB of physical memory. It provides both 4-node clustering and load-balancing services. Datacenter Server is a good candidate for large-scale server consolidation projects.

According to analysts at D.H. Brown Associates, Inc. (Port Chester, New York), the scalability and reliability improvements introduced in Windows 2000 Datacenter Server helped greatly in narrowing Microsoft's enterprise credibility gap and underscored the Windows platform's price/performance advantages over UNIX. The analyst group believes that Windows 2000 Datacenter Server is especially good for large data warehouses, econometric analysis, large-scale scientific and engineering simulations, and online transaction processing for customers with large-scale server needs.

While many users are attracted to Datacenter Server's server consolidation potential, Microsoft has developed several other ways to soup up its data center operating system. Winsock Direct allows standard Winsock applications to operate in a clustered environment using TCP/IP (Transmission Control Protocol/Internet Protocol) without having to be modified. This boost to system I/O and interprocess communication (IPC) increases response times while allowing more users on the system.

The value of these Windows 2000 Datacenter enhancements has been substantiated in various enterprise tests. For instance, testing of a Datacenter Server cluster on the Transaction Processing Performance Council's TPC-C database benchmark reached a stable peak throughput of 505,303 transactions per minute. During peak throughput, the cluster handled queries and updates from 432,000 simultaneously connected users while maintaining response times of under 2.3 seconds for 90 percent of requests. Dozens of other benchmarks have been done showing similar or even better scores.

Datacenter Server User Study

One company that found success implementing Datacenter Server (with two-node clusters) is FreeMarkets of Pittsburgh, Pennsylvania. FreeMarkets conducts business-to-business online auctions for industrial parts, raw materials, commodities, and services. Over 7000 suppliers in the Americas, Europe, and Asia compete in real time for orders from the likes of BP Amoco, the U.S. Defense Logistics Agency, John Deere, and Alcoa. FreeMarkets' business-to-business (B2B) E-marketplace conducted 1690 auctions of industrial parts during a single quarter, representing $3 billion in goods and services. This was an increase in market volume of 34 percent over the previous quarter and 302 percent over the same period the previous year. The number of hits has soared to over 400,000 on a busy day.

According to the IT director of FreeMarkets, the need for a stable, reliable system with the scalability to keep pace with expansion determined the choice of Windows 2000 Datacenter Server. The company began by replacing NT servers with Datacenter Server. Two-node clusters utilized Compaq ProLiant 8500 machines with 550-MHz processors and 16-GB RAM. Each cluster was attached to a Compaq StorageWorks EMA 12000. One two-node cluster replaced on average about six noncluster NT servers. The company consolidated almost two dozen NT servers onto three Windows 2000 Datacenter Servers.

As FreeMarkets already experienced a 99.999 percent uptime rate, it is difficult to envision a Datacenter implementation improving upon that figure, but, according to the IT director, it is not that simple. In the real world, maintaining that rate required a high degree of system maintenance. On NT, each server received one to two hours of scheduled downtime each month. With more than almost a dozen machines, that amounts to almost a day of work each month dedicated to keeping the system performance at its peak. Due to Windows 2000 Datacenter Server's clustering and load balancing, however, FreeMarkets finds that scheduling downtime for routine maintenance is no longer necessary. Despite a substantial increase in traffic load, the company is using no more than 20 to 25 percent of the CPU power of the Datacenter Server during peak times. The system has also contributed to an increase in IT efficiency of around 20 percent, according to FreeMarkets, with an overall payback for the system of about six months.

In addition to the operating system's stability and reliability enhancements, Datacenter Server's new Process Control tool allows system administrators to tweak system performance by allowing them to assign a process or groups of processes to be handled as a single unit. This feature makes it possible to assign or specify limits of system resources for specific applications and processes. The Process Control tool enhances management and allocation of critical server resources. Scheduling priority can be assigned to processes, CPUs can be used for dedicated functions, and administrators can define how individual processes are handled within clusters. Application of this feature also allows administrators to place a limit on CPU or memory usage for a process or group of processes which prevents resource-intensive applications from depriving other programs of needed system resources. The Process Control tool was not available on any earlier Microsoft operating systems.

Additionally, Datacenter Server has built-in features that enable the system to utilize much larger quantities of RAM than previous Windows versions could support. The Enterprise Memory Architecture (EMA) of Windows 2000 Datacenter Server, for example, increases the Physical Address Extension (PAE) capabilities. Whereas Windows 2000 Advanced Server supports 8 GB of physical memory, Datacenter Server will support up to 64 GB. To help developers fully utilize PAE, Microsoft has developed a new application programming interface called Address Windowing Extensions (AWE). With these APIs, the applications can access 64 GB of memory. The additional physical memory is mapped within an AWE window automatically after four system calls. Loading data into RAM reduces response time that would be slowed by writing and reading the data to and from a page file on the disk.

Unlike earlier efforts by Microsoft to enter the enterprise arena, the Datacenter Server Program is designed as a complete hardware, software, and support service package, as discussed in the previous chapter. It is only available through a partnered dealer and is preloaded on third-party hardware. A rigorous training and certification process is undertaken prior to an OEM becoming licensed to sell and support Datacenter 2000. As a result, the newest Windows 2000 operating system is never going to be on sale in every mom-and-pop computer store in the neighborhood. For certification, an OEM must minimally ensure 99.9 percent uptime for customers and a four-hour response time window, 24/7. OEMs are also responsible for handling updates and change control. Another requirement for the OEM is that it must set up a joint support center that will be staffed by both Microsoft and OEM personnel. In this way, a single point of contact is used for support issues. The call is then routed accordingly for resolution.

Several renewable support/service level agreements are available for the Datacenter program. The idea is for customers to be able to make just one phone call for any problem, whether it is hardware or software related, something that signifies a big change from the old finger-pointing days. But, to enter the higher end, Microsoft had to provide the same level of consolidated service to which UNIX, and especially mainframe customers, have grown accustomed.

Datacenter Server, though, does have some drawbacks. Initial costs are very steep, and it is still a relatively very young OS. Below are some important points for those considering Datacenter Server:

- To achieve higher levels of scalability and reliability, Microsoft has narrowed its areas of compatibility. Rather than providing an operating system that works with a large variety of hardware configurations, its focus is on performance. Thus, it is proving more difficult for hardware/software designers to utilize the breadth of functionality on this OS compared with previous Windows versions.
- The shortage of available device drivers certified for Windows 2000 Datacenter Server must be taken into account, although this issue is not as critical as it was a couple of years ago. As the product has matured, driver availability has become a relatively minor issue.
- Many applications may have to be tailored to fully utilize Datacenter Server; however, certified or not, even untailored applications will likely show better performance or stability.
- It will be difficult to find support resources outside such certified OEMs as Hewlett-Packard and Unisys; however, this is not a problem as long as the service agreement is in force.

In a recent profile, technical research and consulting firm Aberdeen Group, Inc. (Boston, Massachusetts) warned that Datacenter Server will require a large investment in new hardware, software, and services. If IS managers are unprepared to make this financial commitment, then they should not attempt to deploy Datacenter Server. According to Aberdeen, although Datacenter Server solutions beyond eight-way clusters are likely to cost twice that of a cluster with equal processing power, many IS managers are expected to be willing to pay the price. The payback for the high ticket is more processing power for large-scale applications and simpler manageability of multiple distributed systems.

No doubt Datacenter Server is a much-improved product over NT and other versions of Windows 2000; however, prudence would dictate a thorough evaluation of the compatibility of any needed applications before making the jump. When hardware and software manufacturers start designing products that adhere to the strict requirements and better harness the capabilities of Datacenter 2000, the decision to migrate will become much easier to make. Meanwhile, Datacenter Server should be stringently evaluated before jumping into an ill-considered upgrade. Poor planning could turn an envisioned fairy tale into a data center nightmare. But, for those who can comfortably afford the price of admission, Datacenter Server goes a long way toward providing a Windows-based platform that functions well in mid-range and some high-end environments.

The Rigors of Windows 2000 Migration

It is never easy to switch an enterprise over to a new operating system, and Windows 2000 is no different. Such deployments typically take six months to two years to execute, especially where one is implementing Active Directory, the crown jewel of the new operating system, according to Gartner Group. At the same time, Windows 2000 has become the most widely deployed server operating system in the Microsoft arsenal, while still grabbing a big share of the enterprise desktop space. So, while the migration path is not an easy one, many have followed it. What does it take to realize the full benefits of Windows 2000? Essentially, success depends on proper deployment.

One must realize from the outset that the Windows 2000 operating system is a mix of Microsoft technology and many bits and pieces licensed from other vendors. For example, Windows Terminal Services (WTS) is based on technology licensed from Citrix Systems, Inc. (Ft. Lauderdale, Florida), and the Active Directory Migration Tool (ADMT) is licensed from Net IQ Corporation (San Jose, California). Some of these tools are good enough for enterprise use but others are inadequate. In many cases, third-party migration products are a necessity for successful Windows 2000 migrations.

Anyone moving to Microsoft Exchange 2000, for example, is forced to deploy AD, as that system is designed to operate strictly with Active Directory and lacks its own directory. AD compatibility is also a requirement for third-party products applying for Windows 2000 certification. Similarly, Microsoft made AD an integral part of the Windows 2000 network architecture to serve as a single location to store, access, and manage information. This eliminates the multiple user accounts and passwords associated with multiple directories, as well as the duplicative steps and middleware needed to manage them.

Active Directory incorporates a hierarchical, object-oriented structure. Related network objects, such as users, machines, devices, and applications, are grouped in "containers" that are organized in a tree structure. Objects within a container can have attributes assigned to them as a group, rather than individually. For example, all personnel in the engineering department may be given access to a CAD application at the same time. They would share the privileges of any higher containers within which the engineering department is contained. Then, because the engineering department is part of the manufacturing division, if all people in manufacturing have access to the ERP system, anyone in engineering would have access to it. The engineering staff would also have privileges for companywide applications such as e-mail.

When a user is created within a container, that user automatically assumes all its attributes. When someone leaves the company, deleting that person from one location automatically removes each point of access, thus eliminating a common security hole: former employees still being listed within an overlooked directory. Transferring an employee means a drag and drop from one container to another.

Active Directory has several additional advantages over NT's directory. For one thing, it can accommodate many more objects. While an NT domain has a 40,000 object limit, 85 million users have been placed in one AD domain on one server. AD also uses a multimaster structure, as opposed to the Primary Domain Controller/Backup Domain Controller of NT.

Another valuable AD feature is assigning limited administrative privileges; that is, a manager can reset employee passwords within one office without having the authority to reconfigure servers. Other features include single log on, remote software installation, remote desktop access, and the ability to access applications from anywhere in the network rather than being tied to a certain machine.

The Three Active Directory States: Native Mode, Mixed Mode, and Parallel Mode

Migration nirvana, when it comes to Windows 2000, is manifested in a state known as *native mode*. In Windows 2000, few users have attained this hallowed state, which involves complete utilization of AD; most have had to settle for lesser planes known as *mixed mode* or *parallel mode*. Following is an explanation of these various states and their default settings:

- *Native mode:* Allows all domain controllers to run Windows 2000.
  - *Pluses* — Native mode offers all the benefits of all AD features.
  - *Minuses* — Native mode requires upgrade of all domain controllers; once you flip the switch, falling back to mixed mode operation or support for NT domain controllers is not possible.

- *Mixed mode:* Supports both Windows 2000 and NT domain controllers under AD.
  - *Pluses* — Administrators can roll domain controllers back to Window NT, which is useful when some servers, such as application servers, cannot be upgraded immediately to Windows 2000.
  - *Minuses* — Advanced features such as universal groups, interdomain group membership, and group nesting are lacking.
- *Parallel mode:* Creates separate domains for different groups of servers.
  - *Pluses* — Parallel mode can operate the Windows 2000 domain in AD native mode without migrating all enterprise domain controllers to Windows 2000.
  - *Minuses* — Separate domains are difficult to administer and support.

Mixed mode is the default server setting. It is used when only some of the domain controllers have been fully upgraded to Windows 2000, while the rest are still using Windows NT. The switch to native mode is made when all the domain controllers have been upgraded to Windows 2000, at which point all the new Windows 2000 features are available. The third option, parallel mode, involves setting up separate domains running in either NT or Windows 2000 which allows the servers in the Windows 2000 domain to be in native mode, but it also requires the added work of running the separate domains.

Unless the enterprise simultaneously migrates all servers to Windows 2000, a risky choice at best, it will have to get used to the idea of spending quite some time in mixed mode. Mixed mode has the advantage of being able to roll the server back to NT when something goes wrong during the migration. But, an organization still will want to minimize mixed mode time as much as possible, because the full benefits of Windows 2000 are not experienced until the network is completely translated into native mode. For example, users cannot take advantage of AD's ability to create universal and nested groups. Similarly, verifying dial-in IDs and applying static routes will not work.

Additionally, mixed mode creates new security problems in terms of administrative privileges for NT domain controllers. One administrator, for example, gave help desk personnel access to the Windows 2000 Admin Tools pack so they could change passwords in AD. Unfortunately, he also inadvertently gave the help desk the ability to do DHCP scopes and WINS entries on the remaining NT 4.0 servers.

On top of these considerations is the major headache of simultaneously managing and supporting multiple operating systems, separate directories, and different versions of certain applications. For some, mixed mode is a tough place to be, and one they are glad to have behind them.

Beyond native mode and mixed mode is the third AD state, parallel mode, which consists of running separate mixed mode and native mode Windows 2000 domains. Part of the organization can then run in native mode if everything cannot be switched over right away. The drawback is having to maintain separate domains and operating systems. If the goal is to arrive in native mode, get there as quickly as possible.

For these and other reasons, a fast and complete migration, including setting up AD, is generally the best option. Now, let us take a look at the tools used to achieve native mode.

Windows 2000 Migrations Tools

To help organizations make the switch, Microsoft has included the ADMT utility with Windows 2000. The lack of enterprise functionality of this tool, however, is demonstrated by the fact that a Giga Information Group survey determined that 70 percent of enterprises using Windows 2000 were having trouble implementing AD. Giga strongly recommended the use of a third-party migration tool to ensure success with the AD migration. After all, ADMT is really just a stripped-down version of Net IQ's Domain Migration Administrator. It can be used for simple migrations, but it lacks features that are part of the full-featured, third-party migration suite. Among these are the ability to model the migration beforehand and ways to efficiently migrate user passwords, exclude disabled/expired accounts, and clean up the security ID (SID) history. If one is migrating anything other than the simplest small network, therefore, it is simpler and less expensive in the long run to purchase a third-party migration tool. The administrative burden incurred by attempting to use the free ADMT tool makes it unwieldy in an enterprise of any size.

What are the choices? In addition to Net IQ, several other vendors offer excellent migration tools. These include Aelita Software Corporation's (Powell, Ohio) Controlled Migration Suite and Quest Software, Inc.'s (Irvine, California) FastLane Suite. Using these tools, of course, means higher migration costs overall. Factor in about $10 extra per user migrated, sometimes a little more.

Making the Transition to Native Mode

Before you purchase migration tools, several steps should be taken to ensure a smooth transition to AD. The first step to native mode is not technical, but organizational. Active Directory will not straighten out fundamentally flawed organizational structures or policies. These must be addressed before proposed changes can be modeled and tested. Next, directories must be prepared for the shift, including clearing out old identities, resolving conflicts, and updating SID histories. Finally, for anything but the simplest organizations, migration to native mode requires migration tools in addition to well-trained resources.

The recommended steps are:

1. *Thoroughly study AD.* Various courses and books are available that adequately cover this subject. Newsgroups, user groups, and conferences may also provide the necessary information.
2. *Acquire a consultant experienced in AD migration.* So many variables are involved and the repercussions of getting it wrong are so severe that it is best to bring in someone who has been through it all and can advise you on the best way to go about it. Select someone who can provide numerous references who can verify his qualifications and record of success.

3. *Select and install a migration tool that meets your needs.* Dozens of these are out there so it is easy to choose the wrong one. Speak to the consultant you bring in as well as current users of the migration tools on your short list, and ask enough questions to determine which tool would work best in your environment. Price is one factor to consider, certainly, but you also want a tool that is robust enough to handle thousands of users with ease during a migration.

4. *Plan the migration.* This may involve redesigning aspects of the network or setting new policies. Again, talk to your consultant, speak to those who have been through it, and make the changes that add the most value to both the migration and the organization.

5. *Model and test offline.* Roll back failed migration tests and work out what went wrong before proceeding. Many who have been through a native mode transition strongly recommend establishing a test area where everything is piloted prior to executing anything on the corporate systems.

6. *Clean up existing directories.* Get rid of old or expired passwords and accounts. This is an essential step — why move these old vulnerabilities to the new system?

7. *Create and populate the AD.*

8. *Install Windows 2000 on servers.*

9. *Promote domain controllers to native mode when everything is running well.*

The above sequence is only a general guide, so be sure to discuss your systems with peers and industry experts and make sure your homework is complete.

Consolidating Directories

Another factor must be taken into account in a native mode migration — the reality of multiple directories. AD will reduce the number of directories, but it will not consolidate everything into one directory; therefore, it is recommended to implement some kind of metadirectory or directory synchronization software to reduce the time and expense involved in manually populating and updating directories. Numerous options are available, such as Microsoft Metadirectory Services (MMS), Novell's DirSync, or Computer Associates' Unicenter TNG Directory Management Option. If Unicenter is already being used, its directory management module may be best, whereas a Microsoft shop might lean toward MMS, just as a Novell NDS business would opt for DirSync. To consolidate directories:

1. Consolidate or eliminate any excess directories.

2. Install a metadirectory or directory synchronization tool; this may require restructuring some directories into compatible data structures.

3. Eliminate "orphan" directories that must be manually updated or, if some are necessary, establish and enforce policies for updating them.

4. Review security procedures on a regular basis.

Windows 2000 Migration Case Studies

Cincinnati State Technical and Community College

Windows 2000 Active Directory deployments can take much longer than expected. Cincinnati State Technical and Community College, for example, started planning the switch to Windows 2000 and AD in November 2001, before moving 6000 student users over spring break 2002, but the migration for the administration departments was interrupted by a million-dollar storage equipment donation. Cincinnati State configured the new storage first, before consolidating the entire school, including upwards of 8000 students and staff accounts, into a single AD in the fall of 2002. In the interim, the school had a native mode Windows 2000 domain for the students, and the school administration has Windows 2000 application servers running under Windows NT 4.0 domain controllers.

Such time frames are not unusual, as AD migrations take a lot longer than most organizations anticipate, but until all domain controllers are upgraded to Windows 2000, enterprises are in the state of directory limbo known as mixed mode, in which directory features from Windows NT domain controllers remain enabled while new AD features, such as the ability to create universal and nested groups, are unavailable. New security problems arise when administrative privileges for NT domain controllers are operating in mixed mode. AD dial-in options — such as verifying caller ID and applying static routes — will not work. In addition, network administrators must support multiple operating systems, multiple directories, and, in some cases, multiple versions of applications. Due to the complexity of managing mixed mode domains, experienced IT managers say it is best to make the switch as quickly as possible. The proper tools and methodologies can make the transition to native mode faster and easier and help to manage a mixed mode domain.

Cincinnati State received consultant help from Quest Software, Inc. (Irvine, California) to model the college's migration. As a result, the organization set up backup domain controllers (BDCs), replicated the domain structure on these machines, upgraded them to primary domain controller status, and created a duplicate domain. The duplicate domain was used to model different scenarios. This allowed the college to write a comprehensive domain migration plan within a few days.

The college did not utilize Windows 2000's built-in Active Directory Migration Tool utility, as it is primarily designed for simple migrations. Theoretically, it can scale up to 10,000 users, but Cincinnati State did not find it feasible to utilize ADMT. The college initially modeled the change with ADMT then moved to Quest's FastLane tool as it was easier and faster and could scale better. FastLane also included roll back and recovery functionality that proved necessary during the migration. Whenever a mistake was made, it proved relatively simple to roll the system back to a previous state and eliminate the error. ADMT also lacks such features as user password migration, migration modeling, exclusion of disabled/expired accounts, and the ability to clean up the security ID history. Also, it supports only native mode AD servers. If an enterprise wants to consolidate its NT directories in preparation for an AD migration, for example, ADMT will not oblige; a third-party tool, in this case, is essential. AD domain migration and policy-based management tools are must-haves, not options, in many AD migrations. Unfortunately, they are not inexpensive. Some are reported to add about 25 to 30 percent to overall upgrade costs. Others say $10 per user should be added to costs to cover the purchase of migration tools.

CVS Corporation

Managers can reduce the time spent in mixed mode by thorough planning and testing and by using domain migration tools. At least that is the experience of pharmacy retailer CVS Corporation (Woonsocket, Rhode Island). Prior to migrating 5000 workstations and 120 servers at CVS headquarters in 2002, the IS manager set up a lab to test migration. He opted for Controlled Migration Suite by Aelita Software Corporation and used it to model the directory migration before it began. The result was a smooth domain controller transition to Windows 2000 and AD over two weekends followed by an in-place upgrade of other NT servers to Windows 2000 Server. During the process, however, the company discovered a security problem. The account operators group had access to the Windows 2000 administrative tools for password changes, and the IS manager realized that those users were able to create DHCP scopes and WINS entries on NT 4.0 servers. CVS immediately upgraded the servers to Windows 2000 to eliminate the problem.

Pioneer Hi-Bred, Inc.

Even the best-laid migration plans sometimes go astray. Despite extensive planning and design, nothing turned out exactly as envisioned by the senior network engineer at Pioneer Hi-Bred, Inc., a biotechnology firm in Des Moines, Iowa. He set up a test lab to review migration tools but was not able to fully model his network's 18 domains and 4000-plus groups and test all the procedures prior to beginning the implementation. He wished he could have done so, but he also realized that until the actual process has begun it is impossible to predict exactly how things will pan out. His company spent many months in the middle of an AD migration that encompassed 5000 users at hundreds of locations. For a long time, Pioneer ran in parallel mode: one NT domain that covered one group of sites and another Windows 2000 domain running AD in native mode for another group. However, this setup led to confusion by creating two structures for controlling shared resources. Security administrators had trouble determining which structure a given user fell under and what groups/object access rights they should have. These issues were eventually resolved using Domain Migration Administrator (DMA) by Net IQ Corporation to manage the changeover.

Mt. Sinai NYU Health: Managing AD in a Hybrid Network

While administering a network in mixed mode can be tough, it gets even more complicated with hybrid networks. Take the case of Mt. Sinai New York University Health (MSNYU), a healthcare organization composed of six hospitals in New York City. It manages a network that includes AD for Exchange 2000, Windows 2000 workstations accessing mainframe applications through IBM's Systems Network Architecture (SNA), and servers running NetWare, as well as a few storage area networks (SANs) and some virtual private networks (VPNs). The MSNYU network contains 6000 workstations, 300 to 400 servers, and 12,000 users spread out among the hospitals. The entire system is tied together with Novell Directory Services (NDS) eDirectory. Because the main applications are mainframe, rather than client/server, and most of the servers are running NetWare, MSNYU does not intend to make the switch to native mode. It uses Novell's DirXML synchronization tool to coordinate the user IDs in AD and NDS so users can enjoy single sign on. As the organization adds additional products that use AD it will use DirXML to keep everything in sync. MSNYU also uses bvAdmin by BindView Corporation (Houston, Texas), which provides a single view of an entire network operating on different directories. With this tool, it is possible to manage both NDS and AD trees from a single GUI. BindView can also provide a single management interface for both the Windows NT and 2000 portions of networks undergoing Windows 2000 migrations.

No Universal AD Panacea

At this point, no directory panacea exists, but things are moving in the right direction. Considering the explosion in the number of applications the typical enterprise now supports, it would be disastrous if each application required its own unique directory. However, we may never reach the point where a company uses a single directory. Given the nature of the computer industry, as soon as a directory standard becomes widely accepted, some vendor comes up with its own proprietary enhancements or competing system. But, by using Active Directory, metadirectories, and middleware, the directory management task on Windows 2000 Server is at least rendered more manageable.

Chapter 14

Windows Present: Windows XP

Although Windows XP is not a server system, it is included here due to its prevalent desktop in many corporations. System administrators are likely to find themselves managing XP machines and XP disks for many years to come. This chapter includes a discussion of the differences between XP Professional and XP Home editions, the many tools built into the operating system, new features such as Fastboot and Fast Resume, and security enhancements. A brief look at the underlying architecture of XP is also presented.

No More DOS

The release of Windows XP actually marked a significant event at Microsoft — it was the first time that the entire Windows product line moved completely from DOS and onto the Windows 2000 kernel. This represents a major improvement in system stability compared with Windows 9x and Me, and less work for IT support staff. When Microsoft Chairman Bill Gates formally released XP in 2001, he symbolized the end of the era by typing "exit" and logging out of DOS for the last time. Microsoft's DOS-based operating systems date back to 1981, with version 1.0 through to Windows 95, 98, and Me. That said, 400 million people still use products built on the DOS code base, compared with fewer than 100 million people using Windows NT/2000. These demographics are rapidly changing, however. Seven million copies of Windows XP were snatched up in the first two weeks of its release, and OEMs have made it the default installation on their new desktops and laptops. For those users running Windows 2000 Professional as a desktop system, there is probably little incentive to switch to XP. As the kernel is essentially the same, the decision revolves around whether the added features are enough to justify an upgrade. For most business users, the answer is often no.

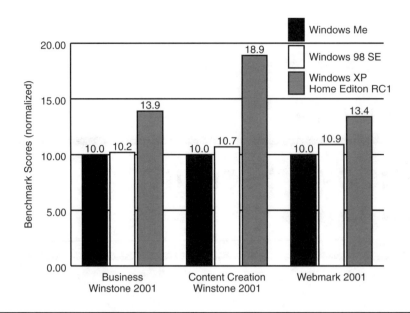

Exhibit 1   Overall System Performance (Normalized) for Windows Me, Windows 98 SE, and Windows XP

Note that, for organizational usage, it is vital to deploy only XP Professional, *not* the home XP version. XP Pro contains every feature of the home version, plus a number of added features that are crucial to operating in a business environment. Among the key differences are support of dual processors, roaming profiles, client-side caching, dynamic disks, Simple Network Management Protocol (SNMP), Intellimirror, and Internet Information Services (IIS). It has a built-in fax utility and allows for Active Directory log-ons. It has both a backup utility and Automated System Recovery (ASR), while the home version has only ASR and no backup. The Professional version also allows for remote access and provides additional security. Although both versions contain a firewall, the Encrypting File System is only available with the Professional version. So, while the home version of XP is much more stable than anything built on the Windows 9*x* core, it is of no real value in a networked environment. It should only be used, as the name states, at home. The Professional version, however, is suitable for both power users and network installations.

How does XP Pro compare with Windows Me, 98, and 2000? For one thing, it is faster. Testing by Ziff Davis Media's eTesting Labs showed that XP Pro outperformed Windows Me and Windows 2000 Pro in overall system performance, startup time, application launch time, and time to resume to an active state from hibernation or standby modes. In terms of run-time performance, for example, the average application startup on XP is 25 percent faster than Windows 98 SE and equivalent to Windows 2000 Pro (see Exhibit 1). System startup performance is also noticeably better on XP due to a feature known as Fastboot. Anyone currently using NT or Windows 2000 knows just how long these systems can take to boot up, especially compared with a Windows

Exhibit 2   XP Benchmark by eTesting Labs

Performance Measurement	Windows XP Features	Performance Improvement
Commercial benchmarks (averaged)	Overall system improvements	36% faster than Windows 98 SE; equivalent to Windows 2000
System startup time	Prefetching and elimination of unnecessary network delays	27% faster than Windows 98 SE; 34% faster than Windows 2000
Resume from standby	Overlapping device initialization; maximizing parallelism	19% faster than Windows Me; 21% faster than Windows 2000
Resume from hibernate	Optimizations in the compression algorithms and overlapping compression with Direct Memory Access (DMA) transfers to disk	13% faster than Windows Me; 9% faster than Windows 2000
Application startup (average)	Prefetching	25% faster than Windows 98 SE; equivalent to Windows 2000

Note: eTesting Labs of New York City compared Windows XP with earlier versions of Windows. The lab compared performance on nine desktop systems including high-end desktops and notebooks, mid-range desktops, and an older desktop. Several memory configurations were also used. It used three well-known benchmarks (Business Winstone, Content Creation Winstone, and BAPCo WebMark 2001). In terms of startup, for example, eTesting found Windows XP to be 27% faster than Windows 98 and 34% faster than Windows 2000.

98/Me machine that might be used at home. The eTesting study showed that XP starts up on average 34 percent faster than Windows 2000 and 27 percent faster than Windows 98 SE. Furthermore, it is much quicker at coming back to life from standby or hibernation mode (see Exhibit 2).

XP Fastboot

Booting up is a complex process that begins from the moment a machine is turned on and continues through BIOS initialization, loading the operating system, and initializing various devices, system functions and services until the user is ready to enter a log-on. Once entered, the user desktop appears. The term *boot* comes from the phrase "pulling yourself up by your bootstraps." In essence, the PC is bringing all its components alive long enough to launch the operating system. Once launched, the operating system takes over, as it is capable of far more complex tasks.

Windows XP has decreased the time required for the system to boot through a series of changes to the boot loader, several key drivers, and the registry initialization and network interaction processes. Further, the higher throughput capabilities of XP mean that the operating system can deal with larger I/O requests. During boot up, I/O can be overlapped with device detection and initialization. These features are collectively known as Fastboot.

The design goals behind Fastboot were:

- Operation resumed from standby in less than 5 seconds
- Operation resumed from hibernation in less than 20 seconds
- Boot time not extending beyond 30 seconds

In total, Fastboot addresses nine stages of the bootup process, all the way from BIOS initialization through loading the operating system to loading the shell. It includes improvements such as initializing multiple device drivers simultaneously and starting the Winlogon process before completing network initialization (Winlogon, therefore, no longer has to wait for network initialization to complete). The overall concept is straightforward: Use available memory and CPU resources to accomplish as much as possible in a minimum of time.

With Fastboot, two key features work together — prefetching and layout optimization. Both are unique to XP and were not available in older operating systems.

Prefetching

Under Windows 2000, every I/O requires the head to move and the disk to rotate. Typically, fewer than 100 I/Os per second can be completed (on desktops, this number is even smaller). Windows XP reorganizes and speeds up I/O by the process known as *prefetching*, which is basically a read-ahead cache. It reads ahead into memory information or files before they are requested. Thus, it reduces page faults and eliminates delays in I/O processing. This is accomplished by analyzing the underlying architecture in order to determine which files to fetch. A device driver built into XP monitors file access activity and builds a list of files required to boot the machine or launch an executable.

Consider the example of launching an application. Microsoft Word, for example, is launched by winword.exe. Before the application appears on the screen, associated DLLs, font files, and more must be loaded. These files and their precise request order are captured and passed on to a prefetch file. Every time winword.exe is launched, this file is triggered and speeds up the launch process by placing associated information into memory. Prefetch files (.pf extension) are referred to as *scenario files*. They are filed in the % windir%\ prefetch folder (notosboot-B00DFAAD.pf is the boot prefetch scenario file). Monitoring file access (as in prefetching) is expensive in terms of system resources. Fortunately, XP's built-in file filter and added hardware requirements reduce the toll on resource consumption.

During the boot process, prefetching also comes into play. Pages accessed during boot are logged in the %windir%\prefetch\notosboot-B00DFAAD.pf file. This file logs eight prior boots and is updated one minute after every boot. XP uses this file to determine which pages to prefetch. These files are then loaded before they are called so the boot process takes less time. Do not expect, though, to turn on a machine and 20 seconds later it is ready to go. XP is also a lot larger than Windows 9*x* or NT workstations, so the speed gains from Fastboot are relative. The end result on many machines is that the bootup process takes slightly less time than these other systems.

Layout Optimization

Layout optimization works hand in hand with prefetching to enhance boot time performance. Those files required to boot a machine are listed in the layout.ini file in the order in which they are needed. After observing several system boots, Windows XP determines the code/data needed for the boot and the optimum placement of those files on disk. To speed up the process, these files are strategically placed contiguously (in one piece) on the disk in the sequence in which they will be called. If the small number of files needed to boot the machine are fragmented, a rapid defragmentation is done to make them contiguous (note that this defrag is done only once every three days). The files involved are mostly system files that rarely change, so the same files are loaded every time and in the same order. Each file involved in booting can now be read with a single I/O operation.

Layout optimization provides a relatively small improvement — it adds another 10 percent to the gains achieved through prefetching. As it affects only the boot function, it does not replace the need for regular file defragmentation. After all, Fastboot technology impacts only a tiny fraction of files on a hard drive. The operating system, all applications, most system files, and all user files are unaffected by Fastboot and remain subject to a significant performance decline due to fragmentation; therefore, regular defragmentation should be conducted on all Windows XP systems.

Boot Optimization versus File Optimization

Optimization itself is an old concept that dates back to the OpenVMS system. During the 1980s, several software developers investigated the theory that placing files in an optimum location could reduce the amount of fragmentation. Although the idea has marketing appeal and provides a pretty pattern of file colors on visual disk representations, file optimization tends to utilize too many system resources for the minor performance benefits it can sometimes return. Why? The algorithms used in the operating system and file system act to scatter newly written or revised files throughout the disk in available pieces of free space. Thus, file optimization is sometimes working 180 degrees opposite the file system and operating system. The optimization algorithms dictate a set pattern on the disk for files that the operating system and file system algorithms ignore when data is written to or deleted from disk (see Chapter 8).

One or two vendors still advocate file optimization on Windows systems. They will dispute the statements made here regarding the value of optimization and come up with convincing arguments for the value of file placement; however, the acid test is real-world deployment, and file optimization just is not that popular in the enterprise marketplace. Those networkable defrag-menters that bundle defragmentation with file optimization do not seem to do as well as those that stick to standard defragmentation.

Boot optimization, however, is a different matter. The technology is aimed at producing faster system boots on XP and does not compete for system resources. It addresses only a few files (some system files, DLLs, etc.) which are rarely modified. Prefetching to speed up access, therefore, supplemented by layout optimization does produce some small benefit. The potential gains, though, will not be fully realized unless disks are regularly defragmented.

Here is an example to illustrate why regular defragmentation must be carried out regardless of Fastboot. Consider a Word file called bio.doc. The winword.exe and related files used during boot up may have been well organized in a precise location on disk and fetched in advance to make them more quickly available, but if bio.doc is fragmented into hundreds of pieces, all the gains achieved during application launch will be lost due to the excess I/Os required to open the document.

As mentioned previously, optimization procedures can lead to overcon-sumption of system resources. To guard against this, Windows XP makes sure a machine has been idle for at least 30 minutes before it attempts to optimize the boot files. Accidentally touching the mouse aborts the layout optimization.

XP Fast Resume

Windows XP has a feature similar to Fastboot that speeds the time it takes to resume normal activity in a computer that is in standby or hibernate mode. Standby and hibernation modes are most applicable to laptop users and are intended to conserve battery life. Instead of turning off a computer, the user has a choice of standby or hibernate. In the newest laptops running Windows XP, resuming from standby can take as little as two seconds or less. Standby is a low power condition from which the user can quickly resume work. When the system is in standby, the memory contents are stored in volatile RAM. When resuming, the operating system informs the computer devices of a change in state. Some devices must return to an active state ahead of others. Windows XP has sped the process by overlapping device initialization using a new algorithm that eliminates blocking interactions among key system drivers or with other system activities. This does not, however, eliminate all delays in resuming. Page faults, for instance, might occur that cannot be remedied until disks are completely initialized, or a delayed program might not be released until that program is allowed to continue. Further, device driver quality can sometimes slow the resume.

In hibernation mode, memory contents are compressed and saved to disk in the system hibernation file (\hiberfil.sys), and the computer is turned off completely. When the user resumes, these contents (desktop and applications) are restored intact. The contents of the hibernation file are read into memory and used to restart the system and associated devices. High-end laptops can return from hibernation in less than thirty seconds, although this is highly dependent on what was in memory at the time of hibernation.

Improving hibernation mode compression algorithms and overlapping compression with Direct Memory Access transfers to disk have heightened hibernation speed in Windows XP. Hibernation resumption also benefits from the Fastboot improvements, especially prefetching and changes to device initialization routines used in resuming. Note, however, that resumption times can vary considerably and consume as many system resources as booting the computer. If too little RAM is installed and/or large applications were running when the computer went into hibernation, it can take longer for the machine to resume.

Tips To Improve the Impact of Fastboot and Fast Resume

While Fastboot and Fast Resume are welcome features in any system, they suffer from the usual limitations. By far the biggest factor is having adequate RAM and a fast disk drive. In order to prefetch, for example, the system must have sufficient RAM to prefetch into. Unfortunately, 64-MB systems generally prove inadequate to take advantage of XP prefetching. At least 128 MB is recommended, although for some this is nowhere nearly enough. Additionally, the speed of the disk can make a big difference to prefetching gains. As the operating system image must move from the disk to memory, the faster the disk drive the better. A switch from a 5400- to a 7200-rpm disk will probably save several seconds during boot time. Larger disk drive buffers may also help. It is interesting to note that a 128-MB/5400-rpm configuration gives better performance than 64 MB/7200 rpm. Lack of memory leads to more paging and this slows the boot process. Enough memory, therefore, is essential with XP. It should also be noted that high-end PCs with high-capacity, multiplatter hard drives may take longer to boot up and resume. Further, due to their architecture, SCSI systems tend to boot slowly.

What about the processor? Regardless of the size of CPU, performance will barely be impacted during the first half of boot. A faster CPU, though, does help speed the Winlogon phase of the boot, as the processor is typically operating at 100 percent utilization at this time.

As noted, Windows XP has been enhanced to provide speedier boot ups, as well as faster resumes from standby and hibernate modes. Fastboot techniques, in particular, have been found to increase performance by as much as 40 percent. Over 90 percent of the gains, though, come from prefetching — fetching and loading files in advance in a manner similar to caching. Layout optimization, on the other hand, is a minor enhancement to prefetching. Because the layout optimization process is being conducted on a small number of files that are always run sequentially, these files can be placed in specific locations on the drive to good effect. File placement optimization technology, however, should only be used in such limited environments. When attempted more widely, it sometimes consumes more system resources than it saves in terms of reduced disk I/O.

Underlying XP Architecture

Windows XP represents the death of DOS, at least on any Windows platform. For the first time, all versions of Windows (including the server, workstation and home PC versions) are running on the same kernel. This simplifies administration, particularly because Microsoft built the new operating system on the Windows 2000 kernel, its most stable kernel yet, which means fewer blue screens and reboots and fewer calls to the help desk than from clients running NT 4.0 or, worse, Windows 95, 98, or Me.

Windows XP, therefore, has several key advantages: (1) fewer crashes, (2) one basic code for all PCs, (3) compatibility with over 90% of the 1500 most popular Windows applications, and (4) support for over 12,000 devices. Microsoft's newest operating system also offers such features as a built-in firewall, CD Writer software, Windows Media Player, Movie Maker, an extremely limited defragmenter that functions poorly in the enterprise, and System Restore.

System Restore addresses the subject of those multiple error messages that plague NT. I used to receive two per hour due to an incompatibility with Norton Antivirus, as well as several alerts after startup for various reasons. System Restore makes it possible to remove this hassle by reverting to a previous system state if a new application creates errors. Essentially, it is a combination of file system filter driver and user-mode services that provides a way to revert to an earlier configuration.

Another recovery function built into XP protects against the installation of driver updates that create problems. A hardware installation wizard backs up replaced drivers so that system restore is effectively made available if the driver update goes badly. A Last Known Good recovery option accessed through the boot menu allows users to revert to the previous drivers.

The defragmentation APIs within Windows XP have also been revised. For some years NT file systems have used exposed APIs that allow the querying of files in order to defragment files. The NT APIs do not address directories, the Master File Table (MFT), or paging files; in Windows 2000, they do not address the MFT or paging files. Now, with XP, only the paging file is untouched by these APIs so the results of regular defragmentation are more thorough than ever when using a third-party defragmenter.

Another significant shift in Windows XP is support for 64-bit computing. The 64-bit version of XP runs on the Intel Itanium processor. The IA-64 platform offers improvements in terms of floating-point performance to speed up activities such as three-dimensional modeling, human genome analysis, and special effects. Because it can access up to 16 TB of RAM, entire databases can reside in memory at access speeds 100 times greater than disk I/O.

Unfortunately, IA-64 lacks supporting applications at the moment. Computer Associates, BMC, SAP, J.D. Edwards, IBM, SAS Institute, VERITAS, and others have ported 32-bit applications to the new platform. Early pioneers include Wells Fargo's use of a 64-bit version of a SAS Institute database. Some of the tables used for quantitative modeling in this application have 600 million observations and performance is much better on a 64-bit platform.

Note, however, that many of these enhancements are available only on XP Pro, not the consumer-oriented XP Home version, which has no place in the enterprise. Professional extras include a backup utility, Remote Desktop (which allows administrators to access PCs remotely and users to pull up files while out of the office), dual processor support, Access Control (which restricts access to selected shared files, applications, and resources), roaming profiles, client-side caching, dynamic disks, SNMP, Intellimirror, and IIS. Additionally, XP Pro has a built-in fax utility, allows for AD log-ons, and features the Encrypting File System (EFS).

Security, in fact, has been given considerable attention in XP Pro. It contains several security improvements not available in Windows 2000 such as multi-user support for EFS. Based on public-key encryption, EFS encrypts and decrypts files using randomly generated keys. This enables multiple users to access encrypted files. The inclusion of security features, however, has not transformed XP into the desktop Fort Knox. Holes that make it possible to take over XP at the system level have been discovered by hackers. While patches have been issued, third-party security products should be relied upon in an enterprise environment.

On top of security shortcomings are several additional points to be aware of to minimize user complaints. Microsoft could perhaps be accused of optimism in its minimum system requirements: 233 MHz CPU, 128 MB of RAM (64 MB minimum is supposed to be supported, with the warning that this setup may limit performance and some features), and 1.5 GB of available hard disk space. When it comes to memory, XP surely needs a lot of it. Microsoft recommends 128 MB RAM minimum, but this is not really enough. One of my machines has 128 MB RAM and it rarely has more than 14% physical memory available. As a result, the paging file is under heavy use — constant usage at 85 percent or greater, even with little running. It is advised, then, to load typical workstations with at least 256 MB RAM and far more for high-end workstation users.

A 233-MHz CPU will not work with XP, as even my old 400-MHz machine could not take the load. Although a 1-GHz CPU was a big improvement, a few months down the line, CPU utilization was often topped out. So, 2 GHz is probably the minimum for XP. A 1-GHz CPU may be enough for some users, but it may be better *not* to load XP on older machines and to delay the XP installation until the lower powered desktops are ready to be replaced. For high-end machines running graphics-intensive applications or which are used for such things as software development, a faster CPU should be considered an absolute must.

When it comes to hard disk space, XP is a monster. The operating system alone takes up most of the 1.5 GB of recommended available disk space. So, if users have old systems with small hard drives in the range of 4 GB or below, their choices are simple: Forget about XP, upgrade the hard drives, or purchase new machines. Realistically, a 10-GB drive is the minimum, and with hard disk prices so low 20 GB assures that user complaints about running out of space will be few and far between.

So, is XP Pro for you and your many users? If Windows 2000 is already on every desktop, possibly not. The differences between XP and Windows 2000 are relatively minor in comparison with XP versus Windows NT or 9*x*. With budgets being tight, it is likely that Windows 2000 desktops will stay right where they are for another year or two. For everybody else, though, there are plenty of reasons to move to XP. Help desk operations will benefit enormously from the stability, reliability, and remote management features of XP. User calls should be less frequent, and those that come in can be dealt with remotely much more easily.

Beware XP's Consumer Features

While consumer-like features built into XP Pro may not have any real business value, they could very well make XP popular among users and even some IT staff. After all, buying an operating system is a lot like buying a new car. Each year a new model comes out with new standard features that a person used to have to get from an aftermarket supplier. Stereos, air conditioning, seatbelts, GPS systems, cup holders, and even rear view mirrors are all third-party products that are now incorporated as standard equipment. Many sales-people can tell stories of cup holders being the decisive element in the sale of a $35,000 vehicle. It is the same with PCs. They now come with all sorts of bells and whistles built right into the operating system. XP, for example includes media players, CD burning software, firewalls, and a whole lot more.

The XP Windows Media Player

Windows Media Player (WMP) is now bundled with the operating system and is set to operate as the default player. OEMs can, however, make other arrangements. With WMP, users can play CDs and DVDs, watch analog and digital TV, create music disks, and listen to Internet radio through a single interface. With XP Pro, system administrators can lockdown the media player features to provide a consistent look, configuration, and feature set. Admin-istrators can also use restrict functions and playback features for certain individuals or groups to save bandwidth.

The major criticism raised about WMP is that it works better with Microsoft's own media formats — Windows Media Audio (.wma) and Windows Media Video (WMV) — than it does with competing formats such as MP3 or QuickTime. A user can create an MP3 file with WMP, but only at 64 kbps. Microsoft promotes this lower baud rate as a feature, saying that it allows for faster CD burning and cuts down on storage. For higher audio quality, users need to purchase and install third-party software. WMP is, however, adequate for most business uses. Third-party software, such as RealOne Player, J. River's Media Jukebox, or Sonic Foundry's Siren Jukebox, lets users create MP3s at the higher quality 320 kbps, in addition to offering a more complete range of editing and copying functions. Those in the marketing or public relations departments might need better tools for creating content, but for most people in the company the question is whether they even need a media player. It may just prove to be an unnecessary distraction.

The XP CD Burner

When a user has compiled a music list with the Windows Media Player, it can be recorded onto a CD without buying additional software. Roxio, Inc. (Milpitas, California; spun off from Adaptec in 2001) has licensed portions of its Easy CD Creator technology to Microsoft. This tool has been incorporated into Windows Explorer, making it as easy to record files onto a CD as onto a floppy. The XP software, however, lacks the label-printing, audio enhancement, editing, and video CD creation features of the full Roxio software. The CD-burning application that comes with XP probably will not need to be replaced by any third-party software currently being sold, however. Most computers that come with CD-R or CD-RW also include basic CD burning software. Roxio's "lite" software, for example, has shipped with tens of millions of recorders from Compaq, Dell, Hewlett-Packard, IBM, and others, bundled with the operating system. Typical business users have little need to create CDs, other than for occasional backups or to transfer files to a laptop, and for such users the XP CD burning software does the job. But, for those in IT, marketing, and public relations, who are more likely to require full functionality, an upgrade should be considered, such as Easy CD Creator 5 Platinum ($99.95) by Roxio (www.roxio.com).

The XP Defragger

Like Texas, everything is bigger about XP. That means bigger files, bigger disks, more memory, and a whole lot more trouble with fragmentation. High levels of fragmentation, in fact, manifest as soon as the operating system is installed. Right after I loaded XP, XP Office, and a couple of applications, I checked out the amount of fragmentation. The result shocked me. System files were badly splintered, making up 189 fragmented files in 559 pieces. Fragmented directories were also scattered all over the disk, severely restricting the availability of free space. If I had loaded something like SQL Server 2000 along with a large database at that point, it would not have found enough contiguous space to be written in one piece.

Fortunately, as the benefits of defragmentation have become better known in recent years, this technology has become an important performance addition for many networks. Microsoft, therefore, wisely added the built-in utility Disk Defragmenter to Windows 2000 and has added some minor upgrades to the XP version, targeted at greater thoroughness. Amended APIs for XP allow the MFT to be safely defragmented by Disk Defragmenter (in Windows 2000, Disk Defragmenter ignored MFT fragmentation, resulting in a gradual degradation in performance of the utility over time).

Although the new Disk Defragmenter is a little better than the previous version, it is still woefully inadequate for any type of enterprise application. According to recent tests by NSTL, the built-in utility is three to five times slower than a good third-party defragmenter and a whole lot less thorough. Paging file fragmentation, for instance, is not addressed by Disk Defragmenter. As a result, fragmented memory resources lead to sluggish reads and writes within a few months of enterprise usage. Even when Disk Defragmenter is run regularly, steadily worsening paging file fragmentation will impact system performance.

Disk Defragmenter is also found lacking as an administrative tool. A system administrator needs a robust scheduler to manage defragmentation on all machines throughout the network. The Microsoft defrag utility comes with an elementary scheduling script that is not adequate in an enterprise setting. In particular, the XP scheduler works only on XP boxes; therefore, any company containing a mix of Windows 9x, NT, 2000, and XP machines has to resort to SneakerNet, with the system administrator marching from box to box to manually defrag them one volume at a time. As this scenario is not likely to happen, the result will be a steady buildup of fragmentation across the network and significantly deteriorating performance due to neglect.

Even in XP-only enterprises, this scheduler is an administrative nightmare. The system administrator has to know the names of all systems and their volume configurations. Further, schedules have to be set blind; that is, the system administrator has to guess how long defragmentation will take on each machine and schedule it accordingly. If it takes longer for one volume to defrag than allocated, the process will shut off midway without notification, which means that any remaining volumes will also not be defragmented. And, as this utility runs only at high priority, in most sites it will have to be scheduled off-hours, but it takes far longer than a third-party tool to run and does not function at all on large disks, so it is largely useless in an enterprise setting.

A business of any size, then, requires the purchase of a third-party defragmenter for each workstation and server on the network. When it comes to Windows XP or 2000 tools that impact every file in the machine, it is important to deal only with reliable products. The Windows Certified Program is an effective tool for judging the quality of products, as it is based on stringent standards for reliability, scalability, and manageability. Executive Software offers networkable defragmentation software that is currently certified for Windows 2000 Server and Windows 2000 Professional, as well as Windows XP and Windows Server 2003. Try Diskeeper ($49.95 for workstation edition) by Executive Software (Burbank, California; www.execsoft.com). Other networkable defragmenters are offered by Ratco, Winternals, and O/O Software.

XP Security Features

According to Microsoft, one of the top reasons for upgrading to XP is new security features. These include its Encrypted File System, a built-in firewall, configurable Access Control Lists (ACLs) and Group Policies, and Smart Card support. With the EFS, individual files and folders on NTFS volumes can be designated with an encryption attribute. When an administrator turns this attribute on, EFS automatically encrypts all new files created in the folder and all plain text files are copied or moved to the folder. As an option, all existing files and subfolders can be designated for encryption. XP includes predefined templates to establish security levels during creation of a resource, applying ACLs and establishing Group Policies. Administrators have the option of accepting the defaults or using any of the thousands of individually configurable security settings.

The biggest XP security news has been the new Internet Connection Firewall (ICF) that works as a packet filter to block unsolicited connections. It does this by using the Network Address Translation (NAT) flow table. It allows incoming data flows only when there is an existing NAT flow table mapping. ICF works only when a computer is part of a work group or is operating as a stand-alone device. If it is operating as part of a domain, the IT administrator sets the protection features. So, should an enterprise rely on the ICF? Probably not. Gartner Group believes that pulling complex application software into operating system software represents a substantial security risk. More lines of code mean more complexity, which means more security bugs. Worse yet, it often means that fixing one security bug will cause one or more new security bugs.

Not surprisingly, it did not take long before the first XP security hole was discovered. Within three weeks of its release, eEye Digital Security, Inc. (Aliso Viejo, California) had already located three major flaws, one of which would let hackers take over a computer at the system level. Although Microsoft quickly released a patch, the FBI's National Infrastructure Protection Center still recommended that users disable XP's Universal Plug and Play features to avoid any problems.

According to Gibson Research Corporation (Laguna Hills, California), ICF only masks the machine from the Internet in order to block inbound packets. Because many worms spread by users clicking on an e-mail attachment, XP would not block spyware or prevent the computer from being used in a denial-of-service attack. XP's built-in firewall, in fact, does not attempt to manage or restrict outbound communications at all; therefore, a good third-party personal firewall will still be necessary to manage and control outbound connections from a system.

To adequately protect the network, then, a third-party software or hardware firewall is an absolute must in any enterprise. The XP firewall feature is worth using on laptops or home computers that do not have an enterprise-strength version already installed, but mobile users can achieve far greater security by installing any of several products on the market. One of the better ones is McAfee Personal Firewall ($29.95 for a one-year subscription) from McAfee.com Corporation (Sunnyvale, California; www.mcafee.com).

XP Task Manager

Windows Task Manager can be useful in diagnosing slows and other problems on XP. Accessed via CTRL + ALT + DEL, Task Manager now has five tabs:

Applications, Processes, Performance, Networking, and Users. Two of them are particularly useful. The Applications Tab indicates which applications are running and provides an easy way to kill any of them. The Performance Tab graphs memory and CPU usage. Keep an eye on it after loading XP to see if the system really does have enough CPU power and physical memory or a large enough paging file. This feature can also help users spot such things as programs that are hogging memory or improperly coded programs that may be the cause of memory leaks. Overall, this is a good tool for debugging a specific desktop or server.

XP Performance Tool

The Windows XP Performance Tool is a combination of the old System Monitor and Performance Logs and Alerts that allows users to collect and view real-time memory, disk, processor, network, and other activity in graph, histogram, and report form. Users can configure the logs to monitor such data and to send alerts if values go beyond a specific threshold. It is accessed via the Control Panel by double-clicking on Administrative Tools and Performance. When a system is upgraded to XP from an older operating system, this tool indicates whether the old CPU and memory are up to the task or require an upgrade. Do not rely too much on Performance Tool, however. Trying to keep track of too many metrics at once can drain system resources. Again, home users, road warriors, and some small businesses can probably get by with Performance Tool, but a well-priced upgrade for small and mid-sized operations is WebNM by Somix Technologies (Sanford, Maine). It utilizes polling techniques to create a centralized performance database so users can see what is happening across the network and detect the cause of slows.

XP Quotas

Windows XP Professional has a built-in quota system that limits the amount of storage a user can have on an NTFS volume. When a user exceeds the preset limit, that individual or the administrator or both are notified. Alternatively, the limit can be set so the file cannot be saved until other material is deleted (be aware, though, that this option might not be popular with users). This utility is accessed through My Computer: select a drive and click on File, then Properties. Basically, it alerts users who are starting to fill up their disks and places limits on disk usage per user. This feature should be more than enough for a home or mobile user. Like other disk and file management tools in XP Pro, XP Quotas may be adequate for simple quota management of a few users but lacks enterprise functionality. For something better, try Storage-CeNTral by Precise/W. Quinn Associates, Inc. (Reston, Virginia; www.wquinn.com).

XP Backup

XP Backup is accessed via My Computer in a manner similar to that for Quotas. This time go into the Tools tab and select Backup. A wizard walks users through the process and allows selection of individual files or folders for backup. If a zip drive or tape drive is hooked up to the system, that drive should show up automatically in the wizard, which makes it easy for users to set up a simple backup schedule. As expected, XP Pro comes with all the backup functions the home office user or mobile professional will probably need. On the other hand, it is not designed to be a corporate backup system that encompasses thousands of systems. As a result, it does not come with tools for media/device management, alerting, virus scanning, remote server protection, and disaster recovery. But, what it does, XP Backup does well. For a more sophisticated environment, try BrightStor Enterprise Backup or ARCServe by Computer Associates (Islandia, New York). For systems that have more than a couple of servers, such backup programs save a lot of administrator time going from box to box to run manual backups.

Backward Compatibility of XP

When designing Windows XP, Microsoft wanted to make it easy to implement the new operating system without having to rip out and replace earlier elements or embark upon extensive customization. The company invested significant research and development dollars to address reasons why applications would run on older down-level platforms but not on later ones. Microsoft's developers found, for example, that many applications were hard-coded to look for a particular operating system version. If the program checked the registry or memory and did not find the release it expected, it simply would not run. To get around this, XP developers programmed XP to "lie" if an application insisted on, say, Windows $9x$, so the program would run without problem. This improvement translates into potentially significant cost savings, as an agency can leverage its current applications while also gaining the added features of the latest operating system. As a result of this feature, some organizations have chosen to bypass Windows 2000 and move desktops directly to XP. That way, they could run more of their existing applications on Windows XP than on Windows 2000 without having to write customized middleware.

Extending Hardware Lifespan

In addition to extending application lifespan, it is also vitally important to gain additional mileage out of hardware. Corporate America's three-year refresh cycle for PCs appears to have become a thing of the past in organizations struggling under the burden of massive IT budget cuts. The public sector model, for example, is sometimes characterized as a run-to-failure one; that is, system administrators replace items when they stop working. This operating basis is starting to creep into various enterprises that are strapped for cash. The downside of tighter belts is the resulting mix of networks ranging from 386s to Pentium IVs running every version of Windows released over the last decade — in other words, a nightmare for support personnel. While it might be easier to upgrade everything to a single platform, such a sweeping change is rarely in the budget. XP, therefore, incorporates Windows Terminal Services (WTS) to preserve the value of current investments until new equipment can be procured. With WTS, end users obtain the benefits of XP applications even if they have older PCs and do not have the resources to run XP itself.

Improved XP Management

Windows XP Professional also offers administrators a range of new tools to manage workstations. In addition to simplifying administration, these tools also cut the overall cost of ownership. Features include:

- *Additional extensions.* XP has over 300 more extensions than Windows 2000 Professional, allowing policy-based management of the entire user environment, including desktop appearance, wallpaper, access to applications, and which items appear on the Start menu.
- *Windows updates.* Workstations contact an internal server on a scheduled basis and download any new patches.
- *SysPrep.* This feature is used to build a system image for remote deployment.
- *Remote Assistance.* This feature, which allows help desk staff to take over control of a workstation, extends the reach of support staff to any computer out in the field.
- *Remote Desktop.* It is Saturday night, and the department head is scheduled to give the keynote address to the National Governors Association, but he forgot to download the PowerPoint presentation onto his laptop before catching his flight. No problem. With Remote Desktop he can dial into the network, take control of his workstation, and drag and drop the file onto his laptop.

Only Room for So Much

Because XP is already a 1.5-GB download and the number of lines of code number in the tens of millions, Microsoft has had to compromise on the quality of its built-in tools. If the company added top-of-the-line utilities it would have to charge a lot more and the operating system would become bloated, which is why almost all of the tools are rather basic versions licensed from other software developers. While Microsoft should be applauded for attempting to satisfy the user community by building so many tools into its operating system, these tools are mainly of value to mobile and home office users. When it comes to systems and network management though, most users are better served by proven third-party utilities that are specifically designed with the enterprise in mind.

Chapter 15

Windows Present and Future: Windows Server 2003, 64-Bit Computing, and Beyond

As the last two chapters demonstrate, many changes in Windows have particular relevance to the enterprise. The transition from NT to Windows 2000, the addition of Advanced Server and Datacenter Server versions of the Windows 2000 family, and the arrival of Windows XP have all served to make Windows a far more viable platform for mid-sized and large enterprises. The immediate future holds the promise of even greater change. The impending release of Windows Server 2003 and future releases such as Longhorn and Blackcomb, as well as the arrival of 64-bit architectures on the scene, demonstrate that Microsoft is dead serious when it comes to providing enough scalability to match mid-range stalwarts such as Sun and Hewlett-Packard, and possibly even take on IBM with mainframe-class Windows platforms. Certainly, Windows platforms will keep getting bigger, more reliable, and more scalable. Our look down the road begins with an examination of .NET and Windows Server 2003. Then we cover 64-bit computing, still a nascent technology but one destined to render 32-bit computing a thing of the past within a few years (who uses 16-bit these days?). Finally, we try to predict what lies ahead for Windows to see how the enterprise computing landscape might unfold.

Microsoft's .NET

Never shy of promising Hall of Fame numbers from fresh-out-of-high-school rookies, Microsoft is touting its .NET strategy as being *the* way to seamlessly link applications running on the complete range of computing platforms. A wide array of Web services allows applications to communicate and share data over the Internet; employees and customers are able to access data any time at any place on any device. So, is .NET a swish or an airball when it comes to living up to the hype, and what is it exactly? Representing a fundamental shift away from the client–server architecture, .NET applies to everything from desktop operating systems and handhelds to the way enterprise-class servers talk to each other. Windows Server 2003 is the first to incorporate .NET features.

Just imagine if corporate or government online services were connected and integrated. This would make it so much easier for the consumer, the business customer, or the citizen to find out the information needed and the services available, and the key to achieving that level of functionality is integration of applications. But, how is it possible to integrate when so many platforms are running amid a sea of conflicting standards and architectures? Although companies may like the idea of complete integration of applications, they definitely do not want to have to deal with replacing multiple systems or converting everything to one single platform. So, let us investigate how Microsoft's .NET vision relates to solving the integration puzzle.

What Is .NET?

The first thing to understand is that .NET is not a single technology or even a group of technologies. Based upon specific standards, it is essentially a brand name for Microsoft's business strategy. By giving it a single name and trumpeting it from the rooftops, Microsoft has done a good job of grabbing mindshare in the Web services arena, according to Giga Information Group (Cambridge, MA). This is not to say, however, that .NET is no more than a marketing gimmick. Behind the name is a wide-ranging view of the role the Internet plays in the future of computing, as well as concrete actions to bring that vision to fruition. The strategy recognizes the rise in the Internet as a platform of operations, along with the decline of the PC as the sole or primary computing device. It defines how Microsoft is adapting to and promoting that change.

According to Microsoft, the .NET integration strategy consists of four main elements:

- *.NET Framework.* The .NET Framework is the element that builds in Web services standards throughout the Microsoft product line, from VisualStudio.NET developer tools to Windows Server 2003 and the Windows XP desktop operating system. The .NET Framework basically allows for greater interoperability with the products developed at Redmond as well as those applications created by other companies.

- *.NET Enterprise Servers.* Microsoft has released the first of the .NET Enterprise Server line — Windows Server 2003. The company is incorporating Web services standards into all of its enterprise servers starting with Windows Server 2003. Following on its heals will be .NET-enabled versions of other Microsoft server products, such as Exchange, BizTalk, SQL Server, and Commerce Server, among many others.
- *.NET Services.* Both .NET Framework and .NET Enterprise Server exist in order to facilitate the third part — .NET-based Web services. The first of these services, Microsoft Passport, has already been released, with numerous others under development within the .NET services banner.
- *.NET Clients.* Clients for .NET include PCs, laptops, workstations, phones, handheld computers, the recently released Tablet PCs, game consoles, and other smart devices. In short, anything that can access Web services will be made compatible with the .NET platform. These clients will all incorporate software that supports XML Web services and allows users to access data regardless of the time, place, or type of client used. The long-term goal is to have all applications communicating while leveraging existing assets in a flexible way.

.NET and Web Services

The core of the .NET strategy (and that of the rival integration platforms of competitors such as Sun and IBM) is Web services. These are a step toward what World Wide Web creator Tim Berners-Lee refers to as the "semantic Web" — that is, users can search and access not just Web pages but actual data. Web services mark a shift in computing away from a client/server to an Internet-based platform, with seamless integration of applications running on different platforms. Current applications are typically built on the Component Object Model (COM), where an application is assembled from smaller blocks of reusable code. Rather than writing everything from scratch, programmers harness preassembled code packages to accomplish routine functions in a manner similar to building something with Legos, where all the pieces are designed to work together and can be used in different configurations to build anything from a house to a spaceship. Web services take this concept one step further. Although COM allows an application to be built of components running on a single machine and running a particular operating system, Web services permit these applications to be assembled out of components running on different machines and operating systems connected using Internet standards. Four standards make up the procedure.

The .NET Starting Roster

Any new technology has its own set of unique terms and acronyms, and Web services are no exception. The four key terms and technologies and the standards organizations involved are as follows:

- *Simple Object Access Protocol* (SOAP) creates a method for one program to communicate with another program, even if they are on different operating systems, through the use of HTTP. It solves the problem of getting code through firewalls, as most firewalls allow HTTP to pass through while blocking other types of applications. With SOAP, computers can call each other and exchange information. Originally developed by Microsoft, DevelopMentor, Inc., and Userland Software, Inc., SOAP is now a standard of the World Wide Web Consortium (www.w3c.org).

- *Universal Description, Discovery, and Integration* (UDDI) provides an online business registry, similar to the phone book, that allows people to search out a Web service. The same standard can be used by an individual organization to create its own internal directory of Web services. To access the public online directory or for further data on UDDI, go to www.uddi.org.

- *Web Services Definition Language* (WSDL) is an XML-based format for describing a Web service in a way that other computers can locate it and interact with it. WSDL was submitted to the World Wide Web Consortium in March 2001 (see www.w3c.org).

- *Extensible Markup Language* (XML) is a way of exchanging information over the Web. It is similar to the HTML used in creating Web pages, but while HTML is limited to describing how items should appear in a Web page, XML describes data so that applications can exchange information with each other. XML is a formal recommendation of the World Wide Web Consortium (www.w3c.org).

Other formats are also used. For example, Microsoft has developed another type of XML document called Discovery of Web Services (DISCO) for querying a particular URL to discover what Web services it offers. Only the above four, however, have attained widespread acceptance.

What does this all mean? More than anything, Web services hold the promise of better data and application integration. As well as providing the opportunity to shuttle data between different departments, systems, and services without the usual integration tangles, this utility gives applications the ability to call application logic in different entities, without regard to operating system or development environment. Consequently, .NET offers the ability to integrate internal systems and databases, as well as linking up easily with other companies, partners, databases, agencies, vendors, and customers. Of itself, this ability is not particularly revolutionary, as countless middleware solutions are available to accomplish just that. Simply stated, the Web services do not do anything that could not be done previously. What does make the Web services unique is that cross-platform integration is being built into every step of the software process. Microsoft includes .NET features in Windows XP, and the same Web services standards are built into IBM, Sun, Hewlett-Packard, and BEA/Bowstreet server software. This takes middleware out of the realm of customized one-on-one hookups and brings it much closer to Plug and Play functionality.

Middleware, in fact, is a massive industry. Companies such as IBM and Candle Corp. make millions tying together disparate systems, and consultants galore swarm across the systems of Fortune 500 companies attempting to make E-business applications function and to cobble together back-end and front-end systems. Instead of customer integration, Web services will make rapid integration feasible by adhering to one of the standards covered above. Microsoft is hoping that its .NET initiative becomes the *de facto* standard for IT. With the release of Windows Server 2003, it hopes to greatly expand its share of the integration and data availability market.

Although customers and the public will experience obvious benefits when applications talk to each other, perhaps the biggest effect of .NET will be felt internally. Many IT departments have been tied up for some time trying to put everyone on a single platform. With .NET, that may no longer be necessary. The bottom line is that Web services will make it easier to achieve interoperability without any kind of common architecture. One organization using Microsoft, for example, can integrate with one using the J2EE programming language without the need for expensive middleware and months of endless consulting to do so.

As .NET also makes it easier to integrate with applications running outside the organization, this could eventually eliminate the cost of maintaining duplicate databases. At a government level, for instance, state and local government agencies would be able to talk to federal government Web services (and vice versa) to share information instead of storing it in several places.

Consider the area of crime prevention. Currently, most local police forces have their own individual systems that record crime in one city or county. Small amounts of data sharing take place between the city and county systems and federal policing entities such as the FBI, as well as state law enforcement agencies. Yet, it is quite common for a criminal to be perpetrating crimes in several jurisdictions without anyone realizing it is the same person. Early pilot programs with .NET in California, for example, have demonstrated that it is feasible to tie these systems together with ease to improve performance among the agencies concerned. The King County Sheriff's Office (Washington State), for example, is developing an information sharing system with a search engine exclusively for police to use for local coordination. By typing in the name of a suspect or his *modus operandi* or the kind of car he drives, it is possible to obtain matching information from around the county. Currently, the fact that similar crimes are being committed in two or more cities may not be detected (e.g., a serial burglar in one town doing similar jobs in a neighboring town), but police networks are now being established to eliminate the need to make special requests to state and federal agencies for local matters. The pilot program is ongoing in the King County Sheriff's Office and two other police agencies. The plan is to hook together all of the county's police departments.

Case Study: Making the Case for Information Sharing among Police Departments

The front pages have been filled with tales of how the September 11 attacks might have been prevented if only the FBI, INS, CIA, and other agencies had shared their information in a timely manner. While the terrorist attacks are a spectacular example of the costs of information-sharing failure, they are far from the only example. Information-sharing failures, in fact, occur every day in law enforcement jurisdictions throughout the country, resulting in unsolved crimes committed by repeat offenders. Combining the description of a car used in one robbery with the description of a suspect in another robbery may lead to a quick arrest. For example, it is not unusual for two apparently similar auto thefts to occur only a half mile apart, yet because they occurred on opposite sides of a city boundary, the data is never shared, thus hampering the investigation. Now factor in the typical patchwork of municipalities making up most metropolitan regions, and with so many separate police departments and jurisdictions the task of information sharing can become daunting. Police records indicate that it is quite rare to have robberies that do not occur serially; however, without integrating IT systems and cardfile databases across jurisdictions, police forces often do not have access to information regarding where a suspect may have committed other robberies. Further, the dream of uniting this information has been thwarted for many years due to the sheer amount of funds that would be involved.

Fortunately, this situation is about to change. An information-sharing committee for the King County Police Chiefs Association (KCPCA) in Washington State is working together with Microsoft to develop and implement a .NET-based system allowing simultaneous real-time access to information contained in the Records Management Systems (RMS) of all the county agencies. This system will bring together the Tukwila Police Department and another three dozen law enforcement agencies that serve the 1.7 million residents of King County. According to the police chief of Tukwila, law enforcement efforts, like those of so many other industries, have been too concerned with their own territories and have not been able or willing to share information to the extent required. In King County, however, a core of leaders has been assembled who believe strongly in allowing other agencies to access their data to make law enforcement more effective.

The KCPCA members already had access to the FBI's National Crime Information Center (NCIC) as well as the state's crime database, but the NCIC only reflects convictions and the state database does not list someone until an arrest is made. What was needed was the means to share operational data impacting ongoing investigations at a local level. To begin, the KCPCA put together a secure Web site (WIRE, for Web-Based Information for Regional Enforcement), where agencies could post crime bulletins and analyses available to other agencies via a search engine. Only information on major crimes was posted, with data being uploaded perhaps once a week. While this was better than nothing, overall, it proved too limited and too slow to meet the needs of the officers.

Just imagine the extent of information available in every jurisdiction. The information collected on suspects, locations, and vehicles has been stored for years, so databases are uniformly massive. Literally mountains of useful information must be sorted through, and systems such as WIRE reveal just a tiny slice of that data. The KCPCA, therefore, started investigating information-sharing systems used in other parts of the country but found little that approached the functionality it sought. Then in stepped one of King County's more famous companies, Microsoft, to lend a hand. The company offered to donate the expertise necessary to link the different databases being kept by the county's agencies using its .NET platform.

A pilot of the new system, called the Regional Information Sharing System (RISS), has already begun. Initial participants include the Tukwila Police Department and the King County Sheriff's Office, which provides contract services to 14 cities in the vicinity. Rather than having to combine all the data from the different agencies into a huge centralized database in a specialized format, RISS utilizes Microsoft's .NET architecture to link the data that the agencies are already keeping no matter the format (see Exhibit 1). This technology is indifferent to what platform any agency is using. Whether agencies are using IBM's DB2 on a mainframe, an Oracle database on a UNIX server, or one of many Microsoft platforms, the information is in same basic format so that everyone is talking the same language.

To participate, all the agency needs is a server running the Windows 2000 Server operating system and Microsoft's Internet Information Server (IIS), together with Microsoft's .NET framework software, which makes it possible to share information between the databases. Combined cost for the hardware and software is about $3500 per participating site. RISS consists of one central server hosted by the county and separate servers at each of the participating law enforcement agencies connected via .NET Services. The central server (County LSJ Server) contains a UDDI directory, which is a catalog of the types of services that are available online. The catalog listings are designed to be read by a machine, rather than by a person. In this case, the different agency computers contact the UDDI directory to find out what type of information is contained in the other agencies' databases and how to access this information.

Each agency maintains its own server to hold its own records database as well as a Data Access Component, a piece of code that allows users to conduct queries on that database. A second server acts to translate the information into a common format so it can be shared by the other agencies using XML, which is similar to HTML, the language used to create Web pages, but has stricter formatting requirements that allow for the sharing of raw data. The XSLT (Extensible Stylesheet Language Transformation) translators shown in Exhibit 1 refer to a language that translates the XML documents into other formats such as HTML for viewing on a Web page or Portable Document Format (.pdf) for printing. All the computers connect to each other through the county's Inter-Government Network (IGN).

Each agency will continue to store and maintain data in the usual way, but they will be able not only to search their own records, but also to conduct a browser-based search that will access the data in all the other participating

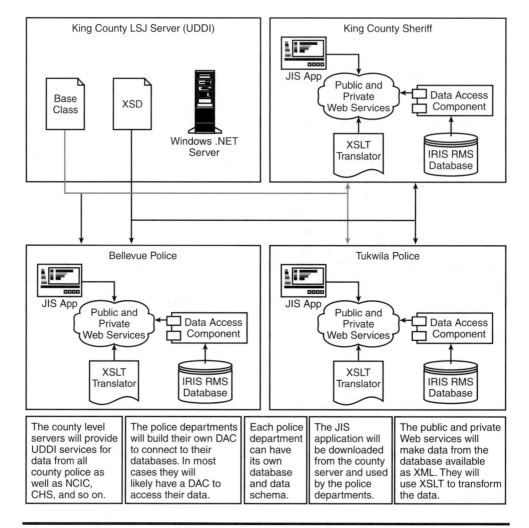

Exhibit 1   Diagram of King County Program

agency's RMSs. Initially, officers and staff will perform the searches from terminals in the stations, but eventually access will extend out to patrol cars and handheld devices. As each agency comes on line, it will make it easier for all the rest to do their jobs. The system will generate more leads and will make it possible to solve crimes to a much greater degree than was previously possible. RISS is now being opened up to the other 36 law enforcement agencies in the county, with the complete rollout scheduled for completion sometime in 2003.

Nothing but .NET: What Are the Alternatives to .NET?

Although Microsoft is grabbing the headlines, other companies offer Web services software. IBM (Websphere), Sun Microsystems (SunONE), BEA/Bowstreet

(WebLogic), and others have mature products on the market, but typically it comes down to Microsoft versus the rest of the development world. Microsoft critics accuse it of being too proprietary in its Web services implementation. They believe that the focus on .NET or COM components makes it a limited integration platform. As a result, IBM and other companies have built their products using the Java 2 Platform, Enterprise Edition (J2EE). Developed by Sun Microsystems and its partners, it is a Java programming language platform designed for enterprise-scale computing. In contrast to Microsoft's products, J2EE is designed to build applications on a platform-independent "Write Once, Run Anywhere" model.

VisualStudio.NET, the development component of the .NET platform, though, has one big advantage — it is very easy to use; thus, it could be simple enough to bring the power of the Web services programming model to the masses. Yet, from a development platform perspective, J2EE is farther along and is more widely supported. Although it is the more favored solution at the moment, Microsoft could easily grab significant market share in a short time and garner support from a wide range of partners.

So how is this canvas going to unfold? Even though these competing systems will talk to each other, as they all rely on the same set of standards, they will probably each develop various flavors with exclusive features to carve out market share. Compared with the others, .NET may ultimately offer enough advantages to win the war. To begin with, all the components come from a single vendor, which should guarantee greater compatibility and eliminate vendor finger pointing when problems arise. Also, because Microsoft is incorporating Web services support right into operating systems and server applications, this eliminates the need for an additional layer of middleware to convert these applications into Web services. And, with over 90 percent of the desktop market in its pocket, as well as 25 million developers trained in Microsoft tools, Microsoft's offering is going to be difficult to beat.

The downside, of course, is a familiar refrain. Microsoft products tend to work better with each other than with competing systems. For exclusively Microsoft shops, this is an advantage, but some may want more options. J2EE advocates say this platform lets users select from a wider variety of operating systems and hardware platforms and provides greater scalability. Additionally, the issue of third-party software and tools cannot be overlooked. Simply put, a greater number of innovative vendors offer tools for J2EE than for .NET.

Whatever format prevails, Web services represent the next evolutionary stage in distributed computing. They are catching on quickly and will become widespread within a few years. While the technology is still in the early adopter phase, now is the time for developers to learn about it and experiment with its application. Free toolkits are available to help Microsoft and Java developers become familiar with these technologies. As Web services can be implemented one at a time, IT staff can begin with simple internal-facing applications. Once these have proven their worth, they can be moved to the Internet.

.NET Slam Dunk

So is .NET a swish or an airball? Unfortunately, too few applications are currently available to know for sure. Based on early indications, however, it has at least hit the rim. .NET's defense still needs some work, because it is vulnerable to the occasional steal (security issues), as are other Web services, and it faces stiff competition from other teams which took an early lead. But, because it is backed by the 7-foot, 300-pound giant Microsoft, you know it is at least going to make it into the playoffs, where it will be very difficult to beat.

Windows Server 2003

Windows Server 2003 has now been released. According to early indications, it offers significant performance, productivity, and security improvements over previous Windows server operating systems. Windows Server 2003 contains core technologies that build on the strengths of Windows 2000 Server. It is a multipurpose operating system that has been designed to take care of a wide range of different server functions. It has been built to work well in either a centralized or a distributed fashion. For example, it can be deployed as a simple file and print server, Web server, Web application server, or mail server. Additionally, it has been optimized to run well as a terminal server, a remote access or virtual private network (VPN) server, or a streaming media server. When it comes to directory services, the Domain Name System (DNS), the Dynamic Host Configuration Protocol (DHCP), and Windows Internet Naming Service (WINS), Windows Server 2003 will also be found to perform well.

What has been improved?

- *Availability.* The Windows Server 2003 family has enhanced clustering support to provide improved availability. The clustering installation and setup of .NET Server is easier than before, and enhanced network features offer greater failover capabilities and higher rates of system uptime. Server clusters for up to eight nodes are supported by Windows Server 2003. If one node becomes unavailable because of failure or maintenance, another node provides failover capabilities. The Network Load Balancing (NLB) of Windows 2000 Server has been improved to better balance incoming Internet Protocol (IP) traffic across nodes in a cluster.
- *Scalability.* Like Windows 2000 Server, the Windows Server 2003 family can operate within a scale-up architecture using simultaneous multiprocessing (SMP) or a scaled-out model using clustering. According to initial tests, Windows Server 2003 delivers up to 140 percent better performance in the file system compared with the Windows 2000 Server and significantly better performance in AD (Active Directory), Web server, and terminal server components and networking services. It scales from single-processor solutions all the way up to 32-way systems and supports both 32-bit and 64-bit processors.
- *Security.* Bill Gates recently staked the company's reputation on a commitment to provide reliable, secure, and dependable computing. As a result,

a lot of work has gone into heightening the level of security offered by Windows Server 2003. Developers spent hundreds of thousands of hours attempting to identify every possible fail point or exploitable weakness. Though this may prove to be as fruitless an endeavor as a camel trying to get through the eye of a needle, Windows Server 2003 does represent several important upgrades in security. The common language runtime is a software engine that reduces the number of bugs and security holes caused by common programming mistakes. Fewer vulnerabilities, therefore, are available for attackers to exploit. The common language runtime also verifies that applications can run without error and checks for security permissions, making sure that code performs only appropriate operations. Another security plus is Internet Information Services 6.0, which is now configured for increased Web server security with fault tolerance, requesting queuing, application health monitoring, automatic application recycling, and caching.

■ *Active Directory.* The AD has been improved in Windows Server 2003 to make it more versatile, dependable, and economical to use. A beefed up version of AD offers such upgrades as: (1) removal of the group size limitation of 5000 objects per group; (2) elimination of the need for a global catalog at each site; (3) ability to load directory content from media (tapes, CDs, or DVDs); (4) support for the inetOrgPerson class (a popular means of identifying users); and (5) better replication conflict solutions for multivalued attributes when replicating between domain controllers. One caveat, however. Just as for a migration from NT to Windows 2000, all Windows 2000 domain controllers must be upgraded to Windows Server 2003 before the new features can be made available. Windows Server 2003 can still be installed, but when it detects the presence of any Windows 2000 domain controllers on the network, it shuts off its own AD features and runs in the usual Windows 2000 AD mode. So, are the changes worth waiting for? According to the Gartner Group, these are all good AD changes, but for the most part they will have a relatively minor impact on an enterprise. However, if an enterprise is planning on deploying Windows AD in the immediate future, it may be best to wait a few months and deploy the Windows Server 2003 version rather than going back and upgrading all the domain controllers later.

■ *Management Services.* Windows Server 2003 contains several new management automation tools including Microsoft Software Update Services (SUS) and server configuration wizards to automate deployment. The Group Policy Management Console (GPMC) enables organizations to set group policy and better utilize the AD service. Note, though, that GPMC is a separate component from Windows Server 2003.

■ *Storage Management.* Microsoft's efforts to forge alliances with all the leading storage vendors can be seen in Windows Server 2003. The new server operating system introduces enhanced features for storage management, making it far simpler to manage disks and volumes, to backup and restore data, and to connect to Storage Area Networks (SANs) and Network Attached Storage (NAS). These features include snapshots, various ways for users to recover lost files, and the ability to conduct complete backups in minutes (see Chapter 11).

XML Web Services and Windows Server 2003

As mentioned previously, .NET-based Web services are deeply integrated into the Windows Server 2003 family. This feature offers developers the ability to quickly and reliably build, host, deploy, and use secure and connected solutions through XML Web services.

Members of the Windows Server 2003 Family

Windows Server 2003 comes in several flavors, depending on the function intended for it. While Windows 2000 comes in standard, advanced, and data center versions, Windows Server 2003 has four versions: Standard Edition, Enterprise Edition, Datacenter Edition, and Web Edition.

Standard Edition

Windows Server 2003 Standard Edition is a flexible server that is best suited for small businesses and usage within organizational departments. Though it should not be deployed to house the company's massive database or mission-critical applications, it is good enough for most functions. Among its many features, it supports file and printer sharing, offers relatively secure Internet connectivity, and allows centralized desktop application deployment.

Enterprise Edition

Enterprise Edition is intended for businesses of all sizes as the platform for applications, Web services, and infrastructure. It offers higher reliability and performance than the Standard Edition, supporting up to eight processors, eight-node clustering, and up to 32 GB of memory. Enterprise Edition is available for Intel Itanium-based computers and will come out in a 32-bit version as well as a 64-bit version capable of supporting eight processors and 64 GB of RAM.

Datacenter Edition

Datacenter Edition is intended for business- and mission-critical applications demanding the highest levels of scalability and availability. It is the most powerful of the Server family, supporting up to 32-way SMP and 64 GB of RAM. It also provides eight-node clustering and load balancing services. A 64-bit computing platform will be made available capable of supporting 32 processors and 128 GB of RAM.

Web Edition

No doubt spurred on by the immense popularity of the Apache/Linux combo, Microsoft has come up with its own specialized Web server. Windows Server 2003 Web Edition is suitable for Web serving, as well as Web application hosting, Web pages, and XML Web services. It is primarily designed, though, to be used as an IIS Web server.

64-Bit Windows

Microsoft successfully made the leap from desktop operating system dominance to grabbing a hefty share of the server market. Now it is setting its sights on high-performance workstations and servers. After six years of development, Intel released its 64-bit Itanium processor and Microsoft shipped beta versions of compatible server and workstation operating systems. Compaq, Hewlett-Packard, Dell, and others followed up with the necessary hardware. The whole idea was to create high performance at a good price; that is, offer the performance of Reduced Instruction Set Computer (RISC) at the price of Intel servers. This new platform, IA-64, offers significant improvement in terms of floating-point performance to speed up activities such as three-dimensional modeling, human genome analysis, and special effects. Because it can access up to 15 TB of RAM, entire databases can reside in memory at access speeds 100 times greater than disk I/O.

64-Bit at a Glance

What is it? 64-bit Intel Itanium processors running 64-bit Microsoft Windows. The advantages include:

- Larger addressable virtual memory (up to 16 TB)
- Larger addressable physical memory (up to 64 GB)
- Larger file systems
- 64-bit wide data paths for increased processing speed
- 64-bit or 128-bit floating point and integer register so that larger number quantities can be manipulated for technical and scientific applications
- Higher availability
- Use of the familiar Windows operating system
- Backing from Microsoft, Intel, Dell, Hewlett-Packard, Compaq, SAP, PeopleSoft, Oracle, VERITAS, and others.

Who needs 64 bit? Enterprises using high demand applications, including:

- CAD/CAM/CAE
- Geographic information systems
- Movie editing and special effects production
- Large databases
- Data mining
- E-commerce
- Genome sequencing
- Fluid dynamics
- Encryption
- Multimedia serving

- Web caching
- Software development

While 64-bit processing is not new to Linux/Unix, bringing Microsoft into the loop adds development strength. Fortunately, developers were smart enough to leave IA-64 on the standard Windows programming model. That way, 32-bit developers and independent software vendors do not have to learn a new platform. The 64-bit architecture also employs the familiar 32-bit user interface.

Early IA-64 releases were geared primarily toward developers and early adopters. Wells Fargo Bank, for example, ran a pilot to optimize a 64-bit version of a SAS Institute database. The company used a 64-bit Windows 2000 Advanced Server LE on a Compaq ProLiant 590 server with 8 GB RAM and dual 650-MHz Itanium processors. The results were compared with a 32-bit version of the database running on another server with dual 650-MHz Xeon processors. The company has not noticed much difference in small databases, but with larger ones the 64-bit version is running faster, although it is not yet fully optimized. This project demonstrated some of the high-end strengths of 64-bit. Some of the tables Wells Fargo used for quantitative modeling had 600 million observations. By optimizing the SAS code, the bank saw increasingly better performance.

Microsoft released 32-bit and 64-bit versions of several Windows Server 2003 versions, and Intel has released its 2-G Itanium processor, McKinley, which will have enhanced compiler capabilities. The first 64-bit applications are now beginning to appear. Vendors such as Computer Associates, SAS Institute, BMC, SAP, J.D. Edwards, IBM, and VERITAS have ported 32-bit applications to the new platform.

The next two 64-bit processors, code-named Madison and Deerfield, are scheduled for release late in 2003 and will be built using the 0.13-micron fabrication process, but that does not mean that the 32-bit processor will disappear overnight. Microsoft and Intel intend to continue releasing 32-bit products for several more years. The sheer weight of independent software and hardware vendor support for Windows should mean that it gains acceptance quickly; however, 32-bit applications are likely to predominate for some time. Aberdeen Group predicts it will be at least 2004 before 64-bit Windows gains mainstream support. By that time, the marketplace will feel more comfortable that it is a hardened platform that is fully tested and ready for mission critical applications.

The Next Few Years of Windows: Longhorn, BlackComb, and XP Second Edition

With Microsoft having developed Windows Server 2003, we will be hearing a lot more about three new operating system products: Longhorn, BlackComb, and XP Second Edition. So what should we expect in the coming years? The .NET platform and Web services will continue to dominate future releases for the foreseeable future. As the technology matures, we can look forward to better and simpler modes of integration and greater information sharing.

XP Second Edition

On the desktop and enterprise desktop side, the successor to Windows XP is looming on the immediate horizon. Microsoft's new licensing program, Licensing 6, puts pressure on the company to issue a new enterprise desktop version over the next two years or face the wrath of customers who have been paying ahead for upgrades on an annual basis, under two- or three-year contracts. This means, though, that Microsoft has to come up with the goods, and that is where XP Second Edition comes in. XP Second Edition should be available either late in 2003 or early in 2004, though, historically, such estimates are undependable. The XP operating system was once going to represent the integration of the operating system code used for servers and desktops, but that goal appears to have been shelved once again in favor of getting an improved desktop operating system out in the required time frame. The amount of work required to align desktop and server code bases means that it is unlikely to happen for another few years.

Longhorn and BlackComb

Depending on whom you talk to, Longhorn is either the next major upgrade of the Microsoft server arsenal or it is will be a purely client-side release. The consensus appears to be with the latter option, however. Another area of uncertainty is the time line. Longhorn is scheduled for release around 2005, but it may possibly be delayed until a little later. Longhorn is expected to provide new features for intelligent auto configuration, such as BIOS and firmware, self-healing technology, a more "componentized" architecture, filter-type monitoring services, a new file system, enhanced storage capabilities, new graphics capabilities, and more APIs.

More than likely, then, Longhorn will supercede XP Second Edition as an enterprise desktop system, while the BlackComb release will be later and will focus on an overhaul of the server operating system. BlackComb is slated to encompass a complete revision of the Windows user interface while fully embracing XML Web services. The releases of Longhorn and BlackComb may or may not tie into another project that Microsoft has going, code-named Yukon, an upgrade to SQL Server that appears to be a key component in plans to offer a unified storage architecture foundation. XML and file streams will be introduced as native types for storage designed to improve storage functionality and enhance management.

Over the long term, Microsoft intends to create a federated operating system infrastructure where all operating systems are built on the same basic code with variations to suit their functions. The XML protocol framework, GXA XML, will be the main driving force in this federation strategy. GXA XML will provide a consistent model for building protocols for Web services and applications. The intention is to achieve interoperability among Microsoft products as well as competitive offerings.

Chapter 16

Asset Management for Server Hardware and Software

Because so much technology is now in use in just about any company and due to the sheer size and extent of today's enterprise IT department, managing server hardware and software has become more important than ever. In particular, attention must be given to inventory and license management, often referred to as IT asset management. In this chapter, we first take a detailed look at the asset management field and its value, the installed base, leading products, and more. We take a look at various asset management approaches, including the deployment of Microsoft Systems Management Server, as well as simple tools that take care of server hardware and software asset management without taking up much in the way of time and resources. This is an area anyone involved in server disk management really needs to know about; otherwise, you are unlikely to know exactly how many disks you have, where they are, and what type they are. Asset management software helps IT staff stay on the top of the game and in touch with the current deployment of disks, space quotas, and more throughout the enterprise.

The Asset Management Explosion

An explosion in the adoption of IT asset management software has occurred over the past few years. According to International Data Corporation (IDC; Framingham, Massachusetts), this market will grow from $1.1 billion in 2000 to $2.8 billion by 2004. A cursory search on the Web for vendors in this category revealed over 50, and that includes just those that were immediately findable. With so many vendors operating in this space, it is not surprising to learn that the installed base is already around the 40 million mark. About 85 percent of the large-site market, in particular, is already owned by tools such as Computer Associates' Asset Management Option (AMO), Microsoft Systems Management Server (SMS), IBM Tivoli, Novell ZenWorks, and Intel LANDesk Management, among others. These products include functions such as software distribution and configuration management. Among small to medium-sized organizations, however, only about one third have adopted asset management.

Hot Spots

Although asset management is not a new activity, two aspects of it still should be closely monitored: (1) keeping track of licenses in order to stay legally compliant and (2) accurately recording the hardware/software inventory for each machine. Without a means of automation, the load on system administrators is often so great that these actions are either omitted or not carried out thoroughly, and that presents a problem. Neglected asset management can really come back to bite you. Trade groups such as the Software and Information Industry Association (SIIA) and the Business Software Alliance (BSA) have become quite militant in enforcing software licensing. They have staged surprise audits and have levied hefty fines for unlicensed software use regardless if the cause is a simple recordkeeping error or unreported user installations anywhere on the site. They even have whistle-blowing hotlines for disgruntled and former employees to report violations.

According to the BSA, the value of pirated software comes to $3 billion annually in North America. Via surveys conducted each year, the BSA grades states on license compliance. The ten states that experienced the largest percentage point reduction in piracy from 2000 to 2001 were California, Colorado, Illinois, Maryland, Missouri, Nebraska, Nevada, New Hampshire, New York, and Utah. Such studies also serve to forward the BSA's message regarding the negative impact of software piracy on the nation's software industry and economy, including lost jobs, wages, and tax revenues. The BSA also emphasizes how piracy brings about a depletion of available funding for research and development.

According to one study, the U.S. software piracy rate was 25 percent in 2001, up one percentage point from 2000, and piracy was costing the nation $1.8 billion in retail sales of business software applications and more than 111,000 jobs. The BSA Web site advises businesses and consumers to take the following steps to adopt a corporate policy on compliance with copyright laws: audit company computers, document software purchases and understand licensing agreements, beware of prices that are too good to be true, and educate management and employees on their obligations under copyright laws.

The BSA takes a hard line on licensing violations, sweeping around the country, city by city and state by state. In the vanguard are often press releases announcing an amnesty for license violators; if users get their license payments

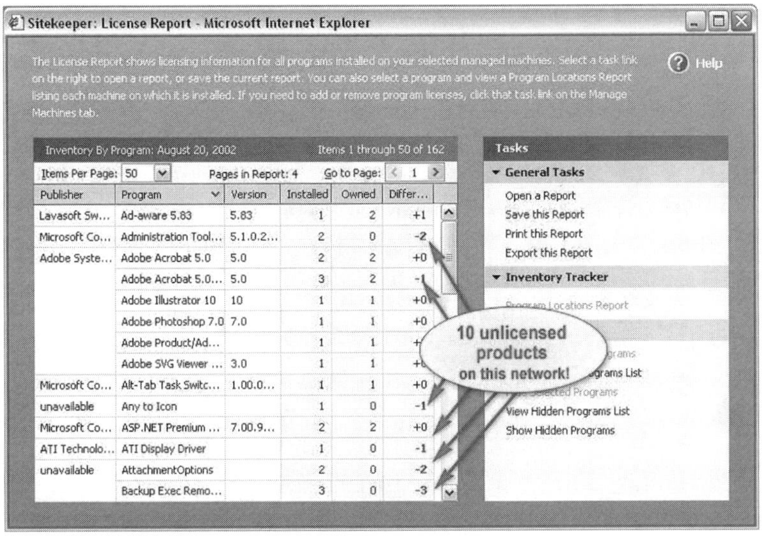

Exhibit 1   Unlicensed Software

in order before a specific date, they will not be held liable for any violations. After that date, however, enforcement actions come in to play. When a tip comes in, the BSA can take one of two paths to enforce compliance: (1) request a self-audit of the organization concerned or (2) stage an unannounced raid. Fines regularly exceed $100,000, and lawsuits are frequent. Also, the firms still have to pay out funds for the unlicensed software. Over the past decade, the BSA has collected about $80 million in penalties.

Unfortunately, too many organizations assume that if they get caught with unlicensed software on their computers, they will face the equivalent of a traffic ticket. In reality, federal copyright laws allow for up to $150,000 in damages for each work infringed. A visit to the BSA's Web site (www.bsa.org) and their press release section reveals document after document regarding the various companies that have settled with the BSA to avoid heavy penalties, and every one of them also paid in full for software licensing (Exhibit 1).

Piracy and Asset Management

As just discussed, software piracy is big business, although progress is being made in the fight against it. According to the BSA, worldwide software piracy rates dropped from 46 percent in 1995 to 37 percent in 2000. But, even so, the value of the software involved comes to $11.75 billion. In countries with lax copyright enforcement, such as China and Vietnam, over ninety percent of applications in use are illegal compared with 25 percent in North America, which is why some of the largest vendors, combatants on most other fronts, formed the BSA: Apple, Microsoft, Novell, Adobe, Macromedia, Symantec, and Network Associates, for example. The BSA, then, could be likened to the Internal Revenue Service of the software world in its aggressive pursuit of any violators. The BSA conducts public relations and advertising campaigns to promote the idea that unauthorized use of software constitutes theft and results in the loss of thousands of jobs, and it holds seminars and lobbies politicians to strengthen the enforcement of laws. But, what the BSA is best known for is its pursuit of businesses that do not have licenses for the copies of software they are using.

The BSA has adopted a "big stick" approach to enforcement and is not shy about publicizing its enforcement actions. And, bolstered by the penalty provisions of the Digital Millennium Copyright Act, the BSA has become increasingly active in enforcing software copyrights. The organization currently maintains hotlines in 65 countries, giving disgruntled employees the opportunity to call in to report violations. A report can lead to a self-audit or raid. Depending on the level of cooperation it receives, the BSA arranges for voluntary payment of a fine (regularly running in excess of $100,000) or initiates a lawsuit. Either way, the firm must still pay the vendor for the unlicensed software. But, some protest, sometimes it is no more than bad recordkeeping, not intentional fraud, or what if the IT staff has neglected their duties with regard to licensing or even falsely reported that all licensing was current? It does not matter. There is no getting off the hook. Take the example of Giroux Glass, Inc. In 2000, Ernst & Young named Giroux's chief executive officer as the Entrepreneur of the Year in the Los Angeles area, and in 2001 the company made its way onto *Inc.* magazine's Inner City 100 list. It also was one of six Los Angeles firms to pay the BSA a total of $450,000 in fines recently. In Giroux's case, it had relied on an outside consultant to manage its software licenses.

Asset Management Strata

In such a dangerous climate, it is understandable that many companies are keen to adopt asset management applications. That has led to an explosion in the number of vendors offering tools to satisfy this need. While greatly simplified, following are three distinct strata that can be identified:

- System/desktop management platforms that include asset management, configuration management, and a host of additional features
- Asset management suites that include software deployment or other features such as remote management
- Dedicated asset management utilities

System/Desktop Management Platforms

In this category, tools are geared mainly to large enterprises. They are packaged with features such as remote control, help desk, support for laptops/PDAs, and security. Most are priced around $100 per machine, though prices are falling. This echelon of management encompasses Radia Management Suite by Novadigm, Marimba's Software Management, On Command CCM by ON Technology, Argis by Intraware, Vision64 by SWAN Technology, Computer

Associates' Unicenter with AMO, LANDesk Management Suite by Intel, and Microsoft's SMS. Gartner Group notes that Novadigm's Radia Management Suite is the overall leader with the highest license growth rate. The company appears to be taking steps to monopolize the market, or at least a part of it. It has established several agreements with Hewlett-Packard to include Radia inside every commercial server sold and anything managed by Hewlett-Packard's Outsourcing Services Division. Other vendors have followed suit. Altiris software was included on Compaq desktops and laptops (10 million a year). With the Hewlett-Packard/Compaq merger, Hewlett-Packard offers Altiris software as part of its Client Management Suite. ON Technology software offered by Dell is an option that can be preinstalled on all commercial computer orders. IBM Services and Consulting recommends Tivoli to all its clients, while Computer Associates' huge Unicenter user base is a ready market for AMO.

New York City's Fordham University, for example, implemented Unicenter's AMO module to simplify asset management. The school has over 3000 faculty and staff spread among three campuses. All desktops are upgraded every three years as part of a lease agreement with Hewlett-Packard, but managing the software proved to be a nightmare. While Fordham had an asset management application, the IT staff still had to go around to each box and inventory the installed software and settings before manually entering the data into the asset management program. Needless to say, this was a seriously time-consuming task, and the data was frequently inaccurate. Fordham University decided to install Computer Associates' Unicenter AMO, which has a desktop agent that performs the inventory and sends the data to a central database. With AMO, Fordham can inventory the installed software at each user's desktop to find out which users have what applications and to determine the rate of frequency with which each client is utilizing the software. AMO gives the college an accurate representation of licensing needs without technicians having to leave the IT department.

By implementing AMO, Fordham is now able to conveniently collect a full inventory of all the hardware and software elements from every desktop machine running the AMO client. The data is automatically uploaded to a comprehensive resource where a complete history is kept and transferred to a comprehensive resource database. From that point, Fordham's IT team can conduct a wide range of queries to isolate systems by specific criteria and determine what upgrades and maintenance services should be performed. AMO provides IT with complete knowledge of desktop configurations, without their spending a lot of time physically tracking assets or manually inputting data that might very well be inaccurate. When IT personnel are freed from the data collection process, they can focus on providing technical support to university faculty and staff.

Note that the products in this category tend to be focused on the higher end of the market — the large enterprise where asset management tools have to include software deployment, systems management, configuration management, change management, and more. Mid-sized and smaller companies are more attracted to simpler asset management tools or mid-tier suites with a lower price tag.

Asset Management Suites

The middle-level applications consist of products that do asset management/ licensing as well as software deployment and sometimes remote capabilities. They are priced around $20 to $50 per node, although some are higher. Several products within the mid-market seem to be out in front in terms of user base. NetSupport TCO, LANutil32, Blue Ocean, Tally, and Vision 64, for example, each boast a user base of several million. Prices for some of these products are as low as $3 per license on large-site purchases. Other vendors with promising offerings in this area include Asset Management Suite by Altiris and Sitekeeper by Executive Software.

Asset Management Utilities

In this category are a host of companies that offer asset management/license management for $1 to $20 per node. Vendors include Peregrine Systems, Tangram, Centennial, E-Z Audit, TrackBird, Somix, and Blue Ocean. At least fifty products perform asset management, although some of these may lack the robustness demanded by an enterprise environment.

Microsoft Systems Management Server

In terms of cost, a quiet revolution is taking place inside this industry segment. Aggressive as ever on pricing, Microsoft is driving a price war by significantly lowering the going rate for SMS. According to one analyst, SMS has made this a commodity-type market. Officially, SMS costs $889 for 20 desktops, and server nodes are $1779 for 25 servers, but some users report obtaining licenses for one or two dollars as part of larger package deals. LANDesk is priced similarly. Just about everyone is following the SMS lead to lower prices, except Marimba, which remains over $100; however, vendors like to keep discounts close to their chests, so these prices may actually go much lower during negotiations.

Lack of simplicity, though, seems to be the bugbear of SMS and other high-tier and many mid-tier products. Novadigm, LANDesk, and SMS are all accused of excessive complexity by users and analysts. Marimba has made a play against the Novadigm market share by saying it is much simpler and more accurate. Microsoft SMS, too, suffers from complexity. Despite each SMS release stressing how it is far simpler than the previous version, Microsoft still has a long way to go to make SMS truly user friendly.

Nevertheless, Microsoft has been successfully using its market clout to penetrate the systems and software management markets. By offering its SMS at low cost, sometimes free with the purchase of other products, the company has made some progress in expanding the SMS installed base. Although Internet Explorer grabbed more than ninety percent share of the browser market from Netscape, Microsoft's SMS has largely failed to capture the imagination of systems managers primarily due to such factors as complexity and lack of functionality, but that may be changing, as Microsoft has been working hard to address these faults and produce an easy-to-use, full-functionality version of SMS

Microsoft SMS 2.0 addresses software distribution, asset management, and remote troubleshooting:

- *Software Distribution*. The software distribution function deploys applications, software updates, and operating systems over the network. It can also remove already installed software. Rather than having to deploy the software to all desktops from a single server, it can send the software package out to site servers to distribute the packages locally, reducing bandwidth requirements. It works with most Windows client versions with the exception of Windows XP Home Edition, 64-bit Windows XP, and Windows XP Embedded (see Chapter 14).
- *Asset Management*. The asset management function of SMS inventories all Windows-based software and the machines it runs on. This includes servers, desktops, and laptops. It collects the hardware data using Win32, Simple Network Manage Protocol (SNMP), and the Desktop Management Task Force's Desktop Management Interface (DMI) protocol for centralized inventorying and managing of desktops. It inventories the software by checking each installed executable for version and other information rather than looking at a specific database such as the registry. It also includes a software metering function for monitoring and controlling usage to avoid licensing violations, something that Microsoft is particularly interested in even if its customers are sometimes less concerned about it.
- *Remote Troubleshooting*. The SMS troubleshooting functions allow support staff to remotely troubleshoot desktops, laptops, and servers, eliminating the need to visit the units in person, thereby cutting down on costs while providing faster response time and higher first-call resolution rates.

The main problem with SMS, some say, is that it is not exactly what you would call an out-of-the-box tool. A study by NerveWire, Inc. (Boston, Massachusetts) found that it took mid-sized and large enterprises an average of four full-time employees working 36 days to pilot SMS 2.0. After that, it took five personnel fifty days, on average, to roll out SMS. Anyone planning to deploy SMS, therefore, should be well versed in the application by taking Microsoft courses on it and conducting thorough research on how others have fared during the implementation stage.

Microsoft Press offers a host of texts and courses. The Systems Management Server 2.0 Training Kit is one example. It contains an 800-page training guide, plus a CD with supplemental course materials. Alternatively, instructor-led classes, such as the one-day Microsoft Official Curriculum course, are available, as are three- and five-day courses on how to administer, deploy, and support SMS.

Microsoft's efforts to simplify SMS appear to be paying off. While SMS 1.2 required the user to be something of a rocket scientist, the learning curve on version 2.0 is not nearly as steep. That said, the best bet is to hire a Microsoft Certified Solution Provider to assist in implementing SMS and offer advice on best practices, which may take some of the complexity out of the deployment.

Although SMS certainly beats deploying software manually, the NerveWire study found that it still takes about four days of preparation to deploy one update to a thousand workstations. On top of that, its takes a day or two to address machines where installation has failed. Veteran SMS users, however, refute these findings, stating that once users know what they are doing, SMS is much faster to utilize.

So, those who have already purchased SMS or are planning to should make sure to have a realistic estimation of the effort required to deploy it. There is no substitute for know-how, obtained by enrolling in courses, hiring well-trained SMS specialists, or bringing in consultants to deploy it. SMS also enjoys plenty of newsgroup support for help in getting the product up and running.

As an alternative, Microsoft also offers a free downloadable tool called the Microsoft Software Inventory Analyzer, but it only notes what versions of Microsoft's own software are on the network.

Simplifying Asset Management

One tool that does a good job of solving these installation, cost, and simplicity issues is OStivity by Somix Technologies (Sanford, Maine). This is a hybrid approach to the market, suited to both small and large systems. It costs less than $5000 and can be used on any number of machines. For a business of 50,000 desktops, this works out to a dime per node. For small businesses or enterprises that want to pilot this tool on a branch office or test it for possible corporate adoption, a 50-license version can be downloaded free with no time expiration from www.somix.com.

OStivity is a desktop and server hardware/software inventory tool that works on Windows, UNIX, Linux, and other platforms. It does not require manual loading on every machine, it is Web based, and it answers asset questions such as what software has been installed companywide, how many copies are out there, how many more licenses should be purchased, and which employees are using this software.

Currently, this tool gathers data such as operating systems in use, operating system revisions and service packs installed, CPU speed, available and total physical memory, available and total virtual memory, available and total page memory, available and total hard drive space for all drive letters and partitions, software inventory (including package name, revision, and publisher information), network information (including Hostname, IP Address, DNS information, Gateway, MAC address, Subnet Mask if DHCP is enabled, and NIC), and Routing Table information (including protocol used, TCP/IP port number, and local and foreign addresses). Users can apply filters to all the above information to locate the information they need.

In addition, OStivity can be used to determine if people have installed software that the company prohibits. Software such as network games, instant messengers, and internet radio streamers, for example, can consume bandwidth. Administrators can locate these packages rapidly. Also, in order to inventory a workstation or server, an executable is run from a log-in script.

Exhibit 2   OStivity Screenshot

Systems are inventoried without installing agents or client software and without consuming noticeable overhead. A decent range of report templates is also available (Exhibit 2).

While at first glance, this appears to be a simple software/hardware inventory tool, its designers included a lot more. It locates trouble spots, recognizes trends, and helps resolve network issues. A UNIX CRON-like utility allows users to schedule asset management as well as many other tasks, and it works well in conjunction with third-party alarm monitoring packages such as Ipswich's WhatsUp Gold.

OStivity is packaged with a mySQL database but runs on any SQL-based database. A search engine makes finding answers relatively straightforward. To run advanced searches for specific information, users can type in SQL database queries. Users can also, for instance, schedule an event to search the database every morning for any resources that violate preset thresholds and to notify the help desk before a user experiences performance problems — for example, when hard drives are low on disk space or CPUs are below a certain acceptable megahertz level.

Chapter 17

Software Deployment and Distribution on Windows Platforms

Purchasing software is an expensive proposition for any enterprise, but license fees are only a small percentage of the total cost of ownership (TCO) of software. Deploying it, managing the licenses, and installing patches/upgrades are actually far more expensive than the software itself. And, if software is not kept up to date and properly inventoried, one is vulnerable to legal problems, huge fines, and hacker attacks. With so many challenges inherent in using software, it is essential that companies be aware of these dangers, as well as what can be done to overcome them such as employing the proper tools to minimize risk and exposure. Although the previous chapter addressed one aspect of this problem, asset management, perhaps a more vital activity these days is that of software deployment and distribution. Software deployment addresses the area of how to get new applications, upgrades, patches, and the latest antivirus signatures out to every single server and desktop throughout the enterprise. The "sneakernet" may have been good enough in the mid-1990s, but it has no place in the 21st century.

Deployment Complexity

Software management used to be fairly simple. The enterprise either wrote its own customized applications and took care of a limited number of changes internally or depended upon a company such as IBM to put together a complete package. Changes could be made on the mainframe over a weekend. Nowadays, though, it is more a matter of assembling software from many different vendors and figuring out how to get them to work together in a harmonious fashion. Calls for a return to those seemingly simpler days, however, fail to take into account technology advances and the explosion in the number of applications in use on enterprise networks. Gartner Group reports that in 1996 the average help desk supported only 25 applications, but by 2001 that number had mushroomed to 200. It is not unknown for some companies to possess over 1000 applications. Adding to the confusion, usage of laptops and PDAs has experienced tremendous growth in recent years. Employees not only expect the latest software on these devices, but they also demand access to enterprise applications from their home computers.

Security Breaches

Computer security must take care of threats from both within the company and without. The seventh annual Computer Crime and Security Survey, released in April 2002 by the Computer Security Institute (CSI; www.gocsi.com) and the San Francisco Federal Bureau of Investigation's Computer Intrusion Squad, found that 90 percent of respondents had detected computer security breaches. The losses are staggering. The 223 survey respondents willing to quantify their losses reported total damage at over $455 million (see Chapter 10), and that is just the tip of the iceberg. The CERT Coordination Center at Carnegie Mellon University in Pittsburgh received over 52,000 security incident reports last year, more than double the previous year. Some estimate total losses worldwide may top $100 billion annually. According to the Internet Security Alliance (Arlington, Virginia; www.isalliance.org), three attacks — Code Red, SirCam, and Love Bug — cost corporations more than $13 billion.

While external attacks are serious enough, the threat posed by one's own employees can often be much worse. External attackers are rarely motivated enough to do much damage, do not know what to look for, and are more likely to just stumble into an intrusion detection system. On the other hand, the attacks that tend to hurt most generally come from disgruntled employees who are motivated to do harm. In the CSI survey just mentioned, for example, one third of respondents stated that their internal systems were a frequent point of attack. Another study of 146 companies by Activis (Reading, England) paints a more grim picture: 81 percent of security breaches originated internally, another 13 percent came from ex-employees, and 6 percent came from external hackers. It is these disgruntled current or former employees who steal trade secrets, sell employee lists to headhunters, or plant "time bombs" to bring down the network months after they leave.

In addition to deliberate attacks, employees can compromise a system inadvertently. Seventy-eight percent of the respondents in the CSI survey reported employee abuse of Internet access privileges such as downloading pornography or pirated software. Although doing so represents improper use of company time and resources, it also exposes the company to huge fines from the Business Software Alliance or Software and Information Industry Association.

Securing the Walls

Computer security used to mean that the system administrator had to lock the door to the server room when going out for a cup of coffee or when leaving for the day. Later, it simply meant convincing users not to load copies of their favorite programs onto the network illegally (and without concern for security compatibility issues) via floppies. Now, with Internet connections running into main servers, security techniques resemble the moats and turrets of a medieval walled city. Yet, despite the billions of dollars currently spent on firewalls, antivirus software, and security consultants, new worms and viruses wreak havoc on enterprise systems throughout the world several times a year. Of course, no security patch can prevent some gullible or ill-advised user from opening infected e-mail attachments. According to managed security services firm Activis, though, the underlying problem lies with system management and administration. Activis reports that 99 percent of all attacks are readily preventable because they come from known vulnerabilities and misconfigurations. Many of these problems are well publicized in the media before a major attack hits the firm, and patches or signature updates are usually available.

But time is not on the side of the system administrator, as vulnerabilities tend to show up quickly. Take Windows XP, for example, and its 1.5-GB of code. Within three weeks of its release, Internet security firm eEye Digital Security, Inc. (Aliso Viejo, California) located three flaws that made it possible for a hacker to take over a computer at the system level and use it for distributed denial of service attacks. Because more than seven million copies of XP were sold in the first two weeks of its launch, it is easy to see how much of a potential threat this originally posed to the Internet structure running on these machines. Even the patch Microsoft issued to fix these bugs may not be enough to resolve the problem, as the FBI's National Infrastructure Protection Center has advised users to disable XP's Universal Plug-n-Play feature in order to prevent vulnerability to these attacks. This is not to single out Microsoft. Many other software products have been found to contain security bugs. It is just that Microsoft is an easy target for hackers. Why would someone design something that would attack Apple's percentage of the desktop market when Microsoft's 94 percent share could be hit instead?

So, why do hackers cause such severe problems to the corporate world? In most cases, it comes down to the time and personnel required to keep up with all the necessary patches and version updates. A study conducted by Activis found that, in a company with only eight fire walls and nine servers running common software, an IT manager would have had to make 1315 updates in the first nine months of 2001, which is an average of seven per working day.

XP Patches

Consider again the example of Windows XP. One of the main reasons given for switching to it was the greatly enhanced security features of the operating system, and as just discussed, buyers snatched up more than seven million copies of the software within the first two weeks of its release. Within the first three weeks, however, security firm eEye Digital had already located three major holes, including one that would allow an attacker to take over the computer at the system level. It took another five weeks to develop the patch. Fortunately, in this case the vulnerability was located by a security firm, rather than some hackers, so that the first press on it was when the patch was released, not when millions of computers started crashing. Based on past experience, however, many machines will not be upgraded and someone will maliciously exploit those holes.

Automated Software Deployment

Whether one is concerned with license compliance or keeping hackers at bay, it is impossible to address the problem manually. In the week of January 16, 2002, alone, for example, 50 virus definitions were added to Norton Antivirus. In response to this situation of having to get out hundreds of updates to thousands or tens of thousands of desktops and servers, a fairly new brand of software has evolved dealing with software deployment and distribution. In its simplest form, IT personnel must go from desktop to desktop to load this deployment software. Once it is on every machine, however, new updates and upgrades can be transmitted to each box relatively quickly. A more sophisticated approach to this problem, fortunately, is now starting to become the standard — loading the software onto one server and having it take care of update distribution automatically without IT intervention. Thus, a systems manager can decide to send the latest virus signatures once a day to all users and set up the server to relay the updates without any further effort.

Next we take a look at the main approaches to automated software deployment and software management. Some are appropriate for large organizations, others for smaller outfits. The key is to understand the software deployment marketplace, the tools available, and the enterprise's needs and current infrastructure; at that point, the choice of approach will become obvious.

Frameworks and Software Deployment

Large enterprises have the option of using network management frameworks such as IBM's Tivoli, Computer Associates' Unicenter TNG, or Hewlett-Packard's Openview. For entities that have already installed such a system, it is probably best to utilize the vendor's inventory/deployment modules. New York City's Fordham University, for example, implemented Computer Associate's Unicenter Software Deployment Option (SDO) along with the Asset Management Option (AMO). The school's three campuses and over 3000 desktops represented a significant problem when it came time to load new applications. Thousands of hours were consumed by IT, with deployment of Microsoft Office alone taking a team of two IT staff several months to load on every desktop. Now, instead of loading applications by hand, IT staff use

SDO to automatically distribute applications throughout the university's distributed IT environment, without leaving the institution's primary support facilities.

Microsoft Tools and Software Deployment

For Windows networks, an alternative approach is to use Microsoft's Systems Management Server (SMS) 2.0, which has both inventory and deployment functions. SMS normally requires a dedicated server and is less expensive and quicker to install than a management framework. SMS was the route taken by Los Alamos National Laboratory (www.lanl.gov). In addition to having two of the world's eight fastest supercomputers for modeling nuclear reactions, the laboratory also has 11,000 desktops. Although it needed to ensure its security functions were top notch, labor requirements made this prohibitive. The laboratory's Information Architecture (IA) team for desktop systems calculated that, even if only one updated virus definition, a single operating system patch, and one browser patch were installed each month, it would take 87 staff working full time (at an average of 19 updates per person per day) to manually keep up with the changes. The IA team simply did not have the personnel to do this, so they decided to investigate enterprisewide desktop management (DM) systems. After evaluating several DM products, they piloted Microsoft's SMS and then rolled it out to five sites serving more than 1500 desktops. In a nine-month period, the SMS team produced and distributed over 70 software packages with a total technical resource investment of 210 person-days. To do the same job manually would have required 5530 person-days.

Implementing a DM system, however, involved significant startup costs including buying a server and paying for all the software licenses, as well as hiring the tech personnel. For a 150-user group, these costs came to $272,541, or $1,817 per client. The IA team discovered, however, that as they rolled out SMS across a larger and larger portion of its overall organization, more attractive economies of scale come into play that eventually brought the cost per client down to less than $200. SMS goes way beyond software deployment, into the areas of remote desktop support and network management. This added functionality, however, also means added complexity for deployment and administration. SMS is not something one can take out of the box, load, and put to use. So, before deploying it, an enterprise must make sure it has available IT resources with the experience to cope with it.

Site Licensing/Tracking Software

The above approaches are comprehensive solutions, but can be overkill — too complex or expensive for someone who wants to deal with the immediate problem of managing licenses and updates. A full framework, for example, typically comes with a price tag of hundreds of thousands or millions of dollars and can take over a year to put in place — not the sort of pace

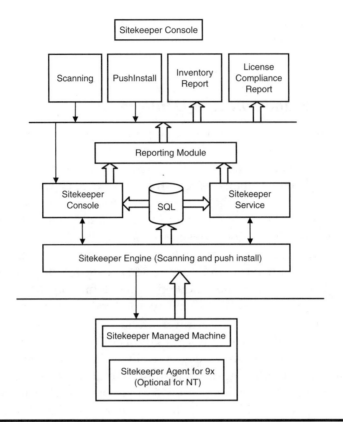

Exhibit 1   Sitekeeper High-Level Data/Control Flow Diagram

required when the BSA might come knocking at any moment. Luckily, several easier and quicker approach to software deployment and licensing are available. Dedicated deployment tools take care of the software deployment and distribution task without burdening users with all the bells and whistles of a framework or SMS. One of the better ones is Executive Software's Sitekeeper. This is a tightly focused tool dealing with automated software distribution, inventory, updating, and license tracking that costs about $15 per machine for large enterprises (Exhibit 1).

After installing Sitekeeper, the first step is to launch Inventory Tracker, which contains a setup wizard to guide the administrator through the process of designating which domains or machines to inventory and how often. It does not install any agents on the workstations but scans the Windows Registry to gather software names, versions (major and minor), build number or patch level, and name of publisher. It typically inventories five to ten machines per second, so a thousand-user network would be done in two to three minutes. Data is stored in a database, and a browser-based inventory report is generated. This shows both the inventory on each machine, as well as which machines have a particular product installed.

Another module, License Tracker, generates a license report based on the completed inventory. The administrator enters the number of licenses purchased, and the report informs the administrator if the organization has excess licenses, if it needs to purchase some more, and if users are installing software locally without permission. From there on out, the module will continue to notify the administrator as licenses expire or new inventories show changes in license status.

Sitekeeper's PushInstall is of most relevance to software deployment. This feature remotely installs and uninstalls software, updates, upgrades, and patches. It works with any Windows 2000, XP, or Microsoft installer-compliant program, as well as most software designed for NT. Software, updates, and patches can be scheduled to use minimum resources, which takes a little longer but has less impact on users. When speed is more important, such as when installing a new virus definition, the administrators can run the program at a higher priority. Once the administrator selects the target machines or domains and the installation speed, the program automatically installs the software and reports the results of each installation back to the administrator.

Sitekeeper is a quick-to-implement, simple-to-run, and inexpensive software management application. For those looking for a "set it and forget it" method of staying on top of licensing and software management headaches, it does the job well.

Software Deployment Case Study

- *Organization* — Unisea, Inc. (Redmond, Washington, and Dutch Harbor, Alaska; www.unisea.com).
- *Business/mission* — Unisea is one of the world's leading fish product companies, with peak production of over 60 metric tons of fish per hour.
- *Goal* — The primary goal was to create accurate hardware and software inventories and ensure license compliance; the secondary goal was to be able to run routine checks for users installing unauthorized software.
- *Scope* — Software is installed at two locations, the headquarters in Washington and the processing facility in Alaska; the company has about 1200 employees.
- *Solution* — Executive Software's Sitekeeper was installed to automate inventorying, deployment, and license compliance.
- *Results* — Inventories are now taken and maintained automatically. Routine deployment of software updates has been reduced to one hour per site during normal business hours (no more coming in early or working late).
- *Cost savings* — Personnel time required for software updates was reduced 85 percent; process revealed that the company had more software licenses than it needed.

For many years, Unisea systems staff performed updates and inventories manually. Administrators tracked licenses using paper and pen, consolidating various notes into an Excel spreadsheet. Similarly, deploying software updates required visits to every desktop every time a new patch came in, and IT staff worked nights going from box to box to install the latest patch. As a result, their workload became backlogged and critical updates were delayed. Unisea purchased Sitekeeper by Executive Software to automate these processes and

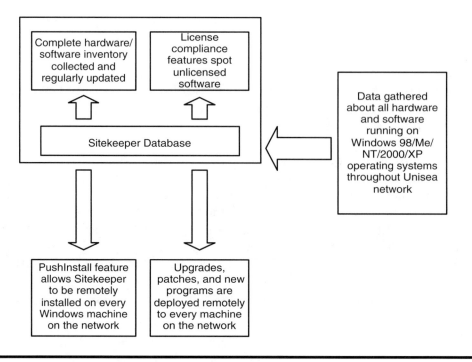

Exhibit 2   Unisea's Sitekeeper Architecture

to add the capability of checking company machines periodically for unauthorized software (Exhibit 2).

Unisea uses a mix of Windows NT 4.0 and Windows 2000 servers running in a NT 4.0 domain. This meant that Unisea did not have to install any agents on these boxes, as Sitekeeper works without agents on Windows NT, 2000, and XP boxes, which greatly speeded up installation because the software had to be loaded only on the host machine in order to automatically inventory all client boxes at a rate of about ten per second.

While many firms are concerned about license compliance because of the huge penalties that could be incurred following surprise audits from policing bodies such as the BSA or SIIA, this was not a concern for Unisea. The company had purchased enough licensing; in fact, initial inventories revealed that the company had actually paid for more licenses on some software than it needed.

The benefits experienced from automated inventorying, though, were overshadowed by the amount of time saved in software deployment utilizing Sitekeeper's PushInstall feature. In one sixty-day period, for example, two critical Internet Explorer (IE) security patches came out. Unfortunately, Microsoft decided to release these IE patches individually by version, rather than one release covering a range of versions. Earlier, an update like this would have meant that Unisea IT staff would have had to go around to each box to apply the appropriate patches. Manually installing patches could require the IT staff to come in at 4:00 in the morning or work late into the evening so they would not have to kick users off their machines. Depending on existing priorities, it could take days or even weeks for every machine receive the update. Using Sitekeeper, however, the system administrator identified the various IE versions on each box and remotely applied the appropriate patch to every workstation and server. This reduced the workload from two days to a few minutes. Today, Unisea updates software as soon as a patch comes in, even during business hours; thus, system security is enhanced as known vulnerabilities are immediately remedied. Further, it means that all needed updates do get done, as opposed to being lost in the line behind scores of other updates.

Do You Feel Lucky?

Perhaps it is not absolutely necessary for organizations to put a software management system in place, and some may never experience a problem. But, with hackers and the BSA on the prowl, it is a little like answering "Yes" to Clint Eastwood's Dirty Harry when he asks, "Do you feel lucky?" Ignoring the problem, then, will not make it go away. Most organizations have unlicensed software lurking somewhere, as well as desktops galore without the latest vital updates. The choice is simple: Take care of the problem quickly or risk hackers bringing the network down and the BSA paying an unexpected visit. If you already have a management framework in place, adding the inventory and deployment modules is possibly the best option, but those without an existing large-scale system would probably prefer to avoid the investment in time and expense typically associated with their implementation. SMS offers a simpler alternative to a traditional framework, but again it is not specifically tailored to software management. If an enterprise is already using SMS as a management tool, it should be a simple matter of activating its software management features or upgrading to a more current version of SMS that contains these functions. Although less complex than frameworks, SMS has a definite learning curve and should only be deployed in organizations with skilled and available IT staff.

If, on the other hand, you are interested in an immediate solution to software inventorying, compliance, and distribution without spending nearly as much, it is probably best to purchase a dedicated application designed for ease of use. With such products, quick downloads and installations take care of software upgrades, updates, and license tracking. And, maybe best of all, you will never have to worry about a recently fired employee or competitor giving the BSA a ring on your behalf.

Chapter 18

The Future of Disks and Disk Management

How prepared are you to meet the disk needs of the future in order to keep up with storage demands? Where exactly is the industry going and how big can disks get? Will disks be around forever? This chapter investigates what is just out or about to come out in the disk management field, as well as what is on the horizon and perhaps just beyond. It includes a discussion of current and expected speeds of hard disks, faster data transfer, and disk densities, as well as the specifics of various disks out there on the market or expected to be soon.

The Storage Industry Is Healthy

The last couple of years have been rather unkind to the tech industry as a whole. PC sales have slumped, actually declining in the United States for the first time. The formerly booming world of broadband has narrowed considerably, highlighted by the demise of such previous high fliers as Global Crossing, Rhythm Networks, and WorldCom. Even traditional industry stalwarts such as AT&T have faltered badly in the telecom shuffle — AT&T has gone from investing tens of billions into broadband via acquisitions and infrastructure buildup to selling its broadband division to Comcast at a steep discount. Further, dot.coms have bombed across the board, leaving few survivors from the wave of hysteria that gripped us only two or three years ago.

But, despite all the bad news, the fundamental requirements for sound basic technology are still there. Nowhere is this more obvious than in the storage arena. Driven by the need for information sharing and increasing usage of multimedia applications, the demand for storage capacity shows no signs of abating. In fact it just keeps rising every year. According to Forrester

Research (Cambridge, Massachusetts) enterprise storage requirements are growing at about 52 percent annually, and the storage industry is responding by coming up with bigger, better, and faster disk drives at a rapid rate in order to keep up with the incredible demand.

In fact, storage capacity is actually outstripping Moore's law, an oft-quoted law that states that CPUs double in size every 18 months or so. The drive industry, in comparison, has been setting a much faster pace. According to a briefing given by Maxtor Corporation (Milpitas, California), drive capacity has been increasing at 100 to 140 percent annually. Other drive manufacturers are making similar claims.

Besides disk size, several other crucial changes are taking shape that will have a major effect on disk performance. Disk speed is going to soar after a period of relative inactivity, and disk management capabilities will be increased once again. During the following examination of advances on each of these fronts, remember that the advancement rate is so fast that very soon the figures and information given below may well be dated.

Faster Data Transfer

Much has been written about how processors and PC buses have kept boosting clock rates higher and higher. Far less attention, though, has been paid to the fact that disk drives, by and large, have matched this pace with ever faster data transfer rates. Just look at some of the advances in the last few years alone. For ATA (IDE) disks, for example, we had the release of the Ultra DMA (UDMA) standard in 1998 which offered transfer modes of up to 33 MBps. That was quickly followed in 1999 by further gains that meant that 66 MBps became the standard. By 2000, however, 66 MBps paled in comparison to the new 100-MBps standard. The end of 2001 again heralded even greater speeds with the announcement of the Ultra ATA/133 interface specification with a 133-MBps data rate.

Not to be outdone, the SCSI drive has also been making great strides. The SCSI Trade Association, in fact, has had a very busy year. Besides recently celebrating the SCSI's 13th anniversary, it released the seventh generation of the standard, Ultra320 SCSI. It is designed for servers, network storage, high-end workstations, and RAID storage applications. This new bus operates at 320 MBps — twice as fast as the sixth-generation spec. The group also reports that Ultra640 is firmly in the works. When that comes out, the data transfer rate on SCSI will double once again.

External hard drives also have advances worthy of note. The 400-Mbps FireWire connection standard (IEEE 1394), for example, is gaining popularity. Because of the improving data transfer rate, these devices are now becoming adequate for multimedia applications, such as digital video editing, as well as backing up internal hard drives.

According to Cahners In-Stat (Newton, Massachusetts), over 35 million PC-based and consumer electronics products supporting FireWire were shipped in 2002, with a predicted annual growth rate of 30 percent. Further, the Converging Markets and Technologies Group at Cahners In-Stat predicts that, because of their ease of use and high performance, we will see continued growth for IEEE 1394 devices. It is expected that by 2005 more than 200 million products will ship with the interface.

On the speed front, though, the actual rotation speed of disks has not improved quite so quickly, as 7500 rpm has been standard in PCs for quite some time, as has 10,000 rpm in many server systems. More recently, 15,000-rpm drives have begun to appear, although they have yet to be made available in the greater than 100-GB sizes of their 10,000-rpm counterparts. What does the extra 5000 rpm buy for the enterprise? For lengthy film or video edits, for example, where the head does not have to move much as it reads a huge block of data sequentially off a disk, a 50 percent improvement can be obtained with a 15,000-rpm drive. But, what about the more common scenario where you have loads of small I/Os with multiple users accessing a server or applications where data is read from all over the disk in quick succession? The good news is that the faster drives still provide a noticeable performance gain — perhaps as much as 40 percent.

Bigger and Better Drives

In addition to speed, drive capacity has also experienced continual growth over the past few years, and the race continues. Everybody knows all about the Intel vs. AMD sprint for the CPU holy grail of the time — the 1-GHz processor. Once the dust settled on that race a couple of years back, another race started up at once to exceed 2 GB of storage capacity. Most recently, the computer world just witnessed another contest to determine who would be the winner of the 3-GB dash. It has been pretty much the same among disk manufacturers, who keep announcing bigger and better disks, with capacities now reaching well over 100 GB. Seagate, for example, has already begun shipping its 180-GB Barracuda 180. By the time you read this, we will no doubt be well beyond the 200-GB barrier. It is not surprising that Gartner Group predicts that, based on the current annual doubling of capacity, 1.44-TB disks will be on the market by mid-2004.

Recent Developments

Recent developments will help manufacturers reach this level. During 2001, Maxtor, Microsoft, Compaq, and others announced a new interface standard for ATA hard drives (called "Big Drives") that will allow the drives to scale from the current limit of 137 GB up to 144 petabytes. Maxtor has released a 10-K SCSI hard disk drive, the Maxtor Atlas 10K IV. This will be quickly followed up with a 15-K class drive. Both drives incorporate Maxtor's second-generation U320 SCSI interface. The 10-K drive has an average seek time of 4.4 ms and a sustained data rate of 72 MBps. At the time of writing it was available in 36-, 73-, and 146-GB capacities. Seagate then set an areal density storage record — over 100 billion data bits per square inch (100 GB/in.^{2}) using a magnetic recording head and multilayer antiferromagnetic coupled (AFC) disc. In effect, this allows 125 GB of data to be stored on a single 3.5-inch platter, compared with the current 40 GB.

Seagate also demonstrated the industry's first native serial ATA hard drive implementation at a recent PC Expo in New York. The companies connected a new Barracuda ATA V hard drive incorporating a native serial ATA interface running at full speed to an Intel motherboard in a PC game box. The serial ATA interface provided a throughput of 150 MBps. This breakthrough is expected to allow more complex, flexible, and intelligent storage systems. This serial ATA hard drive could also see a major change in the data center. Until now, companies preferred disk arrays configured with SCSI-attached drives for the storage of mission-critical data. Lower cost ATA drives were mainly used in PCs but tended to miss out in servers and particularly in data centers due to performance and reliability limitations. That may be changing, as the likes of EMC and Network Appliance are releasing ATA drives inside storage devices using serial ATA technology. This effectively boosts data throughput from 100 MBps for a parallel ATA drive to 150 MBps for the moment, moving up as high as 600 MBps within a couple of years.

Other companies such as 3Ware (Sunnyvale, California) are planning to release serial ATA RAID controllers and drives that offer performance similar to a SCSI while prices remain in the ATA price range; however, it may be a while before serial ATA catches up completely with SCSI, so the use of SCSI-based RAID will likely still dominate for the immediate future.

Fujitsu Drives

Another company at the forefront of disk innovation is Fujitsu. This company has quietly moved up to number two in the enterprise hard disk drive market and is rising rapidly. According to Gartner Group, Fujitsu now ships 21.3 percent of the world's 19 million enterprise class drives. Some of its most recent product offerings focus on removable and mobile disks, while others are suitable for enterprise servers.

2.3-GB MO Drive

A removal storage solution from Fujitsu, the 2.3-GB magnetic-to-optical (MO) disk drive is ideal for backup. It offers a data transfer rate of 8 MBps.

2.5-Inch MHS Mobile Disk Drive

The Fujitsu MHS Series 2.5-inch disk drives feature up to 30 GB per platter data capacity, a 9.5-mm form factor, fast Ultra ATA/100 interface, and 4200-rpm spindle speed.

15-K MAS Series 3.5-Inch Disk Drive

The Fujitsu MAS series disk drive is a high performance enterprise server and high-end workstation type of disk. This drive achieves areal densities of 33.1 GB/in^2 and 15,000-rpm rotational speed. It has an 8-MB cache buffer with 32-bit path for faster data access. An Ultra 320 SCSI interface offers host data transfer rates of up to 320 MBps. Average seek time is 3.5 ms, with a mean time between failures (MTBF) of 1,200,000 (although this does not mean that the universe will end before one of these disks will ever fail; see Chapter 3).

Upcoming Fujitsu Read Head and Media Technologies

Fujitsu also has some exciting developmental work ongoing in the hard drive field. It has developed new read head and media technologies, for example, that will provide hard drive recording densities of up to 300 GB/in^2. Though still in the prototyping stage, they are expected to be in full commercial deployment within two or three years. The new head, for example, features a current perpendicular-to-plane mode, giant magneto resistive (GMR) head that achieves more than three times the playback output levels of current hard drives by allowing current to flow perpendicular to the GMR element. Existing GMR read heads operate in the current in-plane mode and are not expected to scale beyond about 100 GB/in^2 areal density due to their small signal output level. In support of these developments, Fujitsu also just announced a linear density of over 1 million flux changes per inch on synthetic ferromagnetic media with longitudinal recording, making possible greatly expanded areal densities.

What the Future Holds

What does the future hold for hard drives? In addition to major improvements in monitoring tools, we can look forward to even greater storage capacity. Although several exciting new technologies (e.g., using DNA molecules) can greatly boost capacity, traditional magnetic disks will be with us in the enterprise for a long time. So, yes, disks will probably eventually disappear, but it will not be for many years to come, and even then they probably will go on to live far longer than predicted, much in the same way that tape drives are still very much alive and well, over a decade after the industry sounded their death knell.

Similarly, in the area of data preservation, RAID will continue to gain popularity. Until recently its price tag has limited its application to the more expensive and critical servers. That appears to be changing, with RAID now being standard in most mid-sized machines and even appearing more often in lower-end models.

A greater shift toward centralized storage will occur at the enterprise level. Although 92 percent of the market is currently using direct attached storage,

Forrester predicts that by 2003 the use of both Network Attached Storage (NAS) and Storage Area Networks (SAN) will double. At the other end of the spectrum is a growing need for portable disks, such as those used in digital cameras and MP3 players.

One major void still has to be filled, though: heterogeneous disk monitoring tools that can be run across a network. One vendor recently made a valiant, but unsuccessful, attempt to provide this service. It ran afoul of the proprietary nature of RAID arrays and disk controllers. Most manufacturers do a fine job of providing tools that help users run that vendor's own disks; however, these tools rarely do very well with other manufacturers' products. Yet, what organization has only one make of disk throughout the enterprise? As a result, IT managers are forced to go from console to console to read alerting lights and event logs in multiple management systems, not to mention going to various physical locations to check on disk health.

The ideal would be one screen that operates irrespective of disk type or model and that tells users everything they need to know about their disks — their performance (using many parameters such as throughput and error rates), speed, indications of imminent failure, free space, quota information, and more. The SMART standard built into many current disks was a start, but it has too many limitations and was implemented in much too proprietary a fashion to be really useful.

Compaq Insight Manager (CIM) took things a step further. The latest version allows users to monitor drives, CPUs, and other devices on Compaq as well as some other vendor machines. It is hoped that Hewlett-Packard will retain it and expand it, but even CIM left us in the hole when it came to white box servers, and it was not that great with non-Compaq machines. I expect someone will step forward to fill the gap, providing a method that either bypasses vendor proprietary controls or unites the vendors in acceptance of a standard and opening up their architectures (a long shot). Any takers? When, or if, this utility ever arrives, it will offer what IT needs more than ever — a way to easily manage and monitor all the drives and a means of predicting usage and preventing disastrous failures. With that in hand, disk management would become much simpler for all concerned.

Conclusion

In the meantime, armed with the tools and materials covered in this work, the reader should be able to make better headway through the rough waters of disk management. Regular defragmentation will help keep systems stable and disks performing faster and with far fewer errors. Those who keep their disks free of fragmentation report that they experience far fewer crashes and disk failures on Windows. Disk quotas will help maintain order in the challenging world of storage and space management; where systems are constantly short of user space, quota tools can provide a means to predict consumption easily and plan for it. Disaster recovery planning and non-catastrophic contingency plans prepare users for whatever data loss situations they might face, small or large. And, most importantly, a thorough knowledge of the basics of hard disks, file systems, backups, and hard drive reliability provides enough understanding to properly manage an enterprise's disks and get the most out of its servers.

Appendix A:
Glossary of Terms

Access Time: A combination of seek time plus rotational latency. This gives the time it takes to access a cluster. Sometimes, people use the term *seek time* interchangeably with *access time*.

ATA (Advanced Technology Attachment) Drives: First used for the IBM PC/ AT computer; AT, short for Advanced Technology, was a term originally used by IBM in 1984.

Backup: In general English usage, the concept of backup means a reserve or substitute; something extra. When used in computing it can mean a copy of data on various types of storage media or a copy of data kept for safety or emergency purposes.

Basic Disks: The partitions or logical drives that were creatable on Windows NT. Later operating systems such as Windows 2000 Professional and Windows 2000 Server automatically default to basic disks unless set otherwise.

Cache: To store data temporarily to improve access speed or the location where such data is stored. A way to speed up disk operations is to store the most recently accessed data in memory; therefore, drives now come with several megabytes of cache.

Catastrophic Failure: Fires, floods, earthquakes, explosions, hurricanes, terrorist acts, and more are catastrophic disasters that can destroy an entire organization or a portion or branch of it overnight. This type of occurrence requires offsite facilities and data storage to ensure continuance of business activities.

Cluster: The smallest unit of storage that the operating system can manage, usually composed of several sectors. The size of the cluster depends on the size of the disk. On small disks of less than 2 MB, the cluster size is 512 bytes, 1 KB, or 2KB depending on the disk size. On hard disks greater than 2 GB, the NTFS default cluster size is 4 KB. As far as the operating system is concerned, all the sectors in the cluster are a single unit.

Contiguous: Existing in many pieces but with all pieces touching, as opposed to split into many pieces.

Contingency Plan (CP): A plan that addresses non-catastrophic failures that may occur within the organization resulting in some kind of data loss or downtime.

Controller: An electronic circuit board or system in a computer that allows the computer to use various peripheral devices. In addition to the logic board contained in the drive itself, today's disks have controllers. These can come as a controller card or as an integrated controller on the motherboard.

Cylinders: Modern-day platters currently contain in excess of 30,000 tracks. On drives that contain multiple platters, all the tracks on all the platters that are at the same distance from the center are referred to as a cylinder. The data from all the tracks in the cylinder can be read by simply switching between the different heads, which is much faster than physically moving the head between different tracks on a single disk.

Defragmentation: The process of reorganizing the disk by putting files into contiguous order. This combats the tendency of the operating system to store new data wherever space is available, which results in files being splintered into hundreds or even thousands of pieces. Defragmentation consolidates files into one or more pieces, thereby greatly improving access times.

Desktop Management Interface (DMI): A management system that can monitor hardware and software components from a central console. Agents are used to gather data once queries are made.

Directory Quotas: A quota given that controls the amount of data that may be stored in a directory or volume regardless of user. See *Disk Quota.*

Disaster Recovery Plan (DRP): A plan to deal with the operations, technical, and organizational issues that must be addressed to recover rapidly from a disaster of some kind.

Disk Duplexing: Involves using two disks operated by separate controllers and simultaneously recording the data to both disks for reliability and performance. When one disk goes down, the other can still be used for failover. A performance boost can be gotten by setting it up so that a seek operation will be sent to whichever disk offers the quickest turnaround at that time.

Disk Formatting: The creation of the storage layout (file system) on a disk. This is done after the disk is initialized. Without a file system installed on the partition, data cannot be written to it. See *Formatting.*

Disk Initialization: To initialize means to start anew. For hard disks, initialization is necessary to prepare the disk so it is ready for use. This means that the disk is separated into different partitions. A disk can be partitioned into a maximum of four partitions, each of which is assigned a drive letter. Once initialized (or partitioned), the disk is ready to accept the file system and data.

Disk Management Console: The tool used on Windows 2000 to configure disk arrangements. It is a snap-in that is part of the Computer Management function and can be found within the Administrative Tools folder. The Disk Management Console indicates the layout and type of every partition or volume, the file system, the status of the volume, its drive letter, its capacity, any fault tolerant features, amount of available free space, and more.

Disk Optimization (File Optimization): Said to reduce the time it takes to recover data from disks as well as the time it takes to defragment. Disk optimization involves the intelligent placement of files on a disk in order to minimize head movement and process read/writes faster.

Disk Quota: A quota is an assignment limit or amount for something. In regard to disk space, the quota indicates the maximum amount of space assigned to a user or a directory. Disk quotas, then, control space consumption and prevent one greedy individual, for example, from consuming everyone else's space, leading to system crashes and other unfortunate situations.

Dynamic Disk: A physical disk that can contain dynamic volumes created with Volume Manager. A dynamic volume organizes space on one or more physical disks by using a specific type of volume layout. The five types of dynamic volumes are simple, spanned, mirrored, striped, and RAID-5.

Extended Partitions: This is the part of a basic disk that contains a logical drive, which removes the restriction of four partitions per basic disk. Only one of the four basic disk partitions, though, can be extended. Note that extended partitions apply only to basic disks. For dynamic disks having no volume number limit, extended partitions are unnecessary.

Extent: A set of contiguous clusters storing a single file or part of a file. It is best to keep the number of extents for any file to a minimum as each extent requires a separate I/O operation. Reducing the number of extents in a file by the process known as defragmentation greatly improves performance.

Fault Tolerance: Basically, the computer is able to tolerate a fault of some kind, such as data loss or the failure of one disk. Despite such a hiccup, the system is able to continue without impacting the user community. Mirrored volumes or RAID-5 volumes must be created to add fault tolerance to a system.

File Allocation Table (FAT): The part of the file system that keeps track of where data is stored on the disk. The three versions of the FAT file system are FAT12, FAT16, and FAT 32. The numbers used in these versions designate the number of bits used to identify a cluster.

Formatting: Putting the file structure on the disk.

Fragmentation: Allocation of noncontiguous sectors on a disk; that is, instead of placing a file in one location, parts of it are scattered all over the disk. Essentially, fragmentation means that files are broken into multiple pieces rather than residing in one contiguous block on a disk. When a fragmented file is opened, therefore, the head has to gather up all these pieces in order to display the file. Thus, the user experiences delays waiting for a document to appear. If the condition is in an advanced state (it is quite common for server files to be splintered into thousands of pieces), it might even take as long as 15 seconds to open a document that previously was available in one second.

Hard Quota: An enforceable quota limit on disk and directory usage, as set by an administrator. Changes in disk/directory usage are tracked; however, because quota limits are enforceable, the administrator is enabled to exert some control over user space consumption.

Head–Actuator Assembly: Consists of four principal components: *read/write head*, which is the part that takes the electronic 0s and 1s and converts them into the magnetic fields on the disk; *actuator*, which is the device that moves the arms containing the read/write heads across the platter surface; *head arms*, which move between the platters in order to store and access the data; and *head slider*, which is a block of material that holds the read/write head and acts as an airfoil to keep it positioned at the precise height above the surface of the platter.

Initializing (Partitioning): Reserves a part of a disk for a certain function; the operating system considers each partition as a separate drive. Even if the entire disk is to be a single partition, that must be specified. When using dynamic disks in UNIX or Windows 2000, the term *volume* is used rather than *partition*.

Logic Board: Controls the disk rotational speed and directs the actuator in all its motions. To run the various components that comprise the modern hard drive, disk drives contain their own logic boards. Mounted on these boards are a microprocessor, memory chips, and many other more minor components.

Logical Cluster Number: The LCN refers to the location of the first cluster of each extent. Each file has a physical cluster number (PCN) and a logical cluster number (LCN). When no bad clusters are present, the PCNs and LCNs match exactly, but when the system discovers a PCN that is bad the LCN is directed to point to another PCN. Thus, two consecutive LCNs may be widely separated on the disk.

Logical Drives: Drives can also be grouped logically so that the operating system sees them as a single drive. For example, three physical 40-GB drives could be combined logically so that the operating system sees them all as a single 120-GB drive. Also, a physical drive may be partitioned into more than one logical drive.

Master File Table (MFT): On NTFS, the MFT is a map of each and every file on the volume, and it is itself a file. Every time a new file is made, a new record in the MFT file is created. The MFT consists of a series of 1-KB records, one for each file in the partition.

Mean Time between Failures (MTBF): The number of hours a disk can be expected to run, as reflected by the predicted failure rate in the first year; only useful as an enterprise metric. Divide the MTBF rating of disks by the number of disks in the enterprise for an approximation of how many disk failures can be expected during the first year.

MFT Zone: Because the MFT is such an important file, Microsoft reserved space for expansion on the disk immediately after the MFT called the MFT Zone. Approximately one eighth of an NTFS volume is reserved for the MFT Zone.

Microsoft Management Console (MMC): An interface for the use of the different management snap-ins.

Mirrored Volume: A fault-tolerant volume for which the data is duplicated on two physical disks. All of the data on one volume is copied to another disk to provide data redundancy. If one of the disks fails, the data can still be accessed from the remaining disk. A mirrored volume cannot be extended. Mirroring is also known as RAID-1.

Mount Points: All Windows versions assign a different drive letter to each partition or volume on a disk, which limits the number of accessible volumes to the 26 letters of the alphabet. Mount points let the administrator attach other partitions to an empty directory within an already mounted NTFS volume. Rather than being limited to NTFS volumes, these additional volumes can also be using FAT16, FAT32, CD-ROM File System (CDFS), or Universal Disk Format (UDF), which expands the functionality of this feature.

Non-Catastrophic Failure: A subset of disaster recovery that encompasses various types of failure such as accidental deletion by a user, disk controller failure, hard disk drive crash, network downtime, or a power surge.

NTFS (New Technology File System): A log-based file system that is more reliable and recoverable than early file systems. This is the file system used primarily on Windows 2000 and XP.

Partition: A reserved part of a disk that is set aside for a specific purpose. A physical disk can be divided into one or more partitions. Partitions are created before a disk is formatted.

Partitioning (Initializing): Reserves a part of a disk for a certain function; the operating system considers each partition as a separate drive. Even if the entire disk is to be a single partition, that must be specified. When using dynamic disks in UNIX or Windows 2000, the term *volume* is used rather than *partition*.

Physical Cluster Number: Each file has a physical cluster number (PCN) and a logical cluster number (LCN). When no bad clusters are present, the PCNs and LCNs match exactly, but when the system discovers a PCN that is bad, the LCN is directed to point to another PCN. Thus, two consecutive LCNs may be widely separated on the disk.

Platters: The element that actually stores the data. It consists of a substrate coated with magnetic media. The substrate, made out of a non-magnetic material, is there to act as a rigid support for the magnetic media. Hard drives typically contain multiple disks, or platters, stacked on top of each other. PC hard drives generally have one to five platters, while servers will have up to a dozen.

Quota Threshold: A threshold is a point at which something is detectable or observable. In disk management, this can be a point at which a warning is issued (such as X% of the disk quota has now been used) or the point where the limit of disk space usage is reached. Different disk quota management tools permit different types and levels of thresholds. A threshold's being reached triggers specific actions such as e-mail and pop-up alerts, event log notifications, and restrictions.

RAID-0: Uses striping for added performance but has no data redundancy. RAID-0 writes data to more than one drive so as to speed the process. Information is striped to one disk, then others, back and forth, so the data is distributed among multiple disks. If one drive fails, the data is lost because no redundancy is built into RAID-0.

RAID-1: Uses full disk mirroring, with the exact same data being put on two or more disks. Read speeds are higher than a single disk, as more than one disk can be read at the same time. Write speeds, however, are the same as a single disk, as all the data is written to each of the disks. RAID-1 is expensive because twice the storage space must be used to achieve redundancy. In comparison, RAID-3 and RAID-5 are less expensive.

RAID-2: Uses striping for performance and stores error checking codes (ECCs), which allow data errors to be detected and corrected. This is a relatively rare method.

RAID-3: Combines the speed advantage of striping, as in RAID-0, but with the addition of redundancy. Rather than doing full mirroring as for RAID-1, however, it takes the data from two disks, XORs it, and places the result on a third disk, thus it requires half as many disks as RAID-1 to store the redundant data (XOR stands for exclusive-OR). A RAID system will take one bit from each of the two data disks. If both bits are the same (i.e., both 0 or both 1) it will record a 0 on the redundant disk. If the two bits are different (i.e., one is 0 and the other 1), it records a 1. This is also known as *parity*.

RAID-4: Does not use striping; instead, stores parity bits on a separate disk. Like RAID-2, this method is rarely used.

RAID-5: Similar to RAID-3 in terms of striping and replication. With RAID-5, however, the redundant data is interspersed with the user data on the same disks, rather than being stored on separate disks. The read speed is similar to RAID-0 and RAID-3, but the write speed is slower because both the user data and the redundant data must be written to the same disks. This is the most widely used RAID level.

RAID-10: Actually RAID-1,0 as it is a combination of striping (RAID-0) and mirroring (RAID-1). It combines the improved performance of striping with the fault tolerance of mirroring.

Redundant Arrays of Independent Disks (RAID): A disk subsystem that increases performance and/or provides some means of fault tolerance. It is composed of two or more disk drives as well as a controller. RAID is used mainly on servers but is now starting to find its way into PCs, also.

Restore: Retrieve a file from backup; if data loss occurs and the data has been backed up, that data must then be restored from the backup.

Rotational Latency: It is much quicker to access data that is immediately under the head. All the head has to do is move toward or away from the center of the disk to access it. If, however, the head has just passed over the point on the disk where the data resides, it has to rotate almost a complete circle in order to access the data. This is known as *rotational latency*. In a disk spinning at 7500 rpm, it takes a little over 8 milliseconds for the head to complete a 360-degree rotation on the disk; therefore, rotational latency can vary from 0 to 8 ms on such a disk and averages around 4 ms.

Sector: A portion of one of the concentric rings on a hard disk. On PCs, a sector is usually 512 bytes in size. Tracks are broken down into sectors, which are the smallest units of storage on a disk.

Seek: Moving the head from one track to another to locate data on a specific part of a disk or to be in the proper position to retrieve data, program instructions, etc.

Seek Time: The time it takes for the head to move from one track to another. It is the most important factor in determining the speed of a disk and can be broken down into three elements: the time it takes to move the head from a stationary position until it is moving at full speed; the time expended moving the head from one track to another; and the time required to stop the head. Note that if a file is fragmented, many additional seeks are necessary to open the file. Also note that, in its truest sense, seek time really only means the time it takes for the head to move across the disk perpendicular to the tracks; however, some people use seek time to mean the time it takes for one I/O, which includes rotational latency.

Self-Monitoring Analysis and Reporting Technology (SMART): A technology designed to provide data about the health of a disk. The controller takes data from sensors and provides that data, upon request, to the BIOS, operating system, or other software designed to monitor drives. The exact items monitored vary from one manufacturer to another but can include such things as head flying height (predicts future head crashes), disk spin-up time and temperature (disk motor problems), or the number of errors corrected.

Simple Network Management Protocol (SNMP): A widely used network monitoring and control protocol; SNMP agents pass data about devices to the console that is monitoring them.

Simple Volume: Uses free space from a single disk. It can be a single region on a disk or consist of multiple regions that are joined together. A simple volume can be extended within the same disk or onto additional disks. Simple volumes contain no partitions or logical drives and cannot be accessed by DOS or Windows 9*x*.

Small Computer Systems Interface (SCSI): Used widely for a variety of devices, not just hard drives.

Snap-In: A module of MMC that provides certain management capabilities for a specific device. Every administrative tool in Windows 2000 is a snap-in.

Soft Quota: Usage changes are monitored, but quota limits are not enforced. This soft quota mode means that quota violation events are not generated and file operations do not fail due to violation of a disk quota parameter.

Spanned Volume: A spanned volume is created from free disk space that is linked together from multiple disks. A spanned volume can be extended onto a maximum of 32 disks. A spanned volume cannot be mirrored and is not fault tolerant.

Spindle: The platters of a hard drive are attached at the center to a spindle that is directly attached to the shaft of the motor.

Striped Volume: A volume for which the data is distributed across two or more physical disks. The data on this type of volume is allocated alternately and evenly to each of the physical disks. The data on each disk is divided into blocks and data is spread onto all the disks at the same time. Thus, reads and writes are faster — sometimes as much as 300 percent faster. A striped volume cannot be mirrored or extended and is not fault tolerant. Striping is also known as RAID-0.

Track: A concentric ring on the disk where data is stored. Hard drive tracks differ from CD tracks which follow a spiral. CDs are designed for continuous play and the head moves across the disk at a constant speed. Hard disks, on the other hand, are designed for random access to the data on a single track so concentric rings work better.

User Quotas: Allows control over the amount of data any user can store in a directory or volume.

Virtual Cluster Number (VCN): A sequential number relating to each extent of consecutive clusters on the disk that contain the file. If, for example, the file was fragmented into four pieces, the MFT record would list four VCNs (1, 2, 3, 4).

Volume: A storage unit made from free space on one or more disks. It can be formatted with a file system and assigned a drive letter. Essentially, a volume is a portion of a physical disk that acts like a physically separate entity.

Appendix B: Bibliography

The following is a brief list of various books and papers that cover some of the subjects covered in this work in far more detail.

Books

Anderson, D. T., *The Hard Disk Technical Guide*, Micro House, Boulder, CO, 1997.

Bigelow, S. J., *Bigelow's Drive and Memory Troubleshooting*, McGraw-Hill, New York, 2000.

Bodo, M., *Hard Drive Bible*, Corporate Systems Center, Santa Clara, CA, 1996.

Friedman, M. and Pentakolos, O., *Windows 2000 Performance Guide*, O'Reilly, Sebastopol, CA, 2002.

Jensen, C., *Fragmentation: The Condition, The Cause, The Cure*, ESI, Burbank, CA, 1994.

Killelea, P., *Web Performance Tuning*, O'Reilly, Sebastopol, CA, 1998.

Massiglia, P., *Highly Available Storage for Windows Servers*, John Wiley & Sons, New York, 2002.

Minasi, M., *Mastering Windows XP Professional*, Sybex, Alameda, CA, 2001.

Minasi, M., Toombs, D., Anderson, C., and Smith, B., *Mastering Windows Server 2000*, 4th ed., Sybex, Alameda, CA, 2002.

Press, B., *PC Upgrade and Repair Bible*, IDG Books, Foster City, CA, 1996.

Russell, C. and Crawford, S., *Microsoft Windows 2000 Server Administrator's Companion*, Vol. 1, Microsoft Press, Redmond, WA, 2000.

Simmons, C., *Windows 2000 Hardware and Disk Management*, Prentice-Hall, Englewood Cliffs, NJ, 2000.

Solomon, D. A. and Russinovich, M. E., *Inside Windows 2000*, 3rd ed., Microsoft Press, Redmond, WA, 2000.

Zaenglein, N., *Disk Detective: Secrets You Must Know to Recover Information from a Computer*, Paladin Enterprises, Boulder, CO, 1998.

Zobrist, G. W. and Ashar, K. G., *Magnetic Disk Drive Technology: Heads, Media, Channel, Interfaces, and Integration*, John Wiley & Sons, New York, 1996.

White Papers and Reports

American Megatrends, Inc., *SMART Technology and SCSI Drives: A Look at AMI MegaRAID, SMART Drives and GUIs*, 1999, http://www.genitech.com.au.

Comprehensive Consulting Solutions, Inc., *Disaster Recovery Planning: An Overview; Disaster Recovery Planning: Process and Options; Avoiding Disaster: An Ounce of Prevention; Business Continuity Planning*, 2001, http://www.comp-soln.com.

National Software Testing Lab (NSTL), *Comparison Testing: Diskeeper vs. the Windows 2000 Disk Defragmenter*, http://www.nstl.com; *System Performance and File Fragmentation in Windows NT*, 2002, http://www.execsoft.com; *NSTL Benchmarks on Windows NT/2000/XP*, 2002, http://www.execsoft.com.

Precise/W. Quinn Associates, *Quota Management Technologies*, 2000, http://www.wquinn.com.

Quantum Corporation, *Hard Drives and Computer System Performance*, 1999, http://www.quantum.com.

Seagate Technologies, *Estimating Drive Reliability in Desktop Computers and Consumer Electronic Systems; Disc Drive Capacity and Performance; Get S.M.A.R.T. for Reliability*, http://www.seagate.com.

XIOtech, *A True Definition of Storage Virtualization*, 2000, http://www.xiotech.com.

About the Author

Born in Scotland, **Drew Robb** graduated from Glasgow's Strathclyde University majoring in Geology and Geography. Since then, his publishing credits include editing a national magazine in Scotland, an international business newsletter, and numerous technical and training documents. Since 1997, he has focused on magazine articles in the engineering and technology fields. During that time, he published hundreds of articles for such publications as *Information Week*, *ComputerWorld*, *Network World*, *Power Engineering*, *Writer's Digest*, and a host of others. He now lives with his wife and two sons in Los Angeles, California.

Index